Nation-Building and Identity in Europe

Also by Rodanthi Tzanelli

THE CINEMATIC TOURIST: EXPLORATIONS IN GLOBALIZATION, CULTURE AND RESISTANCE

Nation-Building and Identity in Europe

The Dialogics of Reciprocity

Rodanthi Tzanelli
University of Leeds, UK

First published 2008 by
PALGRAVE MACMILLAN

Palgrave Macmillan in the UK is an imprint of Macmillan Publishers Limited,
registered in England, company number 785998, of Houndmills, Basingstoke,
Hampshire RG21 6XS.

Palgrave Macmillan in the US is a division of St Martin's Press LLC,
175 Fifth Avenue, New York, NY 10010.

Palgrave Macmillan is the global academic imprint of the above companies
and has companies and representatives throughout the world.

Palgrave® and Macmillan® are registered trademarks in the United States,
the United Kingdom, Europe and other countries.

ISBN-13: 978–0–230–55199–2   hardback
ISBN-10: 0–230–55199–8   hardback

This book is printed on paper suitable for recycling and made from fully
managed and sustained forest sources. Logging, pulping and manufacturing
processes are expected to conform to the environmental regulations of the
country of origin.

A catalogue record for this book is available from the British Library.

Library of Congress Cataloging-in-Publication Data

Tzanelli, Rodanthi, 1974–
   Nation-building and identity in Europe : the dialogics of reciprocity /
   Rodanthi Tzanelli.
       p. cm.
   Includes bibliographical references and index.
   ISBN 13: 978–0–230–55199–2 (hbk. : alk. paper)
   ISBN 10: 0–230–55199–8 (hbk. : alk. paper)
     1. Nation-building – Greece – History – 19th century.
     2. Greece – Foreign relations – Great Britain. 3. Great Britain – Foreign
     relations – Greece. 4. Greece – Foreign relations – 1863–1917.
     5. Great Britain – Foreign relations – 1837–1901. I. Title.

   DF825.T93 2008
   949.507'2–dc22   2008021566

10   9   8   7   6   5   4   3   2   1
17   16   15   14   13   12   11   10   09   08

Printed and bound in Great Britain by
CPI Antony Rowe, Chippenham and Eastbourne

For Michael Herzfeld
for his intellectual labours and endeavours

For Majid
gia pànta

Contents

List of Figures

Preface

The geographical distance I retained from the political and social changes that took place in Greece in the last decade has certainly helped me to better articulate the theoretical reflections on the process of nation-building that comprise the main subject matter of this book. Today such sociopolitical changes are related by Greeks in formulaic complaints that stress the impact European enlargement had on Greek culture and society, especially after the admission of foreigners into a country that until recently was known as the global 'guest' (stories about the great 'Greek diaspora' of Americas, Australia and Germany come to mind) rather than the 'host' of the unwanted crowds of humanity (North Africans, Albanians and Eastern Europeans, to mention but a few recent examples). The complaints go on to outline how the umbilical cord of European civilization has been severed: Europeans have taken all they could from Greece's Hellenic ancestors (ideas of democracy, philosophy and beauty) and now do not care about its condition any more. The country will now be left to lead an obscure life in one of Europe's dark corners, struggling with alien dangers and challenges.

It may even be suggested that by working primarily with historical materials, I effectively managed to couple my spatial distance with a temporal one. I am only too aware that some groups in the academic establishment regard the disclosure of personal investment as a bizarre occurrence and seek ways to exorcise it at any cost. The justification of this hostility may focus upon the stylistic idiosyncrasies of discursive disclosure: the intrusion of the 'I' in historical narrative is still supposed to be discreetly hidden under piles of formal, pluralized pleasantries. I have no interest in such criticisms: first of all, this is not a history book and I do not aspire to speak as a historian of any establishment. I would prefer to present myself as an anthropological or sociological observer who tries to understand the historical roots of nation-building (especially that of the European margins) and relate it to the realities of global inequalities. More importantly, however, I would argue that the stylistic façade of any academic discourse that emanates from personal commitment is inextricably linked to the commitment itself. *I* write this book, not my academic *alter ego*.

My emerging interest in this project could be related to some incidents that retain their triviality in the grand scheme of European politics but acquire unequivocal significance in the context of the lived national experience. These include my initial puzzlement when realizing that during NATO's bombing of the Federal Republic of Yugoslavia in 1999, former neighbors in my hometown were rather reluctant to talk to any foreigners who spoke a language that vaguely resembled English. It hardly mattered to them if the 'foreigners' were American, British or Australian, defenders or opponents of such aggressive policies. The exclamation that 'if *they* (apparently, foreign visitors and residents were just a uniform whole) want to murder Serbs, then they should do the same to the Turks' helped me make more sense of this identity mayhem. Coming from a place that was founded by Anatolian refugees from the last Greek-Turkish war (1919–22), this reaction occasionally signaled hostility based on local histories of persecution and uprooting (though even this hostility is not a stable denominator for my compatriots, especially those of the second and third generation). Interestingly, the expression *toúrkepses!* (You became a Turk and by extension a foreigner) was often addressed by locals to me. Surely, as a student abroad for years and then resident in the UK, I must have lost touch with my roots and become an *Evropaía*. This sort of indignation mixed with *xenophobia* (I was literally becoming a *kséni*, a guest and a stranger at the same time) was also symptomatic of an inferiority complex I was going to meet in historical sources. The devil of course hides in the detail, and dismissive statements are useful details: the whole of humanity with its perplexing diversity appears to be against Greeks; all outsiders, irrespective of ethnicity, origins and 'color' should be hated, *in case* they hate the Greeks. Cultural insecurities are often translated into hostility that becomes complicit in the creation of internal solidarity and external destruction.

Such hostility found expression in other banal nationalist episodes: it fuelled for example a simultaneous local and national debate on who ought to hold the Greek flag in commemorative parades in 2000 and again in 2003 (Greeks did not want to let children of Albanian immigrants do this, because they were not Greeks by birth). Emotions were running high, and I was becoming interested in their expression. My co-villagers led this debate with style, declaring on the walls of the local school that '*Hellas* belongs to the Christians', a slogan reminiscent of the colonels' regime (1967–74) that tied Greek antiquity to Christian Orthodoxy. When on eve of the 2004 Olympic Games hosted by Athens, the Olympic Torch was crossing the town (Friday 23 July), there was a lot of local debate about a Greek *anástasi* (resurrection) – an incident communicated to me on the phone by relatives. Public talk about national awakening, also reminiscent of the *Athens 2004* opening and closing ceremonies, found a happy continuation in the unexpected victory of the Greek football team in *Euro 2004* that my compatriots celebrated in the streets. There were obvious symmetries between the discourses of triumphant football 'underdogs' and those of the resurrected Greek angels of European culture of *Athens 2004*. Performing small victories concealed unspoken fears of political exclusion from Europe.

This book is about the mechanics and politics of expressing national identity in Europe. By 'mechanics', I allude to the process of nation-building; by 'politics' I refer to the environment in which this takes place and which it produces by turns. I stress the *expressive* dimension of nation-building: first, because it has communicative, dialogical properties of unprecedented cohesive power that I set out to unpack. Second, because the study of emotions *as such* should be considered neither the privileged territory of abstract social theory, nor, inversely, the subject of those who excel at individualizing emotional behavior. Anger, resentment, unconditional love, frustration and compassion, are all emotions that figure in specialized studies of nationalism as a sociopolitical and cultural phenomenon. How can we effectively analyze their productive and destructive nature when we connect them to nation-building in context? More importantly: what happens when the context of nation-building involves collective political marginalization? As many scholars in the social sciences (among them, the significant scholarly voices of this monograph) have explained, in particular inceptions of Europe, the idea of 'Greece' has been productive of exclusive values and practices that promoted the political division of the continent and the rest of the world into two (morally) opposing halves. It was unfortunate that the actual Greece of Europe, the one that emerged from centuries of Ottoman rule and European political feuds, would become a nation on which this binary model would be tested.

I do not claim that this monograph proffers the last word on nation-building and its relationship to European identity. On the contrary, I place it within a debate that started a long time ago but only came to fruition in more recent decades. More modestly, I have tried to bring together different (but not conflicting) schools of thought to produce a coherent theoretical account of the phenomenon. The supporting thesis appears in the first chapter but runs throughout the study, not in a direct line, but in ramified reflections on the multiple facets of national dialogues with significant political others. Less modestly, I do not address this book to historians exclusively, but to academics in the social sciences in general (I place history among them, ignoring any whimpering that it is an 'art' or it belongs to the 'Humanities proper'; such classifications have a political resonance that is contented through this book's deconstructive discourse). Borrowing from social theory, political philosophy, international relations, anthropology, feminist and postcolonial studies, this book aspires to shed light on the *complexity* (in Luhmannian terms I explain in Chapter 1) of nation-building and its future in European politics. The focus on Greece is deceptive: as the analysis develops, more cross-cultural, comparative points are made. These comparisons respond to the suggestion that today the shifting political margins of Europe also dictate an expansion of its cultural borders. It remains to be seen whether such transformations will materialize the tired communitarian rhetoric of 'unity in diversity' or push the reality of political division to an even narrower *cul-de-sac* that has room only for exclusive clientele.

Acknowledgments

Acknowledgments in a book that flags reciprocity as its core *problématique* may put the author's academic decorum to test. Reciprocities may exist *in abstracto* in hydrocephalous academic brains, but they also inhabit, produce and challenge the order of our everyday socialities. It took a long time for this monograph to reach a stage of near-maturation – nine years marked by many productive encounters. As a project, it had at least two lives, a historical and a sociological/anthropological. Like its phantom influence (Bakhtin), it remains polyphonic.

I remain thankful to Martin Blinkhorn for putting up with (and remaining supportive of) a deviant doctoral candidate who stubbornly kept reading anything other than mainstream history; Thomas Gallant for his useful comments during our fleeting encounter in 2002; Paolo Palladino and John MacKenzie for their wide-ranging methodological skepticism; John Walton for the opportunities he gave me to make my work known; Steve Pumfrey and Roger Smith for their dual role as friends and interlocutors; and many peers that I met between 1998–2002 as a 'historian'. I remain grateful for discussions with a Society for Applied European Thought group of young scholars, who questioned my original reluctance to transcend questions of social process and enter the slippery ethical domain. I thank Michael Herzfeld for his performative exposition of 'social poetics' over lunch in 2006; his influence remains formative. Heartfelt thanks to Roger Just for his support and his theoretical suggestions while I was at Kent. Apologies to Martin O'Brien for putting up with my incessant monologues on anthropology's epistemological conundrums; his comments on postcolonial anthropology's shaky commitment to symbolism helped me rethink conceptual categories. Beyond gratitude stand Majid, who remains my emotional home and a companion in ideas (his comments on drafts were very useful), and (the not so 'little') Evelyn, who forced me to understand the dangers of unconditional love early enough.

Aspects of this book emerged from work previously published in academic journals. Chapter 2 benefited from articles that appeared in the *Journal of Historical Sociology* ['Unclaimed Colonies: Anglo-Greek Identities through the Prism of the Dilessi (Marathon) Murders (1870)', 15, 2, 2002, 169–91] and *Sociology* ['Capitalising on Value: Towards a Sociological Understanding of Kidnapping', 40, 5, 929–47]. Chapter 3 was based on three articles published in *The Journal of Modern Greek Studies* ['Haunted by the "Enemy" Within: Brigandage, Vlachian/ Albanian Greekness, Turkish "Contamination" and Narratives of Greek Nationhood in the Dilessi/ Marathon Affair (1870)', 20, 1, 2002, 47–74], *Ethnic and Racial Studies* ['"Not MY Flag!" Citizenship and Nationhood in the Margins of Europe (Greece, October 2000/2003)', 29, 1, 2006, 27–49] and *Nations and Nationalism* ['The Politics of Forgetting as Poetics of Belonging: Between Greek Self-Narration and Re-appraisal (Michaniona, 2000/3)', 13, 4, 2007, 1–20]. Chapter 4 was developed from an article published in the *History of Human Sciences* as '"Disciplining" the Neohellenic Character: Records of Anglo-Greek Encounters and the Development of Ethnohistorical Discourse' (16, 3, 2003, 41–50). Chapter 6 drew upon work published in *Cultural Values* as 'Giving Gifts (And then Taking Them Back): Identity, Reciprocity and Symbolic Power in the Context of *Athens 2004*' (8, 4, 2004, 425–46; www.ingenta.com/ journals/browse/bpl/cuva) and Chapter 7 was structured around themes previously explored in 'Experiments on Puerile Nations or the Impossibility of Surpassing your Father: The Case of Anglo-Greek Dialogue' (*National Identities*, 6, 1, 2004, 107–22). Despite the mandatory acknowledgement to the journals, these studies were significantly reworked and adapted so as to fit the needs of the present monograph.

1
Europe, Nationhood and the Dialogics of Reciprocity

Europe as a system of exclusion

'Lying at the core of the idea of Europe is a fundamental ambivalence about the normative horizons of collective identity in the modern polity', explains Delanty (1995, p. 1). The plethora of myths that fed into the production of 'European-ness' in different epochs did not detract from their essentially divisive nature. Beneath the rhetoric of unity and solidarity, Christianity, Enlightenment rationality and modern nationhood remained proponents of exclusion and conflict. European-ness has always been constructed through negations of otherness (*ibid.*, p. 5) that – in echoes of colonialism – contributed to an active de-humanization of difference (Said, 1978; Said, 1994). These observations are not anachronisms: even at the turn of the twenty-first century the European map continues to be redrawn with borders, buffer zones and dark spots in the place of minority cultures that challenge political and cultural hegemonies.

The conservative communitarian ethos of European identity found its best expression with the emergence of nationalism, an all-embracing ideology of belonging that shaped the continent's cultural destiny. Nationalism offered a new social experience replete with conditional clauses, crafting citizenships as positional goods. All national communities raised claims to pure, unique 'culture'. Nationhood's explicit claims to eternal validity 'rested on the authority of a culturalized nature' (Herzfeld, 1997b, p. 39). In a Romantic fashion, the perennial national spirit could be reborn, reawakened and stroll in human history like any living organism (Gellner, 1998). In a profoundly discordant mode, this spirit lived only in the bodies of those who were born and brought up in such self-contained national communities.

In reality, nationhood produced by a system of political regulation (Parsons, 1971, 1977), which dictated that each nation draws legitimacy for its sovereignty from an imagined European world-center (Wallerstein, 1974, 1980). The operators of this 'center' were the so-called 'Great Powers', influential states that acted as self-appointed guardians of Europe's imagined cultural cohesion, waging wars in the name of universalized European values (Weber, 1985, p. 25; Habermas, 1987, p. 1). During the nineteenth century these 'universal values' were predicated upon Western colonial expansion and often valorized by scientific reasoning that supported discourses of governance. The European system was *autopetic*, as its main aim was to preserve itself by adapting to exigent necessities without any consideration for the social world outside it (Luhmann, 1982, 1990, 1995). Historically, the identification of Europe with the 'West' both produced an exclusivist vision of modern identity and became productive in turn. To recall Hall, 'it became both the organizing factor in a system of global power relations and the organizing concept in a whole way of thinking and speaking' (1992, p. 278).

The discourse of modern Europe was a discourse of progress. Enlightenment ideas had led to a repudiation of the chronicle time and the adoption of linear, chronological time (Fabian, 1983). This development would eventually lead to a projection of the axis of time onto the axis of space and a 'mapping' of time that created hierarchies of 'backward' and 'progressive' species – among them, the 'newly-born' nations (Elias, 2006, p. 110). Nations that could be modernized – comply with the Western European paradigm of socio-political progress – were awarded a bonus. This bonus was nothing other than the successful nation's promotion to a higher level in the civilizational hierarchy. Inversely, nations presenting signs of anomalous or belated development remained in the lower stages. Political disorder, social unrest and public insecurity were all signs of anomaly, instead of being regarded as inherent in the process of modernization – they were the other side of modernity. Practices of classification and accusations of deficiency enabled Western European powers to justify their patronizing attitude towards such nations. It may be dangerous to lump together different European projects as 'Western', for this theoretical umbrella legitimated various collective political identities over the last few centuries. Use of the 'West', whose genealogy is traced back to European military and ideological feuds without any explication of its content, involves adopting a worldview of opposite blocks (Delanty, 1995, p. 31), 'an adversarial self-definition' (Federici, 1995, p. 65). Nevertheless, it was precisely this hazy category of the 'West' that cultivated fears of deficiency that new nations internalized.

Subordinate identities tend to formulate counter-hegemonic agendas too. Returning to Weber's analysis of Calvinism as the precursor of capitalism, Herzfeld noted that bureaucratic systems instill in subjects a form of secular theodicy, 'provid[ing] them with social means of coping with disappointment' (1992, p. 7). Likewise, Western European vocabularies of moral accountability were often turned on their heads: the weak can also accuse the powerful of moral deficiency. Whereas such accusations reify master-slave relationships in the geopolitical arena, they also work to the subaltern's self-satisfaction, allowing space not only for a formulaic grievance of 'gross injustices' but also for the transposition of discourses that demonize difference into the national sphere. Many, allegedly 'lesser', national communities were denied access to family of 'progressive' European nations – a telling metaphor of emotive power I will unpack. The result of this exclusion was not complete resignation, but a turning of the nation-state's efforts inwards, in order to accomplish cohesion and self-recognition. Damaged political reciprocities are useful tools for nation-building.

This book examines the dangerous historical convergence of nation-building as process and 'Europe' as an ideological imposition. The system of European control over 'lesser' nations, a constant surveillance and criticism for their alleged deficiencies, which today continues unfortunately in the politics of an 'enlarged Europe', did not encourage mutual political recognition and cooperation – contrariwise, it nurtured a climate of suspicion, resentment and rebellion. The systemic conditions of historical nation-building serve to shed light on the constitutive mechanism of nationhood. Extending Smith's (1981, 1995) 'nihil ex nihilo', I argue that nations are not created in communicative voids. Their spatio-temporal existence has always been affected by their significant others: rival ethnic groups (Triantafyllidou, 1998), patrons, colonizers, former rulers or supranational systems such as that of 'Europe'. If nations depend on self-narration (Bhabha, 1990a; Gourgouris, 1996, p. 45), they do not narrate only *to* themselves or *for* themselves. Nations are products of collective cross-cultural representations and dialogues: looking *inwards* (forming one's own history and identity) requires also looking *outwards* to meet the world and disseminate national autobiographies (Sampson, 1993, pp. 125–6).

The dialogic relation between the emergent nation and its 'Others' is explored in this book through the encounter between Greece and Britain in latter years of the nineteenth century – a notable instance of nation-formation played out within the heart of a 'modern', 'civilized' Europe that traced its very origins in an imagined Hellenic civilization. Theories of nation-formation have capitalized on various empirical examples, but Greece has been conspicuously avoided. This arises not only from the popularity such case-specific academic discourse may enjoy; the absence of interest is symptomatic of precisely this reciprocal damage on which Europe built its self-image.

The process of Greek nation-building is representative of past and present geopolitical visions of European belonging (Gourgouris, 1992b, 1996). As a state, Greece was institutionalized in the early nineteenth century (1832) with the help of its powerful European patrons (Britain, France and Russia), striving for control in the South-Eastern Mediterranean region. It was a Kingdom with an imported King (Otho) and many socio-economic problems stemming from political divisions and cultural diversities that the state had not begun to understand (Veremis, 1990). As an idea, however, in the eighteenth and nineteenth centuries *a version* of Greece tied to antiquity became constitutive of European identity. Putting therefore European political and economic interests aside, the Western philhellenic desire to liberate the Greek peninsula from Ottoman rule and 'resurrect' the Greek nation from the tombs of history originated in the belief that modern Greeks were descendants of the ancient Hellenes, on which Europe had crafted its 'civilized' self-image (Bernal, 1991). Meantime, the Ottoman sway from the Eastern frontier of Europe, which intensified after the fall of Constantinople (1453) and the collapse of Byzantium (Hay, 1968; Wintle, 1998), dictated the eradication of other contradictions internal to the notion of 'Europe': ideas of Christianity and classical heritage began to coexist in European self-perceptions. These ideas would be reworked into a new exclusivist narrative of national identity.

Soon it became clear that the modern Greeks would answer their patrons' expectations, because of their many suspected shortfalls: they were disorderly, 'Oriental' in habits (like their former Ottoman rulers), and with expansionist ambitions in the region (inconvenient for Western economic interests). As Said (1978) explains, the denigration of the colonized assisted in the consolidation of orientalist projects, which, in turn, supported colonial governance. In Greece's case, this denigration was coupled with an excessive admiration for things 'Hellenic' (Herzfeld, 1987): ancient Greek philosophy, democracy and an ideal of political order associated with antiquity. At various points in the history of modern Greece this past played for the Greeks the role of both the 'other', who lives outside Greek history and in the realm of Western Orientalism, and the 'same', who belongs to the process of Greek *ethnogenesis*. To date, Greeks lay claim to European-Hellenic heritage as 'their own' and insist on their linear descend from the ancient Hellenes. Internally, this narrative serves the Greek imagined community in helping see itself as a uniform entity progressing in linear historical time (Anderson, 1991, p. 193), but also as a unique, self-made community differing from other national communities. Simultaneously, it provides European observers with a familiar reference point that secures the unanimous recognition of Greek modernity. Thus cultural affiliation was translated into racial privilege, a smart hermeneutic adaptation of European exclusivist discourse.

The Greek internalization of such ideological topographies of identity was complemented by constant Western interference in Greek politics between the 1850s and the Second World War. A riotous episode against a Jewish-British subject in Athens in 1849–50 produced a temporary occupation of the city by the British fleet (Gallant, 2001, p. 42). In 1919 it contributed to the outbreak of a Greek-Turkish war, initially supported by Britain and France, and led to the uprooting of Greek communities in Asia Minor (1923). During the Second World War, British confrontation with communists within Greece overdetermined a civil war (1944–49) that still divides Greeks. In the Cold War era Greece was caught between the Western and Soviet spheres of influence. A dictatorship (1967–74) fully revived the narrative of Hellas-as-Europe, bestowing it also with Christian Orthodox, right-wing undertones (Herzfeld, 2002a, pp. 13–15). Gradually, Hellenic excellence became in Greek foreign and domestic policy what Diamantouros (1983) terms 'underdog culture': an inward-looking, Christian-'Hellenocentric' culture, that defensively warns against foreign interventions, alien elements and cultural difference (Eleftheriadis, 1999). The persistence of modern Greeks in calling themselves *Neo*hellenes or modern Hellenes, betrays how the 'curse of philhellenism' (Gourgouris, 1996) continues to cast its shadow, occasionally changing forms, but not objectives.

Western European attitudes towards the 'Greek Question' have been discussed as a manifestation of 'crypto-colonialism' (Herzfeld, 2002b), an indirect form of subjection that impacts on the course of national cultures. Building on earlier elaborations about analogies between anthropology and nationalism (Herzfeld, 1987), Herzfeld argues that nineteenth century Western anthropological writing on countries of marginal status such as Greece and Thailand questioned their sovereignty. The occasional admittance in, or exclusion of such cultures from 'civilization' sanctioned their ever-changing cultural positioning *vis-à-vis* global centers of political power. Even though cultural indeterminacy challenged the primary binarisms of colonial discourse, the crypto-colonial prerogative itself encouraged political dependencies. The internalized discourse of Greek exceptionalism means that Greek culture is politically marginalized and constantly ignored in academic debates on European identity (Gallant, 1997, pp. 210–11; Gourgouris, 1992a; Herzfeld, 1987, p. 3, 2005), despite its historical association with Europe. Greek exceptionalism gives a new twist to Anderson's (1991) endorsement of nationalism's 'modular character' (Chatterjee, 1986, pp. 27–8), supporting the idea that Greekness is just derivative of Western European models of nationhood. In this context, it is tempting to remark that the slow detachment of modern Greek scholarship from an antiquated 'Hellenocentrism', accompanied by a strict enforcement of disciplinary boundaries and a voracious domestic consumption of 'grandiloquent publications such as "History of Neohellenism 1770–2000" and "Abridged Dictionary of Modern Greek History"' (Carabott, 2005b, p. 136), may be the residue of deep-seated national insecurities produced by early Greco-European encounters. It is the sign of a defensive 'banal nationalism' (Billig, 1995) that was forced into a scholarly guise by its European patrons. Perhaps some would recognize in such discomforting connections the aptitude of an anti-Greek conspirator. Marx would mournfully remind them here that 'if the essence and appearance of things directly coincided, all science would be superfluous' (Marx in Cohen, 1972, p. 182).

The empirical focus of this book on Anglo-Greek encounters in the third half of the nineteenth century (ca. 1864–ca. 1881) may offend historical sensibilities. It seems to be an arbitrary incision in time, with no proper justification. Within this period I isolate four important episodes which created long-lasting debates in Anglo-Greek relations: the British cession of the Ionian colonies to Greece (1864), the Cretan Insurrection (1866–69), the Dilessi/Marathon Murders (1870), and the Balkan crisis (1878–81). The Greeks read Britain's cession of the Ionian colonies as the start of a territorial 'redemption' with the contribution of their protectors and an act of recognition of the Greek state's authority. In 1881 Greece's involvement in the Balkan crisis led to the acquisition of further territory from Turkey and Britain was, again, involved in European political negotiations. But I must stress that I do not intend to write a history of Anglo-Greek relations; I do not intend to write a mainstream history at all. Nor do I aspire to tidily cover the episodic nature of the period, ignoring what happened before or after it. Structurally, I examine the most dramatic episodes from the period, defying positivist and empiricist concerns with precision, number and volume. Diachronically, leaps in time enabled me to establish connections and recurring patterns of self-narration that would make no sense if studied within strict chronological confines. In this respect, I reject genealogical linearity and insularity in favor of an appreciation of change, discontinuities or coexisting histories of nation-formation. Nation-building is a term intentionally included in the title, because it alludes to *processes* that take place at least on the level of *la longue durée* – though Braudel's Eurocentric approach to world history issues a warning I take into account. More correctly, I consider nation-building as an ongoing process that ends with the dismantling of the nation and not before that.

Even the institution of the Greek state remained for most of the first half of the nineteenth century a fiction of Western political desire, a series of administrative experiments, not a fully recognized entity. The state's borders expanded and contracted with every new war, assuming a more definite form only after 1923. It goes without saying that the geographical and cultural borders of the nation never coincided, which required re-establishing every time a new territory was added or a social group removed from it. In nationalist discourse 'Greece' did not signify the multiplicity of actual socio-political experiences. The uniform 'Greece' that the Greeks of my texts adduced, was part of a process of self-nationalization. The Greek Kingdom, the Greek-speaking territories of the Ottoman empire, the Greek diaspora and the ontologized neo-Byzantine Greece of the 'Great Idea' (the Greek nationalist project of expansion eastwards) express different facets of modern Greek identity whose incompatibility was suppressed by a state that always struggled to fabricate an image of unity. Hutchinson's (2005) suggestion that we see nations as 'zones of conflict' is an apt metaphor of identity-production, because it draws attention to the internal incoherence of national identity, the coexistence and occasional amalgamation of modern and traditional voices, and the bloody conflict they may eventually induce. Following Hutchinson, this book highlights the diverse origins of these voices and the impact internal ideological conflicts may have on nation-building.

Naturally, one may wonder why Britain was singled out in this study. The French political and intellectual traditions had provided the Greeks with ready-made examples of government and administration and an exemplar of social change (Kitromilidis, 1996, pp. 13–80). Greece's strong religious affinity with Russia, which determined Greek attitudes in historical conjunctures such as that of the Orlov Revolt (1770) and later the Crimean War (1854–56), cannot be passed in silence. One cannot ignore the Bavarian administrative influence on the Greek nation-state during the Regency (1833–35) and Otho's reign (1835–62). It was the Bavarian interest in ancient Greek culture and its survival that officially transposed the myth of European Hellas into the Greek educational system: *Altertumswissenschaft*, the science of 'ancient civilizations' the Bavarians introduced in Greece, reshaped modern Greek identity.

Although reference to other European interlocutors may occasionally appear, I do not intend to measure the British influence against other influences. Instead, I examine the structure of Anglo-Greek exchange as a systemic component of Europe. When modern Greece did not escape the European myth of modernization, Britain made it its mission to consolidate control of the new state, a control that dated back to Greece's institution. British views on the world and themselves, a reflection of economic success, certainly impacted on this patronization. Optimism born of abundance was coupled with a sense of superiority *vis-à-vis* the colonized, and gave birth to the idea of a civilizing mission (Kumar, 2000a). The rationale of this mission was that Britain's ability to produce wealth equipped her as an agent in the improvement of the human condition (Robinson and Gallagher, 1967, pp. 1–2). In the first half of the nineteenth century, when war and social revolutions threatened the very existence of other European countries, Britain remained almost intact. This was regarded as a godly sign. 'Amidst the ruins of the old order, Britain was felt to be specially preserved by God and to have a central role in the fulfillment of purposes now hastening to their climax' (Wolffe, 1994, pp. 42–3).

The missionary spirit of British imperialism, investigated by Kumar (2003), fit perfectly into the nineteenth-century European mindset. The 'British' set out to civilize others, without questioning (or perhaps in order not to question) the dynamics of their own identity. The idea of an essentialized British identity began to unravel only with the devolution of British governance in recent decades, unleashing a universe of cultural voices (Welsh, Scottish, Irish) that were initially silenced in favor of a unitary vision of empire. *English* national identity, Kumar explains, 'cannot be found from within the consciousness of the English themselves' (Kumar, 2003, p. 17). Rather, 'we have to work from the outside in' (*ibid.*) to assemble parts of an identity that was brought to life through external sources. The Whiggish nationalism that extolled English attitudes such as determination and pragmatism alongside English liberties and institutions while elevating English rural life to the realm of essential Englishness contained both the Romantic narrative of European nationalisms and the totalitarian aspects of European ideology (James, 2006, p. 374).

Britain was, for the Greeks, *a version* of civilized Europe, but a very important one. Historically, it stood out as the beacon of philhellenism, even if it was not its sole or strongest source. One of the most 'advanced' European states, with a vast imperial network and a ruthlessness in maintaining global order, Britain figured as a guardian of European modernity. The oscillation of Greek attitudes between admiration and resentment stemmed from insecurity and the fear of exclusion from this modernity. Anglo-Greek cultural exchange was characterized by an apparent political inequality that stood in a reverse relationship to European narratives concerning the superiority of ancient Greek culture. The ideational operation of Greece as the imaginary European center clashed with its actual political marginalization, accentuating the Greek need to project a flawless picture abroad. The split response to European patronage, which incorporated both submission and resistance to foreign hegemony, can be read as a symptom of the normative ambivalence that governed European identity. From an early stage in its political life Greece had to mobilize its various and conflicting representations in search of recognition from those ungrateful Europeans it had allegedly brought to life.

Nation-building and the dialogics of reciprocity

The absence of any systematic analysis of the dialogical nature of nation-building is striking, when one considers that various theorizations of national identity contain elements of a dialogical thesis. One of the most influential works in the area is Anderson's *Imagined Communities* (1991 [1989]), which will open the discussion here. Anderson contends that identities are fostered though imagining, which enables individuals to see themselves as part of an invisible cultural whole. Imagining becomes thus a necessary precondition for the acquisition of national membership. Nations are imagined through language, not racial relations; thus racism and nationalism are separated analytically.

Anderson's thesis came to represent the constructionist paradigm in nationalism studies. 'Imagined communities', he argues, are the product of print-capitalism, which created a popular platform of nationhood through an effective democratization of communication. For Anderson language is addressed to all potential members of the community, because 'it is always open to new speakers, listeners and readers' (1991, p. 146). Interestingly, his engagement with Durkheimian debates on the production of organic solidarity unwittingly sketched a dialogical portrait of national imagination: the conditions of collective self-narration are potentially intersubjective, because 'through language the nation presents itself as simultaneously open and closed' (*ibid.*). The nation operates as a 'closed community' in order to preserve its coherence *vis-à-vis* external change. The fiction of fixity, the myth of an unchanging, perennial and primordial nation is always supported by the construction of *exclusive* histories (also Gellner 1983, p. 125). In short, Anderson suggests that national languages become vehicles for messages and ideas destined to traverse the world and make the nation real for both its members and those who reside outside its territory.

Anderson attracted the attention of postcolonial writers who also acknowledge the dialogical nature of nation-formation. Chatterjee's work on Indian nationalism attacks Anderson's modular argument of nation-building outside Europe, labeling it highly deterministic in the Marxist sense (Chatterjee, 1986, pp. 20–2). Although Anderson maintains that national communities are imagined, he presents this form of imagining as of exclusively European origin (*ibid.*, pp. 27–8). The divide between the material world of Western European colonialism and the spiritual (cultural) world of self-determination (Chatterjee, 1993, pp. 3–5) highlights the presence of different voices in nation-building. For Chatterjee nationalist enunciations are the products of bifurcated discourses addressed to the nation and its rulers, in which different arguments are strategically mobilized for different interlocutors. This conception of nationalist discourse rejects solely exterior constructions of national communities and places their creation in the field of conflict. Violent though this conflict may be, it is *creative*, as it produces for the subaltern dialogically something new (also Hitchcock, 1993). Ultimately Chatterjee's argument is not reducible to instances of direct colonial opposition, because it applies to identity awareness in general – to *subjectivity-as-agency* in short.

This particular debate on agency dates back to Fanon's polemics in favor of the Algerian anti-colonial struggle (Fanon, 1967, 1970). Emphasizing the role of recognition in identity-formation, Fanon urged his compatriots to disengage with their French rulers. The subjection to colonial rule is insidious because it renders itself invisible – it hides in the shadows of etiquette and the need to mimic, to be 'like them' rather than different. The need to wear a 'white mask', to conform and yet never be accepted as a full human being, must be shaken off. As social theorists have pointed out, Fanon equates oppression with non-recognition or misrecognition (Taylor, 1995, p. 255): a repressed community attains national status when it develops an internal, independent, voice. Like Chatterjee, Fanon sees the external colonial voice as a drag in the struggle for independence and prioritizes an internal, national, voice, which helps national communities to re-engage with the world, using their own, unique, vocabulary.

Other postcolonial writers appropriated this argument: for example, Bhabha (1990, 1994) borrows from Fanon's concerns to highlight a dichotomy in cultural self-narration between pedagogy and performativity. Initially, he is concerned with the emergence of culture 'within the nation' (1994, p. 148), recognizing the performative character of national communities in the shift from externality to interiority. The pedagogical character of national narrative is the locus of instruction, as it addresses the cultural community, making collective imagining possible. Contrariwise, the performative consolidates the nation's relationship with humanity (Fuss, 1994). Bhabha's dichotomies suggest the impossibility of viewing the nation as a uniform symbolic force, because 'neither centers, borders, cultural products, nor language can fix national identity' (Bennett, 2000, p. 183). Bhabha's post-structuralist analysis moves away from the problematic of the nation as such and toward 'an articulation of cultural difference in the construction of an *inter*national perspective' (Bhabha, 1990b, p. 5.). Bhabha's argument coincides with Gilroy's (1987) who claims that cultural difference emerges as resistance to hegemonic modes of representation. Gilroy examines cultural difference in the context of dialogical role-making, of fostering an intersubjective engagement of black performance and other-observation. For Gilroy, black culture's own voice offers an alternative to dominant cultural practices. Because the voice of difference comes from within, it generates the predicament of collective self-narration: others are an inescapable condition of collective self-recognition, and they cannot be ignored, as public (self-)presentation needs an audience to be meaningful.

The suggestion that the 'I-for-myself' exists in public only as an 'I-for-others' (Bakhtin, 1990, p. 32) is not discipline-bounded, as Herzfeld's work shows. Herzfeld (1997b, 2005) is skeptical of Anderson and Gellner's understandings of nationalism, because they are inextricably related to the consolidation of elite power. For them national identity is fostered from above and national subjects are indoctrinated to accept it as their ultimate value. Herzfeld pioneers the term *cultural intimacy* to describe the recognition of those aspects of a cultural identity that 'are considered a source of external embarrassment but nevertheless provide insiders with their assurance of common sociality, the familiarity with the bases of power that may at one moment assure the disenfranchised a degree of creative irreverence and at the next moment reinforce the effectiveness of intimidation' (2005, p. 3). He avoids the division of nation into elites (nation-makers) and the rest (passive subjects), explaining that the selfsame need to exclude from intimate understandings occurs both at the level of locality and that of the national center. National stereotyping does not exist independently from local self-stereotyping that may be constitutive of global power relations but can still be creatively mobilized in narratives of identity. The nation reifies itself in discourses of traditionalism in intercultural encounters – the Greeks smash plates to entertain foreigners and bargain for goods in an 'Oriental fashion' to assert their cultural difference – only to 'project familiar social experience unto unknown and potentially threatening contexts' (Herzfeld, 1997b, p. 7). This operates as a 'simulacrum of sociality' (Baudrillard, 1988), projecting outwards an image of intimacy that leaves the core of culture intact. Herzfeld uses 'cultural intimacy' to connect the poetics of everyday interaction with 'the grand dramas of official pomp and historiography in order to break down the illusions of scale' (Herzfeld, 2005, p. 25). It is not difficult to see how Herzfeld's militant middle ground ('between the twin denials of social experience – the extremes of positivism and deconstructionism' [*ibid.*]) may modify a critical social theory that tends to focus on macro-social experience.

It is important to clarify if Herzfeld's cultural intimacy would presuppose the *a-priori* existence of a fixed collective identity under attack by external forces, a defensive argument we encounter in all forms of nationalist discourse. In his earlier work, Herzfeld (1985) already does not separate the tendency to project the desire of others from our own desire to be represented in intelligible ways. A non-relational role of desire would presuppose a clear-cut demarcation of public and private spheres, of performance (what he calls 'social poetics') and the space of embarrassment (that of intimacy). His 'social poetics' corresponds to the Goffmanesque idea of 'self-presentation' (Goffman, 1987), a dramaturgical projection of a coherent self in society. Herzfeld's transition from Goffman's idea of public self-formation, to that of collective self-narration as cultural intimacy begs a number of interesting questions: is there or is there not something behind the scenes, in the 'backstage' of collective performance? How many backstages should we count, given that even internal audiences are culturally fragmented? Could multiple backstages operate as frontstages *within* the national sphere? Is there a single national frontstage, or we should talk about multiple ones, depending on the audience to which the nation addresses itself?

National performance for others is imagined as collective action, because national membership is mediated through imagination. Its cognitive nature has a dialogical mode, because it enables communicative action at its best, transforming 'imagined' communities into real-time nations. Dialogical performance is seen here as nation-building *in practice*, which encourages national agency in the face of adversity and the threat of fragmentation. In reality, imagined communities are akin to Bakhtin's 'conversational communities': they address themselves to internal and external 'others', imagined or real, and through the act of utterance they come into being. As Bakhtin argues, 'to be means to communicate dialogically', because 'a single voice ends nothing and resolves nothing. Two voices is the minimum for [...] existence' (Bakhtin, 1984, pp. 252–3). An integral ideological position requires collective interlocutors who assist in the production of identity (Sampson, 1993; Taylor, 1995, p. 231). Nations only recognize themselves as coherent entities though their significant others: colonizers, patrons and other nations. I borrow the term 'significant others' with caution from Taylor's investigations into the politics of recognition to describe those collective interlocutors that play a crucial part in the formation of identity (Taylor, 1989, p. 38). The achievement of self-recognition through constant performance for others grants imagined-conversational communities with an agency in the world. Identity is realized when the community acquires this agency.

National agency has a Janus-like nature. As Delanty and O'Mahony (2002, pp. 50–3) have explained, agency cuts through the Habermasian lifeworld (the domain of social consensus) and system (the domain of centralized, rationalized power) (Habermas, 1989b, pp. 118–19), enabling both interpretive achievement by independent actors and political mobilization by the national core. This observation suggests that democratic and institutional domains do not comprise watertight compartments – the public sphere is always open to institutional manipulation (Habermas, 1991). The communication of lifeworld with system bears the potential to explain the historical transformation of European nation-building from a mutinous force of modernity to the paragon of substructural stability in the European world-system. The irony of resistance from within: the resentful nationalisms of the weak were destined to become essential cogwheels in that oppressive supranational apparatus they set out to supersede.

My combination of Habermas' hermeneutics with Bakhtin's dialogics should not come as a surprise. Broadly speaking, both thinkers assess the dynamics of modernity through the interplay of agency and structure; both view the modern subject as a historical being produced through social interaction. Their key concepts of dialogism and communicative action 'argue implicitly that the expansion of modern lifeworld solidarities can occur through the mixing of cultures and of differing moral intuitions' (Nielsen, 1995, p. 805). Their profoundly humanist worldviews almost converge upon the defense of a 'radical tolerance' of the other, a precondition for the actualization of a functional 'public sphere' (Bell and Gardiner, 1998, pp. 6–7). Bakhtin's coupling of aesthetics with ethics both holds the key for broadening the Habermasian horizons of rational action (Trey, 1992) and allows us to situate rational action in historical discourse. This is not a banal intimation: the limitations of this study remind us that the aesthetic and ethical forms of historical discourse cannot be separated. Most of the historical actors of this book are long gone; all they have left behind is a pile of texts to communicate their aspirations, desires and actions. Although I am confronted with voices that can only be rescued through their textual traces, the traces themselves bear witness to the drama of history (Smith, 1998, p. 64). I am trapped into the role of a Habermasian 'historian' (Habermas, 1989a, pp. 226–7) who strives to resuscitate those traditions that marked European national destinies, aware that it is impossible to capture them in their entirety. And yet, in the final chapter of this book I use what I salvaged from various archives to reflect on the future of Europe.

The nation's in-built dialogic mechanism allows space for the coexistence and interchange of hegemonization, resistance and reciprocity. My understanding of hegemony transcends the Gramscian thesis that gestures towards the non-violent securing and maintenance of political control by a social group. I align myself with Laclau and Mouffe (1985), who view hegemony as a process through which a dominant ideology institutionalizes itself. What defines a society is its 'kernel', is always missing. What 'fills up' this gap and holds together a society is the act of constant self-definition. Yet, all identities fail to constitute themselves without a constant reference to the 'other', which, in its turn, is never totally internal to itself. But if collective self-narration is always overdetermined by external others, we should not assume that anything is internalized without modification (Bleicher, 1980, pp. 225, 228). Here I share Herzfeld's (1997b, 2005), and Gallant's (2002) concern that a polarization between hegemony and resistance may conceal the political and moral ambiguities of intercultural encounters. I also acknowledge Mackenzie's (1993) critique of Said, which points out that counter-hegemonic narratives may emerge from the utilization of elements of master discourses. Cultural encounters may produce friction, especially when they are based on structural inequalities, but they always involve a form of interaction that leaves lasting marks on both sides. We need our significant others to survive as social beings; waging symbolic and actual wars against them when they reject us betrays how much they continue to matter for us. Misrecognitions, however unjust, hurtful and precarious in their consequences *practically* operate as forms of (self)recognition (Taylor, 1995). To communicate this ambiguity, I introduce in my analysis the idea of reciprocity.

My understanding of reciprocity should not be confused with altruistic acts of giving. Giving and accepting creates enduring bonds of love, gratitude and obligation in various combinations. Reciprocity is not free of purpose: giving, taking and demanding can be vital for both the production and destruction of hierarchies. Whether we choose or are chosen by our significant others, the relationship itself (be)comes ridden with the expectation of respect as well as strategies for gaining this respect.

Reciprocity *is* recognition encompassing self-interest and selflessness, calculation and moral obligation (Mauss, 1954). Reciprocity is part of a more generalized reproductive mechanism allowing social regeneration over time (Weiner, 1980). Relationships are consolidated only after mutual acknowledgement that what circulates between givers and receivers is equal. Imbalanced symbolic exchange violates the unwritten rules of recognition, as one party always ends up being 'in surplus' whereas the other stays 'in debt' (Barth, 1981; Bell, 1991).

Reciprocal and redistributive exchange relations are continuous rather than separate in societies characterized by social differentiation. Whereas reciprocity regulates exchange between parties with different interests, redistribution is applied to the collective as a whole since it is regulated by a central authority (Sahlins, 1972). Redistribution as a politicized form of giving ensures social bonding because it secures recognition in a polity. As Honneth explains, 'only social relations that require an attitude of mutual recognition contribute to the development of a positive self-relation' (Fraser and Honneth, 2003, p. 142; Honneth, 2001; Yar, 2001). Recognition is a necessary precondition for the maintenance of self-worth (Kojève, 1969; Taylor, 1994). The dialogical self is created through an ongoing exchange between real or imagined interlocutors rather than within them (Bakhtin, 1986, p. 106): 'recast as the multiplicity of inner voices or "microdialogues", the dialogical self knows itself through the responses of real, imagined, historical and generalized others' (de Peuter, 1998, p. 39). Not only does the withdrawal of recognition produce damaged cultural selfhoods, it may also lead to an uncontrolled unleashing of frustration and bitterness in the social domain.

In a European *Raum* governed by redistributive inequalities, inter-state social stability was permanently under threat. The rebellious climate that political injustice generated with the division of the continent into worthy and unworthy 'relatives' was further enforced by a monological view of the world that supported the centralization of power (Tilly, 1993). Herein lies the absurdity of nineteenth-century discourse of Europeanness: although *de facto* it created and was supported by a polyphonic community of nations – the paragon of Romantic modernity that hailed the expression of cultural difference (Bakhtin, 1984, p. 7) – *de jure* it ended up scapegoating difference to preserve its very existence. European identity became the centripetal political force *par excellence* when nation-building began to develop into the fierce centrifugal force of modernity. Simultaneously, the production of single national cultures generated a brutal elimination of cultural difference: 'essentialized' national identities triumphantly resurfaced as monologic voices of domination. European nationhoods were destined to function as miniature replicas of Eurocentrism.

Greek nation-building displayed all the alarming signs of systemic integration in the nineteenth century. In search of political recognition, the Greek state strived to evade any association with its Ottoman predecessor or any mutinous political community within or outside Europe. At the same time, however, circumstantial affinities with such communities crept into political discourse, especially during times of crisis that invited interaction with European Powers. Even the slow institutionalization of culture began under the auspices of classical studies, a phenomenon that sealed the future of academic disciplines such as history and anthropology in Greece. National self-narration assumed an epic nature, serving what Bakhtin has called 'the future memory of a past' (Bakhtin, 1981, p. 19; Graham, 2000, p. 89), constructing a past on which the nation was supposed to build its future. In the international political arena, the Greeks mobilized antiquity as their exclusive 'social capital' (Renan, 1990 [1882], p. 12) to stand on a par with other European nations. The ancient European past became the national epic past, not simply as unremitting history projected from one point to another on a *telos* 'but also [as] a world of "beginnings" and "peak times" in the national history, a world of fathers and of founders of families, a world of "firsts" and "bests"' (Bakhtin, 1981, p. 13). Still, emerging polyphonies of Greek-ness allowed space for other traditions to affect national self-narration, constructing a unique picture of Greek cosmology and painting it in indigenous colors.

Organization of the book

The book is divided into three parts, each corresponding to one important facet of nation-building: state-formation, the parallel development of informal (peasant) performances for significant others with the academic institution of culture, and political self-presentation in international politics. Part I explores the role of dialogic engagements in the formation of a rational administrative apparatus at the heart of the national-as-political entity. It suggests that, although the 'state' and the 'nation' are not identical categories, the dialogical process of state-formation *both* reflects *and* reworks the idea of an imagined-conversational community.

Chapter 2 examines how conceptions of 'law', 'order', 'modernity' and 'civilization' are constructed, mobilized and contested in the political encounter between the nation-in-formation and its external others. The case of Greece exemplifies this dynamic, as it has been associated with the very origins of Western civilization itself. Thereafter, the chapter focuses on the uses of 'crime' and internal disorder in colonial discourse that counter claims to nationhood – a discourse in which conceptions of 'civilization' and 'barbarism', the 'Occident' and the 'Orient' figure centrally. This process is illustrated through British discursive associations of Greece with notable instances of anti-colonial, social and irredentist movements, such as the Irish Fenianism and the Indian Mutiny, and the Greek response, which simultaneously contested and endorsed these associations. Chapter 3 concludes Part I by exploring how accusations of 'disorder' and 'barbarity' are dialogically refuted, and claims for the nation's legitimate 'right' to recognition are asserted in the national sphere. These issues will be explored through the key role of Turkish, Albanian and Vlach others in Greek self-narration for internal (Greek) and external (British, 'European') audiences – three cases that still occupy a significant place in Greek nationalist discourse today.

Part II examines the intersecting trajectories of history, anthropology and folklore, and their crucial role in the rationalization of colonial and national pasts of Europe. Moving from the hermeneutic potential anthropological encounters unleashed in peasant societies (often considered as the origins of imagined-conversational communities) to the institution of academic disciplines, it locates the dialogic development of national culture in lifeworld patterns of reciprocity-as-recognition.

Chapter 4 examines how conceptions of historical origins and legacies are mobilized to narrate the unity of the would-be nation. This process introduces us to the role played by 'ethnographic' depictions of the 'People' in the construction of the present on the basis of perceptions of the past. The case of nineteenth-century ethnographic encounters is especially significant, as it represents the very moment in which anthropological categories were formed and cemented as an integral element of Western colonial and 'Orientalist' frames of understanding. *Contra* dominant approaches to nationalism (Gellner, Anderson) as the product of elite hegemony, the chapter explains that the 'nation' takes shape first in the resistance of the peasantry to foreign, proto-anthropological 'intrusion'. Before the institution of national knowledge, self-narration developed in formal and informal interactions of foreigners with peasants, whose reactions displayed the selfsame reciprocal ambivalence that governed Greek nation-building in other contexts. It is in the rationale of peasant resistance to (crypto)colonialism-as-anthropology that theorists of nationalism should trace the very emergence of a modern discipline that studies the nation in relation to its others. The chapter suggests that Herzfeld's analysis of 'cultural intimacy' should be considered as the origins of modern anthropological intimacy.

Chapter 5 develops further the preceding chapter, examining how pre-academic practices of research, classification and exhibition of 'criminal Others' construct and narrate the national character. These practices are dominated by Romantic conceptions of cultural essence but haunted at the same time by Enlightenment understandings of anthropology as a process of objectification and de-humanization of the subject studied. The case of Greek brigands is an excellent example: not only did it play a central role in understandings of the modern Greek folk character, it also enabled European observers and 'proto-anthropologists' of Greece to renarrate the English and Scottish past through the lens of crime.

The last part of the book examines how national identity is produced in international politics and activated in domestic contexts through resentful discourses. It looks into British and Greek narratives of Greek identity embodied in the concept of the 'Great Idea', an irredentist plan that, on a discursive level, represented the modern Greeks as the intellectual beacon of humanity. Chapter 6 explores how the ideas and ideals of the 'nation' are engineered through an inter-cultural dialogue in which strategies of national self-presentation are mobilized to establish a set of legitimate rights and obligations that demand reciprocation on the part of significant others. At the core of the contextual analysis there lies a question: by whom were the Greeks 'chosen' to perform the role of the civilizer in Europe? The chapter explains why Greeks restructured their 'nation' as elected simultaneously by God and European philhellenes, and analyzes the politics and metaphysics of the shift from notions of mutual recognition to those of one-sided 'debt'.

Chapter 7 concludes the analysis by exploring how rhetorical tropes of 'family', duty, debt and responsibility are mobilized in attempts to win recognition of the 'idea(l)' of nationhood. It shows how conflations of familial and clinical tropes appeared to suggest Greek subordination to European patronage. Simultaneously, it explores how Greek responses to external significant others combined mockery and imitation of the rhetoric of protection. The *carnivalesque* of Greek identity was not achieved by an outright rejection of the rhetorical uses of kinship and family but through their creative implementation in the domestic arena to codify the political integration of the nation. Central to this codification was the clarification of the national subject's rights and duties in the Greek national community.

The final chapter puts in perspective the political, disciplinary and ideological dimensions of the analysis through a critical synthesis that furnishes a coherent dialogic theorization of nation-formation. The main aim is to address the subtitle of the study, which examines the possibility of re-visioning identity in Europe. It questions whether struggles for the preservation of European identity can be coupled with theoretical endeavors concerning post-national, cosmopolitan forms of belonging. The endurance of national forms of identity and their continuing dialogical relation to significant others (rather than any European 'system') may hold the secret of post-national cohesion.

Part I
Crime and Disorder

2
Brigands, Nationalists and Colonial Discourse

State-formation, crime and the pursuit modernity

The debate concerning the role political centers, especially nation-states, played in the formation of identities, is as old as the study of nationalism. It is argued that no national culture pre-existed the centralization of power and the political organization of social life into a coherent whole. In its most extreme form, the debate exhibits a strictly Althusserian resonance (Althusser, 1994, pp. 106–7 and pp. 123–32; Poulantzas, 1973, 1978), presenting the state as an impersonal force that exercises control over national subjects (for a critique see Herzfeld, 1997b and 2005). Gellner's (1983) and Anderson's (1991) intertwining of industrialization, secularization and capitalism with the rise of nationalism and the production of national cultures by a political center are two variants of this debate. Their theses present central power as pivotal in nation-building, suggesting an identification of state, national agency and modernity in different combinations.

This theoretical move often results in a conflation of process with condition: modernity is an analytical tool, a product of the sociological imagination that encapsulates procession changes that come under the umbrella of modernization. The political nationalization of cultures by the state and nationalism as state ideology might have partaken in these changes, but do not define modernity unilaterally. We must not forget that modernity is envisaged, produced experientially, when historical subjects and collective agents engage in explanatory understandings (*erklärendes Verstehen*) of their condition (Weber, 1978a, p. 11, 1978b, pp. 18–25). It is equally important to ask why modernity is not immediately observed but is often discussed *in abstracto*. Because

23

abstraction obscures the complexity of process and allows for political maneuver, historically it has worked as both an accessory to power and its most potent enemy. In fact, problematic interpretations of 'modernity' as process, alongside its conflation with state-formation, plague modern Greek historiography. With few exceptions (see Gallant, 2002), from Clogg (1992, 2002) to Koliopoulos and Veremis (2002), the narrative of modern Greece is filtered through the evolution of the nation-state and politics 'from above'. These two otherwise praiseworthy books consider Greek 'modernity' almost exclusively in terms of foreign policy-making and 'westernization', mechanically reproducing an abstraction that erases discursive ambiguities: from the Kapodistrian era to the post-1974 political restoration, fusions of western, native and other ideas are viewed as a form of 'compromise' (Koliopoulos and Veremis, 2002, p. 3) rather than *a* dialogic facet of *modernization*.

I will not cover the entirety of Greek history in this chapter. Suffice it to say that the nineteenth-century experience of modernity and its crystallization in European political discourse already encapsulates such theoretical-political vicissitudes, because the division of Europe into powerful and subordinate regions endorsed, and was endorsed by the colonization of the rest of the world. Empires claimed moral superiority on the basis of their capacity to exercise control over other ethnicities and nations-to-be. More precisely, empires tended to translate their capacity to dominate into an ability to 'civilize' others within and without the European continent. As already explained, this attitude bears the stamp of a missionary nationalism, presenting imperial and national enterprises as mere facets of a state-driven, institutionalized 'civilizing process' that promotes ethnic homogenization or domination (Kumar, 2000b, pp. 578–9). We should view the nation-state as just a state form 'which exists within a complex of other nation states [...] a set of institutional forms of governance maintaining an administrative monopoly over a territory with demarcated boundaries, its rule being sanctioned by law and direct control over the means of internal and external violence' (Giddens, 1985, p. 121).

Reflections on the function of imperial and nation-state apparatuses do not belong to the realm of academic scholarship exclusively. The operators of nineteenth-century European nation-states and empires possessed tacit knowledge of their functional likeness: their mission was to maintain a political-territorial cohesion that would ensure their own preservation (Elias, 1996, pp. 324–5; Tilly, 1984, pp. 129–43). This cohesion was to be achieved at two interlocking levels: that of European 'civilization' (with whose standards all nations and empires had to abide) and that of national or imperial culture (which all subjects had to recognize as dominant). What comprised 'civilization' depended upon geopolitical contingencies: administrative competence, order, refined mannerisms, artistic and literary excellence or democratic principles defined the concept in various combinations in different periods. Although the European-Hellenic narrative served to combine these ideals, Western colonial powers prioritized the project of 'sound' governance. The idea of European modernity was a construct of enormous socio-cultural complexity; its systemic incorporation into state discourse is a tiny part of its story.

The moralization of discourses of governance however is always adaptable to understandings and needs of the subjects. This presents us with a new terrain on which to explore the history of sovereignty, not merely as an ontological ground of power but as an emergent form of authority based on interpretive perceptions of violence (Hansen and Stepputat, 2006). The European monologue of 'civilization' was filtered and interpreted through specific intercultural encounters. Gallant (2002) identified such civilizational processes in the Ionian Islands during British rule and explored them through conflicting understandings of order, violence, cleanliness and respectability. Mobilizing Elias' theoretical investigations into the sociogenesis of rationalization and psychogenesis of self-discipline, Gallant explained how Ionian Greek and British *habitus* were defined and redefined by rulers and their subjects through the experience of colonial governance. The association of Ionians with colonized 'races' by the British granted them an indeterminate status as both insiders and outsiders in European culture. In turn, Ionians expressed their own understandings of 'civilized' *habitus,* establishing with their mannerisms firm boundaries between proximity, visibility and intimacy (their private cultural sphere), and distance, invisibility and propriety (the imposed colonial 'order' of things). I maintain that similar conceptions of 'civilized' *habitus* informed European understandings of modern Greek identity more generally. Drawing on the repository of 'characters' that contributed to the production of imperial and national self-images, British and Greek discourses of national *habitus* actualized particular versions of European modernity. By 'national character' I mean the qualities and characteristics possessed by both the (reified) state and the dominant 'nation' that inhabits its territory (Elias, 1996, p. 2; Kuzmics, 2002; Pickel, 2004, p. 4). I also use the concept however to identify the dialogical merging of the two in European political discourses. Such discourses carried out a policing function in Greek-European encounters, assigning political positions and enforcing cultural boundaries (Foucault, 1980). The specificity and historical remoteness of this case is deceptive: ideas and ideals of national *habitus* inform practices of socio-cultural inclusion and exclusion in contemporary European political agendas.

The historical material of the chapter is drawn from British reflections on the Greek state's inability to suppress a particular type of crime within the Greek dominions. It was commonly held in Europe that anti-Ottoman irredentism drained financially the country and undermined internal improvement. One of the most frequent accusations leveled at Greek governments by the European protectors concerned their incapability to eliminate 'criminal' groups infesting mountainous and remote districts. This phenomenon constituted what Greeks called *listeía* or brigandage, something the British patrons of Greece in particular found unacceptable in a country claiming a European identity. Of course, things were easier said than done. The harrowing political experience of the post-Independence era made Greek brigandage a perfect form of what Gallant terms 'military entrepreneurship' (1999, p. 42) subsidized and supported by the state itself. The 'Bavarization' of the Greek administrative machine, which ignored the actual social problems of the Kingdom, and the European call for rapid modernization, acted as catalysts in the Greek body politic and the wider society of Greece. The failure to compensate the veterans of the War of Independence (Kallighas, 1987, pp. 152–4; Koliopoulos, 1988, pp. 218–19); the pending question of land distribution – especially to penniless Greek subjects that had fought for a free Greece (McGrew, 1985, pp. 9–11); the use of brigand bands to intimidate the electorate from the 1840s (Finlay, 1973, vol. II, p. 313); and their use as an irregular army against the Ottoman empire for the promotion of the 'Great Idea' (Stevens, 1989, p. 12); these were some of the underlying reasons for the transformation of the phenomenon into a social institution *officially* condemned by Europeans and the Greek state itself.

Who was to be blamed for this chaos? As in many other European cases (Dickie, 1993, 1999, pp. 26–51; Hobsbawm, 2000, p. 180), the role played by brigandage in the process of nation-building was controversial. On the one hand, after the institution of the Greek state, *listeía* kept alive the popular belief in the heroic spirit of *klephtism*, the only irregular form of resistance developed by Mediterranean and Balkan peoples against their rulers – whether these be Turks, Albanians, or indeed Greeks – during the ages of 'thralldom' (Damianakos, 1987, p. 78; Jenkins, 1998; Hobsbawm, 1959, 1972). The romanticization of the *klephti-listí* (for the two were inevitably confused in Greek traditions) was further reinforced by its incorporation into the logic of the 'Great Idea'. On the other hand, brigandage subverted the image of modern Greece as the heiress of ancient

Greek civilization – the unifying European signifier of order, harmony, democracy and intellectual rigor (Tziovas, 1985, p. 265). This split response to the socio-political phenomenon of *listeía*, made it stand in the national imagination both for a 'scourge' and a demonstration of Greek irredentist heroism, a dangerous disease and a praiseworthy aspect of the Greek rebellious 'character'. It needs noting that *listeía* and *klephtism* were not necessarily recognized by nineteenth-century folk as separate and distinct categories. When they were, they may have signified practices different from those we tend associate nowadays with these two concepts. As Herzfeld reminds us 'the state encapsulates, but cannot internally suppress, the social world of segmentary relations over which it rules' (1987, p. 162). We may therefore identify in brigandage/banditry a type of 'nationalist mobilization' (O'Mahony and Delanty, 2001, pp. 23–5) performed within the nation's *private* sphere. This mobilization was executed by the state through the manipulation of banditry/ brigandage, an essentially anti-statist type of revolt first directed against the Ottomans, and then against the Greek state itself. The Greek state's aim was to develop and maintain a viable identity project through a systematic rationalization of lifeworld narratives of belonging (Habermas, 1984), and the heroic *klephts* comprised a convenient unitary signifier in an otherwise polyphonic society.

Before examining nineteenth-century debates on state-sponsored brigandage, we must summarize Greek affairs after the institution of the Greek state. Greece depended economically upon its patrons, among whom Britain appeared to be the most dissatisfied with the course things had taken. Objectively, the Kingdom suffered from 'maladministration'. When King George assumed his duties in 1864, the state machine was in ruins. The corruption of the army had its roots in the Ministry of War itself. This slow-moving machine, whose inefficiency was exacerbated by incessant changes of government, could not take on the pursuit of brigands (Vitti, 1990, pp. 210–21). The Greek judicial system, influenced by external factors, was even more inefficient, with courts often releasing criminals because of their powerful backers (Kallighas, 1987, pp. 83–6). Agricultural work had been violently interrupted by brigand raids and foreign visitors observed in shock that across the country fertile valleys in remote, mountainous districts remained desolate. State records show that from April to August 1865, the government had put a price on the head of at least forty brigand chiefs and that in many cases it raised this three and four times, looking for informants in vain (*The Times*, 29 April 1870). Troops were sent to hunt bands, but all attempts proved fruitless: brigands continued to kidnap rich politicians and foreign travelers, smearing

Greece's image abroad. Of course, Greek public insecurity is not a unique phenomenon in the Mediterranean region; nor is it a phenomenon confined to the nineteenth century. In reality, the brigands' silent passage from the illegitimate to the legitimate camp (and vice versa) was a feature of European political life from the early modern years (Thompson, 1994). Historical research shows that the third quarter of the nineteenth century was rich in episodes of kidnapping in other European countries (Blinkhorn, 2000). Britain had its own domestic problems of disorder to consider that regular political contact with the Greeks brought to surface. While speculating on Greek domestic problems, British observers reconsidered all these sources of internal disorder that destabilized or questioned English authority in the British Empire.

It is small wonder that brigands figure in European history as *violence specialists* (Tilly, 2003, p. 35), types of 'political entrepreneurs' who work for legitimate power but can also operate outside it (*ibid.*, p. 233). This both stresses the economic and socio-political identity of banditry, and intertwines them: violence is a profession and an economic enterprise essential for the consolidation of the state. Weber (Gerth and Mills, 1948, pp. 78–9), and subsequently Elias (1982, vol. II, p. 237), saw the control of violence as a foundational principle for modern states. The monopolization of violence by states led to the 'depersonalization' of physical threat: the creation of legislative bodies, police and judicial authorities assisted in the consolidation of such monopolies, but never eliminated threats to the system. Tilly was echoing Weber when he noted how 'the precise boundary of legitimate force remains a matter of dispute in all political systems' (2003, p. 27). So, the state has to exercise violence in order to protect itself from those who threaten its monopoly: to kill, repress and behave like a 'gang'. The use of such contested means transcends the material expression of state power, since forms of physical violence can be substituted by invisible and less direct types of 'symbolic violence' (Bourdieu, 1977, p. 196). Power monopolies are not defended only through binary oppositions (civilized-uncivilized, legitimate-illegitimate) that proclaim the state as the champion of order and protection. The 'state' is present in all types of social 'nomination', institutionalizing social divisions through the ways in which we are collectively trained to think and act (Bourdieu, 1994).

Even contemporary uses of the universally palatable rhetoric of 'terrorism' in relation to kidnapping within and without Europe, present terrorism as a malicious ethnic enemy of state order, 'forgetting' thus that the state is responsible for the 'enemy's' existence. The invocation of terrorism in many cases may be contingent, serving interests of the moment. More often than not, however, it attributes a transnational dimension to violence that deserves attention. There is a significant connection between terrorism, which 'grew out of the failure of some national liberation movements to [...] achieve sufficient political potency' (Miller, 1980, p. 1; Tilly, 2003, p. 32), and kidnapping (Means, 1970; Bauman, 1973; Jenkins, 1974). Terrorism invites the creation of boundaries between legitimate and illegitimate camps (Greisman, 1977; Soulier, 1978, p. 30), pointing to the existence of 'ever-larger political units with an internal monopolization of the legitimate coercive force' (Hess, 2003, p. 351; Kössler, 2003) – only this time, crime is not recurring on a national, but a global scale, threatening simultaneously state and transnational political interests. Examining Greece's trapping into imperial monopolizations of power by other European states in the nineteenth century seems now more germane than ever.

An examination of crimes that blur the boundaries of legitimate and illegitimate violence uncovers links between modernization, the monopolization of violence by the state, identity-formation and the resonance of popular revolt in Europe. Hobsbawm (1959, 1972, 2000) recognized in banditry a symptom of transition from social formations regulated by kinship and tribalism to modern societies characterized by internal stratification and central power. Hobsbawm stressed that 'moderation in the use of violence', rational choice in stealing and kidnapping, have always been essential for the bandit image (2000, pp. 92–3). Although even Hobsbawm remained trapped in classical Marxist approaches, his recognition of banditry as a form of pre-capitalist rebellion within peasant societies presents the problem of authority as a problem of reciprocity. The Robin Hoods of Europe figured in popular legends as folk heroes who redistributed to the poor from the rich. The power to give and take, traditionally related to the state, the social adjudicator, both consolidates and questions relationships of hierarchy, linking justice to reciprocity-as-recognition (Honneth, 1992, pp. 7–11). While the state legitimates socio-political hierarchies (Bourdieu, 1998, pp. 198–200), it also crystallizes a moral order: subjects recognize or rebel against central power, depending on the fairness of the center's redistributive practices (Sangiovanni, 2007). As Bakhtin explains, the oppressed draw upon symbolic resources when resisting codified forms of ideology; such resources may even originate in the domain of officialdom (Gardiner, 1992, p. 12; Herzfeld, 2005). The dynamic relationships between states and their subjects point to a mobile figuration of power, status and governance that remain interlocked in a network of political interdependency (Elias, 2006, pp. 180–2).

Take for example the pre-Independence bandits-*Klephts*: their non-recognition by the Greek state as contributors to national liberation, their non-remuneration, reinforced their resentment towards a political system that condemned them to poverty, thus transforming them into brigands-*listés*. Conflict within and with an unjust hegemonic order is the mark of negative reciprocities (Moore, 1978; Thompson, 1971). Social and political collaboration must be constantly reinforced and recreated under the auspices of a shared moral order (Moore, 1978, pp. 5–8; Weiner, 1992, p. 150). Developments within nation-states, such as Greece, were reflected on the global political plateau: titular and weak states were seeking recognition from powerful empires. European political interdependencies (Tilly, 1975) worked on these premises, with weak countries recognizing or rebelling against master empires, and master empires offering protection or chastising disordered states. Nineteenth-century European cosmology was based on the illusion of a Hellenic modernity. The pursuit of an elusive political order, a precondition for the function of European modernity, haunted the European core and its peripheries, reinforcing durable political inequalities between them. Such inequalities are reflected in the British and Greek political discourses presented in the following sections: on one hand, Greek brigandage (or even the Greek state itself as the supporter of such crime) was likened to Irish protest movements that destabilized or directly questioned imperial authority; on the other, it was related to defensive or emancipatory struggles of the imperial periphery (India, New Zealand), circumstantial revolts against European empires (the Abyssinian episode of the 1860s) and other cases of nation-building that followed de-colonization (Mexico). Coupling the 'rebels' of the European periphery with those of the imperial periphery sanctioned systemic violence within the continent and consolidated modern Greece's indeterminate status in the international political arena.

Greece and Ireland: irredentist violence and colonial discourse

Associations between lawlessness and the state had to be avoided at all costs in Greece during the nineteenth century, but were constantly encouraged in British observations. For the British, brigandage might have been presented to Europeans as a force that subverted state order, but in reality it has always been part of Greek nation-building *and* state-formation. The conflation of bureaucratic organization (according to imperial standards) with nation-building was plausible enough to suggest associations between Greece and Ireland. Irish social unrest and anti-British irredentism were likened to Greek brigandage, uncovering the ambiguous social identity of the crime in question.

The Greeks were aware of these associations' significance. Thus Sir Thomas Wyse, British Minster at Athens between 1849 and 1862, urged the Greek state in the 1850s 'to put all in order, and this law amongst others' (1871, p. 125). At the time, the Greek government was trying to make a 'show of order and security' for an 'Anglos' (*ibid.*, p. 124), who was none other than William Smith O'Brien, a representative of the nationalist organization 'Young Ireland' (Sloan, 2000). Wyse was convinced that O'Brien was treated with respect by the Greek government only because of his declared philhellenic sentiments and the threat of an imagined British derision, not because of his ethnic identity. Government officials struggled to present him with a country free of crime in order to ensure a congratulatory message to Athens that would then travel around Europe. Greek administrators perceived and acted out European 'order' as attention to forms, not content: a performance of security was enough for a passing 'Anglos'. For them Western civilization was a mere mode of public presentation; 'it was not about beliefs, character, and morality, but about decorum, appearance and conduct' (Gallant, 2002, p. 60). Europeans had to be kept at a safe distance from the 'dirty laundry' of the nation-state (Herzfeld, 1997a).

The political significance of Greek associations with Ireland would increase after the Dilessi (Marathon) Murders in 1870. We may consider the affair a 'nation-defining moment', a period of crisis that threatened the nation's sovereignty (Eley, 2000) as well as a European *cause célèbre*. The Dilessi Murders involved the kidnapping and murder of three high-ranking Englishmen and an Italian aristocrat by the Arvanitakis brigand band in a location near Athens. Ransom negotiations failed due to a lack of co-ordination between the Greek government and the British Minister at Athens, Edward Morris Erskine, and the story had a tragic conclusion with the murder of all the hostages (Jenkins, 1998, pp. 47–8, 61–4). One of the missing pieces of the puzzle was the identity of those who had encouraged the brigands to insist that they are granted an amnesty, an anti-constitutional action in Greece (Stevens, 1989, p. 4; *The Government Gazette*, 17 November 1864). From the outset, rumors circulated in London that 'the capture was part of a political movement for embarrassing and affecting a change in the government' (*The Morning Post*, 25 April 1870; *The Times*, 25 April 1870). Over the same days some Greek newspapers began an anti-government campaign, because the Zaimis cabinet had delayed convening the National Assembly for the election of a new government, which 'could solve the vexed question of brigandage' (*Palingenesía*, 16 April 1870). A ministerial crisis followed Zaimis' allusion that the kidnapping was organized by the Opposition (*Mellon*, 28 April 1870): Zaimis had tried to blame the murders on unspecified individuals, refusing to present brigandage as a permanent political malady.

Of course, Greek disorder was connected by external observers to brigandage long before the Dilessi Murders: initially it had more to do with the Greek state's failure to adhere to 'democratic principles' outlined by the new Greek constitution (1864) after King Otho's dethronement (Casson, 1943, pp. 106–7; *The Times*, 22 October 1864). British commentators saw in brigandage the last link in a chain of 'evils': it was the political mentality of the Greeks that had to change (*The Times*, 10 December 1864, 19 June 1866, 11 January 1868 and 19 February 1869). But in the post-Dilessi climate Greece was labeled an 'anarchic' country (*The Morning Post*, 2 May and 28 April 1870; *The Times*, 2 April and 13 May 1870; *The Daily News*, 18 May 1870) in which the '"Constitution" is the sport of contending factions, and statesmanship is identified with buccaneering' (*The Daily Telegraph*, 26 April 1870). By 1872 it would be suggested that Greek administrators' inability to defend their constitution and follow the British in extirpating brigandage had allowed the Kingdom to 'fall behind Turkey, Egypt, Romania and Serbia in the career of material progress' (*The Times*, 27 January 1872). The chronic problem of bureaucratic incompetence simply suggested that Greece was becoming progressively Oriental in its dispositions and should join the world of European colonies and protectorates. Simultaneously, its demotion to the category of 'Balkan' states resembles more recent political debates in the West about the 'Balkanization' of the country's politics, especially in the aftermath of the controversy over the name of Macedonia. This issue is examined in the following chapter at length.

The way the Irish Question was introduced in the discussion on the Dilessi Murders is significant. In many British parliamentary debates (*The Times*, 29 April and 21 May 1870. *The Daily News*, 16 May 1870; *The Daily Telegraph*, 4 June 1870) following the massacre the repeated use of the term *banditti* instead of brigands gave shape to a discourse. Although its root is the Italian verb *bandire*, meaning to exile or banish (Gallant, 1999, p. 26), its nineteenth-century English connotation was usually much more specific. 'Banditti' was the exotic label attached to

Ribbonmen, the early nineteenth-century secret societies that operated within the Irish rural context. These societies were proscribed mainly because they resisted the government's law, although their members were not proper rebels, since they probably had no conception of overthrowing the state. Their protest was for land redistribution in Ireland; their hatred aimed towards the British government; their interest in a 'national cause' was rather ill defined. *Ribbonism* and *Whiteboyism* had an ambiguous political program; they were spasmodic rural movements rather than a nationalist organization (Beames, 1983; Foster, 1988, pp. 14–16; Townshend, 1983, pp. 292–4). However, similarities in Greek and Irish rural social conditions and the criminalization of brigandage in Greece post-independence contributed to such comparisons (Gallant, 2002, pp. 43–4).

The origins of such associations date back at least to the 1860s when the Fenians, an Irish secret brotherhood with branches on the other side of the Atlantic, challenged the political stability at the core of the British Empire. Oriented to winning Ireland's independence by force, the Fenians revealed Irish-American nationalism in its full ambiguity. Fenianism was rooted more in the hard life of the Irish immigrants than in Irish Catholicism in Britain, which unambiguously became a form of Irish self-definition against the 'English oppressor'. Eventually the Fenians became the only organization in the history of the United States that attracted so much public attention. They had even invaded Canada in the 1860s for the purpose of using it as a stepping-stone for the invasion and liberation of Ireland. These developments were not welcome in Britain: in 1868 Gladstone had admitted privately that the existence of this secret 'society' had grave importance for questions of policy-making for Ireland (Boyce, 1988, pp. 19–20). In a contextual approach this organization emerges 'not as a manifestation of indefeasible nationality, but rather as the product of a range of political, social, economic and intellectual-sentimental factors, and of assorted contingencies of personality, time, place and interest' (Comerford, 1998). Fenianism was in fact attributed by historians to the rapid changes in the economic life of Britain in the mid-Victorian era, which made a deep impact on Ireland. The new railway networks, rapid industrialization, the subsequent increase of urban populations and the massive emigration of the Irish to England and North America transformed the social and cultural structures of the country.

Nevertheless, the equation of Greek brigandage with Irish Fenianism shows that the nationalist legend matters more than any accurate historical analysis and interpretation. This legend formed part of Irish and

English perceptions of Irish nationalism and has strongly suggested that Fenianism was only another manifestation of the 'phoenix flame' (Lyons, 1971, pp. 20–1), the awakened, or resurrected, Irish nationhood. Such romantic assumptions of innate Irish national consciousness (Townshend, 1983, pp. 26–8) existed in Greece over the same period and were propagated abroad. It was not only that the Greek nation was seen as an entity resurrected from the flames of the War of Independence, but also that the brigands-*listés* had irreparably been identified with Greek expansionism. Yet Greek brigandage was never an international organization (or an 'organization' at all). Yet British obserververations that saw in it a disturbance of 'Europe's peace' (*The Times*, 8 February 1868) provided the essential starting-point for comparisons with Fenianism. Finally, one should never forget the Fenians' involvement in the Irish Insurrection of 1867, which coincided with the Cretan Insurrection of 1866–69 to shake off the Ottoman rule and become part of Greece. The unsuccessful Fenian rising in 5 March 1867 which was regarded as the beginning of an Irish struggle for independence (Foster, 1988, pp. 390–5), helped British observers to maintain analogies with the 'nationalist' Greek brigands.

This is what the anonymous writer of *Some Notes on Turkey* (1867) informs us, when the Greek government of Koumoundouros negotiated with brigands to send them as irregular forces to assist the Cretans (*Aión*, 9 April 1870; *Cornhill Magazine*, June 1870, p. 702). To further worsen Greek-European relations, Koumoundouros made sure that the Cretan Question would be examined as part of the so-called 'Eastern Question', thus entangling the cause in wider European decision-making processes. Sending financial and military aid to the rebels, something Greek governments repeatedly did, provoked anger in both Britain and France because it was contrary to the spirit of the treaties signed to confirm Greek Independence (Daphnis, 1980, p. 287). 'Anonymous' notes that Greece belongs to the category of trouble-making countries that cannot have a regular army and support their so-called national interests with 'robbers who plunder mercilessly' in the same way that the 'Turks' do instead (Anon, 1867, pp. 29–30). Although the Fenians bear some similarities with the Greek brigands and their protectors, the Greek state, they do not 'represent the real opinions of the intelligent Irish people' and 'do not prove that Ireland is misgoverned' (*ibid.*, 45). Hence, the Greek state appears as a parasitic institution in Europe, *unlike* the British Empire that knows how to control its dominions.

Comparisons between Irish and Greeks were extended beyond political contingencies when they began to involve speculations on respective national characters and dispositions. When following the Dilessi Murders, Greek governmental actors made accusations against the Opposition in the Greek press, the *Pall Mall Gazette* observed the similarity between the state of affairs in Greece and that described by 'the late Daniel O'Connell [who] maintained that whenever an Irishman had to be roasted there was always another hand ready to turn the spit'. Internal Greek discord completes the picture 'the Greeks are unconsciously drawing of themselves. The more we know about them, the better our chance of successfully dealing with a state of things, which is a standing disgrace to Europe' (6 July 1870). O'Connell (1775–1847), commonly known as 'the Liberator', was the leader of Catholic emancipation in Ireland. More importantly, his contemporaries related him to the foundation of the revolutionary organization of Young Ireland. It is held that the movement grew out of his campaign to repeal the 1800 Irish Act of Union with Great Britain. O'Connell's struggle for Catholic emancipation helped him in 1829 to win the right for Catholics to sit in the United Kingdom parliament. Success of the repeal was assisted by the encouragement of constitutional agitation, and by O'Connell's ability to rally around the cause Irish peasants and urban working classes, something that inspired admiration even in pro-British continental liberals such as Mazzini. *The Gazette's* comments may betray a preoccupation with imperial problems, but they also bestow the relationship between Greek politicians and brigands with an organized character. O'Connell's relationship with Young Ireland, which acquired an organized character though Thomas Davis' (1814–45) transformation of O'Connell's utilitarian patriotic rhetoric into an coherent cultural nationalist program that defies constitutional imperatives (O'Mahony and Delanty, 2001, p. 82), suggested strong affinities between Greece and Ireland. Through the construction of homologies between Irish irredentist and Greek constitutional political maneuvers, both the Greeks and the Irish were presented as a nuisance to European stability.

Such British arguments provoked anger in Greece. Immediately after the Dilessi Murders the journalist Jean Lemoinne published a proGreek article in the French-speaking newspaper *Journal des Debats*, in which he attacked the bellicose members of the Gladstone government who wanted to restore British honor after Dilessi with an occupation of Greece. But his comments on the British inability to suppress Fenianist uprisings helped the Greeks to organize their counterblast. On the day Lemoinne published his article, the journalists of *Aión*, a Greek progovernment newspaper, were explaining that the Greek government is not the only one that 'cannot eliminate internal evils', pointing their finger to 'the situation in Ireland' as proof that powerful governments are not always in a position to solve domestic irregularities. 'It is true that there is no rural crime close to London', the journalist continued. 'But if the Fenians want, they can commit massacres even there. Tallaghill is not that far from Dublin, it is very likely that the gangs of Fenians are lurking somewhere in the suburbs of the big cities' (*Aión*, 27 April 1870). Some days later, the same Greek newspaper reported that the agency of *The Times* in London, as well as those of other newspapers, had to be guarded by police forces because the editors had received threatening letters from the Fenian brotherhood. In addition, eight counties in Ireland had to be declared in a state of siege after a series of murders (*Aión*, 30 April 1870). When in May, Woolwich dockyard had to be guarded too from the fear of new Fenian attempts to blow up the powder magazines close to it (*The Levant Herald*, 22 May 1870), the tone of the Greek commentators hardened. 'There are, in the bosom of the most moral, the most civilized and well-organized societies, social plagues, forming the accumulated heritage of history that science cannot heal' (*Aión*, 7 May and 25 May 1870). If the British Empire cannot cope with the 'plague' of chronic disorder, how can its administrators accuse the newly founded Greek state of a similar failure?

The language of morality found creative uses in John Gennadios' *Notes on the Recent Murders by Brigands in Greece* (1870), a pamphlet that became the apologia of the Greek nation during the Dilessi affair. Gennadios' parentage (his father was an eminent Greek scholar and his mother was from the famous Venizelos Athenian family) and foreign connections certainly assisted him in disseminating and popularizing his work. At the time of the crisis he was employed in the commercial enterprise of the Rhallis Brothers in London, but the publication of the notes forced his employers to dismiss him. Unofficially, nevertheless, Gennadios received financial help from his Greek boss after the publication of the *Notes*. Interestingly, the *Notes* were translated into Greek in 1871, something that suggests political connections with Athens and the Greek government at the time of the crisis. Gennadios' interference in the episode attracted the attention of the American ambassador at Athens, Charles Tuckerman, and it may not be coincidental that he was first proposed as a second secretary in the Greek embassy at the United States. In fact, Gennadios' successful diplomatic career after the Murders is often linked to his involvement in the Dilessi crisis (Tricha, 1991, pp. 17–20). Stressing that the British made different moral laws for the strong, like themselves, and the weak, like the Greeks,

Gennadios drew attention to 'England's' inability to consolidate order in an Ireland infested by Fenian crime (1870, p. 135). Gennadios might have seen in Irish disorder a characteristic of disorganized rural protest – undoubtedly providing a more accurate description of Irish popular movements than most of his contemporaries (O'Mahony and Delanty, 2001, p. 76) – but his version of 'England' was stripped of its veneer of *civilité*: the ability of British administrators to govern Ireland is questioned. The way Gennadios associated the Dilessi episode with contemporary British anxieties is illustrated in his attempt to transform British arguments concerning Greek 'constitutional anarchy' into a boomerang. When the British government attacked Zaimis for refusing amnesty to the brigands on constitutional grounds, he observed that:

> An analogous case would have been, if a body of Fenians had carried off to the mountains of Kerry a couple of Americans, and, as the conditions of their release, demanded an amnesty in favor of themselves, and other Fenians in prison – say, Rossa – both for past crimes and for that offence. Would Englishmen grant it, and how would they answer any remonstrances [*sic.*] of the American government, urging such a course? But we forget the bitter truth and there is one law for the strong and another for the weak! (1870, p. 33)

Gennadios further introduces the question of Anglo-American tensions into the picture and transforms British disorder into a potentially global crisis. Some non-metropolitan newspapers defended an argument similar to Gennadios' (*The Scotsman*, 24 May 1870), explaining that an analogous episode in Britain and a demand from another country for unconstitutional action would have presented the British government with a dilemma. The London press, however, chose to react to Lemoinne's comments which introduced the subject of Irish disorder in the Dilessi debate – a reaction that had less to do with his pro-Greek views and everything to do with the fact that he was French (*The Daily News*, 28 April 1870; *The Morning Post*, 29 April 1870). A slur on British imperial honor would not go unanswered: Greek brigands were nothing other than 'Fenians after the continental fashion' and false patriots.

> A man can be a rebel without being a brigand [...] spasmodic and nomadic patriotism has this in common with brigandage – that its beginning is lawless and its end is the subversion of the law [...]
> The makers of little rebellions [...] would do well to take this lesson to heart; and we can only hope that, even as war steamers

have proved adequate to extirpate piracy, and railway locomotives have scattered brigands wherever they have come across them, as the opening-up and development of the moral high roads of civilization of education of progress, of constitutional government, of a freer press, and of justice, may ere long teach 'student cliques' and patriotic associations 'limited', that about the very worst way of helping their country is to break its laws and disturb it [*sic.*] peaceable inhabitants (*The Daily Telegraph*, 4 June 1870).

The account of the virtues of Western civilization given in this passage (education, progress, constitution, technology), place the British in a privileged, civilized position; the division of 'we' versus the 'others', provides reassurance. Again, 'uncivilized' movements, such as the Irish and the Greek, are pictured as backward, even 'rural', phenomena. Simultaneously, the journalist expresses a fear that Greek brigandage is confused with 'nationalist movements'. The journalist's refusal of this identification leads him to draw distinctions between patriotism and outlawry – *klephtism* and *listeía* by extension. The more brigandage appears to be a stigma on 'civilization', primitive 'lawlessness', the more it is disconnected from serious national aspirations, the better the British government's decision on the fate of Greece is legitimized. The chain effect works perfectly – for, if Greek brigands are opportunist rogues and not patriots, so it is for the Fenians.

Contrariwise, the Greek discourse of resistance modified Ireland's subjected status in the Empire. For example, a pamphlet written by Colonel Panos Koronaios displayed this ambiguity in an aggressive way. Koronaios had been appointed in 1869 to suppress brigandage in Acarnania. The report on his efforts was published in the same year as *Reflections on the Establishment of Order*, and foretold the allusions he made to the political extensions of brigandage in 1870 (Koliopoulos, 1987, pp. 176–7). His argument suggested that British interference in Greek domestic affairs was responsible for internal Greek disorder, because it held back the political regeneration of the Greek Kingdom. England had the right to deprive Greece of her freedom as much as France and Russia had the right to interfere in the 'civil conflict between England and Ireland'. For Koronaios, the colonizers of Ireland and their native supporters would never recognize that violence is exercised in the country under the power of a 'minority' of the same 'racial family', unlike the Greeks, who are ready to admit their mistakes and work towards internal reconciliation and progress (*Independence Greque*, 23 May 1870; Koronaios, 1870, p. 29). Thus, the Anglo-Irish conflict is a form of civil conflict for Kornonaios. Not only does the 'family' trope he uses present Irish identity as an essential component for British self-narration, but it also re-admits Irishness into Europe.

Who and what were the Greeks and the Irish then – were they nationalist terrorists or misunderstood patriots? The discursive games of the Greeks and the British show how brigandage and Fenianism worked as sychdoches for Greek and Irish identities. The fact that Greek *listeía* became a problem only post-independence suggests that the British discourse on Greek disorder is a discourse on modern Greek identity – and, through substitution, or slippage, on Irish identity. The discourse was part of the long-standing British colonial tradition. We are informed in the 1933 edition of *The Oxford English Dictionary* that associations of Ireland, Greece and disorder appeared at the beginning of the nineteenth century in British sources. The 'unruly districts' of Ireland were often termed 'Grecian' – a vague reference to Hellenic antiquity that is worth bearing in mind. *The Standard* (3 September 1872) argued that the term 'Greek' was 'colonial slang for the Irish' (*OED*, vol. IV, 1933, p. 395). The Greeks could see in the Irish cause something of their own. The auxiliary role brigandage and Fenianism, and the obtrusive role England played in this cause were incontestable. Greek brigandage and political disorder were read against the role the 'unruly' Irish played in the British Empire: that of an 'internalized other' (Mackenzie, 1995, p. 12), so essential for British imperial self-definition.

The notion of internalized otherness mirrors the role of Irish and Greek identities in the geopolitical map of Europe. Greece's peripherality in Europe, something further endorsed by European fears that the Greeks would never become the worthy descendants of Hellenic antiquity, constructed a narrative of irrevocable fall and degeneration (Herzfeld, 1995, p. 219). Modern Greece was, like other Balkan countries, irrational, backward and contaminated by Oriental-Ottoman vices (Todorova, 1997) – a trope that survived over the centuries and still dominates global political discourse (Herzfeld, 2005, p. 127; Tzanelli, 2004). The British verdict that Greek brigandage and irredentism 'disturbed' Europe is suggestive: modern Greece could not be considered a *fully* European country. It was not coincidental that Ireland, another peripheral country, featured in the same debate. There existed a long tradition depicting Irish identity as non-European, 'black' (Curtis, 1971; Ignatief, 1995). Racial studies have shown that the idea of 'race' and racial oppression can only be explained in terms of a substantive, 'operative element', since 'the distinction between racial and national oppression turns on the composition of the group that represents the ruling elite' (Allen, 1994, vol. I, pp. 28, 35–6). It is common practice for the 'oppressor' to recruit part of the dominant elements of subjected native populations and incorporate them into the ruling apparatus. Most often, this ends with an integration of the recruited into the recruiting element, whereas the rest of the oppressed population remains a different 'race'. In this light, 'color' is a sociogenic rather than a physical category. This idea is supported by the fact that when color differences are absent, the dominant group justifies its authority over peoples or communities by stressing instead their 'uncivilized behavior' (*ibid.*, pp. 31–4). Although the revolutionary Irish (as opposed to their Protestant colonial elites) were not represented as 'black' when compared to the Greeks, they were labeled 'uncivilized' and were likened to a half-Oriental, half-European nation: the modern Greeks (Herzfeld, 1987; Peckham, 2001; Todorova, 1997). The British had managed to kill two birds with the same stone: by talking about Greece, they expressed their concern about the dangerous, semi-European Irish *habitus*. The importance of 'coloring' the discourse on Greek and Irish disorder was great, because both the Greeks and the Irish were white *and* Christian (Gallant, 2002, pp. 16–17, 35–45), but the rationale and the subtleties of this maneuver became more obvious when the Anglo-Greek dialogue placed Greek brigandage outside the safe continental margins and into the blurry extra-European span of vision, in Asia and Africa.

Beyond the pale of 'Europe'

The vast space of colonial dominions included less familiar types of *habitus* that had to be understood and conquered symbolically. Categorization informs knowledge, and knowledge supports administrative control in a monologic imperial universe. Again, both brigands and the Greek state fell into the discursive cracks of Europe: we are informed by the 'Anonymous' of *Some Notes* that the Cretan brigand rebels are loutish 'savages' who aim to destroy everything on which an ordered Europe built its reputation as civilizer of the world. The governors of Europe can only be experienced administrators who will restore the political stability of Crete. The island is therefore in need of an economic and material infrastructure, for 'without roads it is difficult to bring [the brigands] under subjection, as it was difficult to reduce the 700 New Zealanders who made head for years against a force of several thousand British troops' (Anon., 1867, p. 44).

New Zealand had been a British colony since the signing of the treaty of Waitangi in 1840. The misinterpretation of the wording of the treaty by both sides led to conflict between the British rulers and the Maoris, who were not disposed to submit to British rule. The anonymous author of the *Notes* refers to the bloody New Zealand Wars that erupted in the 1840s and continued down through the 1860s. The British experience of initial defeat in New Zealand was so shocking that it led to fabrication of evidence and the generation of a British historical mythology on the New Zealand Wars. Both colonial administrators and modern scholars repeatedly attributed British defeat to the Maoris' 'natural advantages', such as their guerrilla tactics, and the geographical inaccessibility of the country (Belich, 1986, pp. 315–16). The British, who always equated racial superiority with military superiority, ignored or suppressed records on the military skills of the Maoris, who based their attacks on their own, centuries-long, tradition of warfare (*ibid.*, pp. 322–3). British defeat had to be written out of history, because it damaged the British colonial prestige. It is easier for Anonymous to attribute the victories of the Maoris and the Cretans to natural advantages and morphological knowledge of the region than to acknowledge their military skills. At the same time, the absence of technology in Crete and New Zealand (roads) is used to represent both the Maoris and the Cretans as the opposing mate of civilization: savagery.

Organized forms of governing, Western technologies of power, fail in non-European environments then. The Cretan rebels can only be defeated if operations are conducted on European terms. Like rebellious 'races' such as the New Zealanders, the Cretan brigands have a mysterious intuitive knowledge that must be discovered and defeated. When in 1869 the European Powers brought the Cretan Insurrection to a closure, *The Morning Post* observed that 'in war scientific skill is vastly more reliable than haphazard and dash', because it confirms 'the wisdom of the strategy employed in Abyssinia' as much as 'it suggests ideas for the subjection of the Maoris in New Zealand. And [British skills] will, it is to be hoped, help to convince the Sultan and his advisers that in every department of life and government the forms and usages of high civilization are the most economical and effective' (5 January 1869). Nomenclature becomes thus a prerequisite for the implementation of theory on the observed and classified subject. Affirmative action in British colonial discourse involved a call for the restoration of a lost order on subordinate peoples, even at gunpoint. Napier's expedition to Abyssinia in 1868, cited by *The Post*, provided a potential model of British occupation of Greece post-Dilessi. The decision in 1864 of King Theodore, an ex-brigand who had named himself King of the Abyssinians, to detain representatives of the British government in Magdala as hostages was seen by Britain as a serious offence, a disgrace that had to be avenged (Moorehead, 1970). The Liberals tried to avoid a conflict, but British public opinion eventually forced the Conservatives, later in office, to organize an expedition for the restoration of British honor.

Following the Dilessi Murders, the Greek brigands and their relationship with the Greek state were frequently likened to King Theodore's regime in Abyssinia (*The Times*, 26 April 1870; *Daily Telegraph*, 27 April 1870). The impression that the Greek state was the product *and* the perpetrator of anarchy was prominent. The invocation of the Abyssinian expedition intimated that Greece should not be regarded as a European state. The Abyssinian case was compared both to the Irish and the Cretan Question: at least this was suggested by 'Omicron', a *Times* reader rumored to be the politician Sir George Campbell. In 1868 'Omicron' labeled the 14 Cretan generals and leaders of the Insurrection 'savage brigands', provoking the nationalist newspaper *Clió* to remind him that although 'the Cretan Generals have not studied in the great military schools of Europe [are not] rich [...] [and do not] have the genius of Sir Robert Napier [...] who conquered Magdala without losing a soldier [...] they are fighting without soldiers, and still beat the Turks' (*Clió*, 20 September 1870). The *Clió* journalist acknowledged British organization and skills, but he regarded Greek patriotism superior – a nice subversion of the British civilizing narrative that claimed exclusivity over patriotism.

Mexico, a relatively new nation, was also used for comparisons with Greece. Mexico had undergone a Revolution (1810–21) to overthrow Spanish rule and a devastating war in principle related to the constitution of 1857, but in practice connected to a changing balance of power and the emergence of new socio-political forces within the racially, culturally and linguistically fragmented country. Independence brought only a succession of *pronunciamientos* or attempted *coups d'état* on the part of factions eager to acquire power. Pillage, highway robbery, and brigand raids became a mode of expected and accepted behavior (Tannenbaum, 1966, pp. 61–3, 74–83). The immediate Mexican experience reminded the British of the Greek War of Independence, the succession of constitutional changes following liberation and the general political instability of the Greek Kingdom. For example, for the *Times* correspondent and philhellene, George Finlay, Mexico and Greece never possessed the 'inherent strength to deliver themselves from such evils' as 'disorder' (*The Times*, 20 October 1866). Both Greece and Mexico were afflicted by 'chronic brigandage': the Mexican War of Independence destroyed the

Spanish road-system, 'the remedy for organized robbery', and left the country in 'a state of disintegration' (*The Daily Telegraph*, 5 June 1870; *The Pall Mall Gazette*, 16 May 1870). The comment became suggestive when it was linked to Sir Edward Watkins' proposal for the construction of a railway and road system in Greece. Watkins (1819–1901) was a visionary entrepreneur who dreamt of establishing a great rail network linking his own Great Central Railway to Europe via a Channel Tunnel terminating at Marylebone Station. He had already contributed financially to the construction of the first rail line in Greece in 1869 and his plan for its extension in 1870 was immediately put into practice (*Aión*, 18 May 1870). The report on Watkins' endeavors fit into the pattern of incessant preaching to the 'uncivilized' as to how they should govern themselves according to a single standard of economic and political organization to which every nation should aspire (Spurr, 1993, p. 62; *The Levant Herald*, 22 March 1873).

Unsurprisingly, the Indian experience occupied a special place in the colonial taxonomic register, and many British commentators reflected on the days of the Indian Mutiny: for example, the Cawnpore and Delhi massacres of English populations by the Indian rebels, were likened many times to the Dilessi Murders (*The Times*, 26 April 1870; Ball, 1981, pp. 68–104, 302–90). For some, the Greek brigands deserved the same treatment as Nana Sahib and Tantia Trophee (Tope), the leaders of the Indian Revolution ((*The Daily News*, 4 June 1870; Hoppen, 1998, p. 190); the Greeks deserved a Viceroy, just like India, because it was evident that King George could not 'tame' them (*The Times*, 6 May 1870). The natives regarded the Delhi and Cawnpore incidents as part of the Indian resistance to foreign, British, oppressors. Palmerston had managed to present in 1857 Indian 'disorder' as a 'national crisis' to be handled in the light of patriotic duty, and the British army's success in suppressing it as Britain's retrieval of 'honor' (Hoppen, 1993, pp. 194–7; David, 2003). British observations presented Greek brigandage as a form of national resistance, proposing a solution to the problem in Greece analogous to that in India: restoration of order by colonization. Although the suggestion had not come from the headquarters of British colonial administration, the Colonial Office, but from the Foreign Office, the examination of Greek and Indian affairs in the same light continued to preoccupy colonial administrators, such as Sir George Campbell, long after Dilessi. Campbell's long tenure of office as an Indian administrator in the South provinces led him to compare the Greek 'Christian Cause' in the East with the Indian Mutiny, and once again, the Irish cause (1876, pp. 32–5, p. 137).

At other times, the Greek state would cease to be a criminogenic source and be called upon to restore internal order and the country's image in Europe. This idea figures in a report produced by Watson, Secretary of the British Legation at Athens, whose concern was that Greek administrators were unwilling to take immediate action against the damage done to tourism in Greece by the Dilessi Murders. For Watson, 'a little of energy [...] like that exhibited by Englishmen in putting down lawlessness on the northwestern frontier of India, would make brigandage no such easy calling' (*The Times*, 8 May 1872). The recognition of the Greek state as the only source of legitimate power (by analogy to England's regulatory role in the British Empire) does not detract from the fact that Greece had to follow the 'European code of law' (*The Times* of 23 March 1871).

The mechanics of discursive moralization in European monopolies of violence sustained a much more complex system of racial classification than that suggested by Said in *Orientalism* (Mani and Frankenberg, 1985, p. 191; Richardson, 1990). Ironically, the system thrived on a heteroglossic principle that often brews social rebellion in support of difference (Bakhtin, 1981, pp. 290–2), but in this instance it assisted in legitimating systemic control: the Greeks could be *like* the Irish, the Abyssinians, the Mexicans and the Indians at the same time, because all those 'races' were under some form of colonial control or patronage. Underneath the bipolar system of 'us' versus 'them', civilized versus 'uncivilized' a second system was in motion, whose function was to manage racial ambiguity by marrying cultural traits that remained antithetical in the first system. The co-existence of the two systems allowed for hazardous political maneuver: whereas in some cases the Greek state appeared to be a criminogenic source (much like the brigands it harbored), in other cases it was represented as the guardian of order (much like the British imperial center). 'Coloring' the Greek state *and* the brigands also assisted in the manipulation of morally detestable political action. The politics of the moment were informed by the pragmatics of experience: conceptions of order acquired a slippery, elusive quality to sanction the European stability of the powerful.

The slippery nature of political classification both concealed and heightened protest against the European system of patronage, ultimately privileging a 'hermeneutics of suspicion' over a 'hermeneutics of difference' (Dallmayr, 2001, p. 40) that might have supported a dialogically constructed European identity shared by weak and strong parties. It brewed a type of resentment akin to that of more recent eras – certainly that of European enlargement, in which states recently admitted to

Europe assume the role of the uncivilized, disorderly pariah. Although I explore this resentment later at length, it is worth concluding the chapter by glancing at what Gennadios has to say about the 'civilized hypocrisy' of Europeans when he takes issue with the 'cruel' British reactions to the Dilessi Murders. For Gennadios the British attachment to 'civility' serves to ameliorate the adverse public impact brutalities committed against others may have, a practice that constitutes the ultimate betrayal of basic humanitarian principles.

> Such transparent inconsistency will not necessarily wait exposure at the hands of the New Zealander, who, it is prophesied, centuries hence, resting on the broken arch of London Bridge, will moralize upon the fall of the great country. A future and not very remote Macaulay may justly stigmatise the present generation of his country-men as one which with one hand distributes Bibles, but with the other sows misery amongst the poor and weak nations; which deputes missionaries to preach African heathens, but which commissions officers to guide the arms of the infidel against his Christian victims; which sends umbrellas and night-caps to Australian savages, but which sends Snifer rifles and Armstrong guns into the hands of the Mohammedan butchers; which establishes societies for the prevention of cruelty to animals, but which organizes committees for rendering national honours to the greatest slaveholder in the world (Gennadios, 1870, pp. 173–4).

3
Crime, Identity and Historical Legacy

'Civilizing' national memory

What Derrida calls 'anthropological wars' are an offshoot of wars of attrition following colonial and military oppression. The writing produced by such confrontations falls under the spell of a 'violation of the letter', which one culture tries to impose on the other: what the one side classifies as A, rivals label B, and this game goes on until both manage to create powerful, though not always compatible, systems of appellations, divisions and restrictions, continuities and discontinuities. What this system of labeling excludes, refuses to display, or names and renames, is as important as the things it embraces and classifies. In a postcolonial twist, Derrida sees in this 'anthropological war' a symbolic justification of the actual domination of the 'other' by any means (Derrida, 1976, pp. 107–8).

We could easily employ this model to explore European systemic violence. And yet, a combined analysis of the means employed in the process of 'appellation' with the actual outcomes is more important than Derrida's insistence to see in writing the mark of violence. Unequal political relationships may be adversarial, but classificatory devices are produced dialogically in the socio-political environment cultures inhabit. The racial rift that characterized Europe in the nineteenth century somehow tied the political necessities of nationalist programs to colonialism, often producing a relationship of reciprocal determination between nation-state and 'race' (Balibar, 1991, pp. 51–2). This reciprocal determination of racism and nationalism did not necessarily reconcile their conflicting agendas: that of assimilation (for nationalism) and that of isolation and stigmatization (for racism) of ethnic groups. Such conflicting agendas led theorists, such as Anderson, to exaggerate the difference between nationalism, which thinks in terms of historical destinies, and 'racism [which] dreams of eternal contaminations'. For Anderson, racism has its origins in notions of class, manifesting itself 'not across boundaries but within them' (Anderson 1991, p. 150).

The experience of European nation-building may cast doubts on Anderson's categorical separation of racism and nationalism (also Mosse, 1995). European national belonging *is* racially constructed in symbolic ways, in so far as it involves a willful confusion of internal limits with external borders. This is not to conflate racism with nationalist xenophobia: internal limits '[refer] to a problematic of purity, or better, of purification, which is to say that [they] indicat[e] the uncertainty of identity, the way in which the "inside" can be penetrated or adulterated by its relation with the "outside", the foreign' (Balibar, 1994, p. 63). The very origins of the word (*phóvos* or fear of the *xénos* as both the foreigner and the guest) indicates that xenophobia and racism are both practices of exclusion, but the former expresses fear of the alien 'within' (Delanty and O'Mahony, 2002, p. 163). A nation institutes its 'People', its unifying signifier (Gourgouris, 1996, p. 18), 'not by suppressing all differences, but by relativizing them and subordinating them to itself' (Balibar, 1990, p. 347). The People is a fantasy, a linguistic creation introduced into public discourse to legitimize a collective fantasy (McGee, 1975, p. 239). Ideally, national identity should promote the recognition of rights and duties in a shared polity, protecting the public sphere from erosion (Balibar and Wallerstein, 1991; Laclau and Mouffe, 1985). More often than not, however, it emerges as a Manichean figment of cultural characterizations, which are thoroughly politicized: 'us' and 'them', natives and aliens, outsiders and insiders (Hedetoft, 1993). All European nations were constructed through such radical distinctions between members and non-members (Rosoux, 2001, pp. 180–5; Spohn, 2005). It is this matter-as-fact-ness of belonging that colors nationalism in divisive ways.

This discursive eradication of difference is especially apparent in the domain of historical memory. Ethnic identities disappeared from various national chronicles across European history because they ceased to fit into the nation-state's political program. Renan (1990) stresses the production of national commonality through selective amnesia. Forgetting is seen thus as a strategic choice – what rhetoricians call 'strategic public memory' (Bruner, 2005, p. 316). The production of collective amnesia may also become a significant aspect of what Herzfeld understands as 'social poetics' in the nation-state (Herzfeld, 1985, pp. 10–11, 1997b, 2005). I view here social poetics as the grandiose frontstage that *the state* constructs to grant national identity with a fictional uniformity. This frontstage will conceal 'dirty laundry' that may threaten its international image; therefore, it practically operates as the opposite of 'cultural intimacy' (Herzfeld, 2005, p. 49), a mechanism of closure that social theorists explored in different national contexts though different vocabularies.

Take for example Habermas' engagement with the vicissitudes of what I will term 'nationalist solidary amnesia', a state-sanctioned form of national solidarity that supports, and is supported by forgetting. Through his engagement with historical discourse on the Holocaust, Habermas exposed an extreme case of conscious, institutionalized revisionism that mirrored Germany's post-war isolation in the European political arena (Adorno, 1986; Habermas, 1989a; Tzanelli, 2007a, 2007c; Wolin, 1989). Habermas' polemics inflamed conservative historians, mainly because they reopened national wounds: for Habermas, forgetting our moral debts to the past threatens the future of democratic principles as it forecloses the possibility for critical self-appraisal, if not reconciliation with damaged others (Cochran, 2002; Ricoeur, 1999; but see also Jay, 1984). In every culture there are norms that regulate 'the inherent *debatability* of the past' (Appadurai, 1981, p. 201, emphasis in the text). Such norms reside in the systemic environment of nation-building, in which history becomes a property that 'those who exercise power jealously guard and hedge around with rules for its ownership' (Herzfeld, 1987, p. 58). Systemically, national memory operates as 'the epic faculty *par excellence*' (Benjamin, 1989, p. 97), a closed world of formalized story-telling moving through history, trying, with the aid of institutionalized sacrosanct tradition to exclude any other possible approach to the social (Bakhtin, 1981, p. 16). The obliteration of certain social groups from national self-narration may nicely ameliorate external criticisms and restore the nation-state's international image – but at whose expense? (Smith, 2007, pp. 229–32). This type of forgetting, a cognitive, moral and political issue simultaneously, does not simply 'impair reason and knowledge; it also prevents recognition' (Fabian, 2007, p. 68). In an attempt to restore itself in the eyes of significant others, the nation-state, the Hobbesian regulator of difference, begins to destroy internal reciprocities so that it can build and re-build its 'People'. Self-civilizing processes come at a big price for internal others.

The nineteenth-century Greek state was seeking ways to embrace Western civilizational models of governance. Yet, because the monopolization of violence did not assist in the suppression of brigand crime, a climate of suspicion was cultivated in Western Europe concerning Greece's capacity for 'modernization'. A convenient discursive strategy adopted by Greek state actors involved presentation of brigandage as a phenomenon alien to Greek culture. The links between *listeía* and *klephtism* were severed in political discourse addressed simultaneously to internal and external audiences. The attribution of brigand crime to internal social others (Albanians and Vlachs) *and* external enemies (Ottomans) repressed an important aspect of the history of Greek nation-building. This 'monumentalization' (Nietzsche, 1980, pp. 17–18) of national history might have assisted the nation-state in re-arranging the nation's internal limits, creating ideal citizenries and projecting desired types of governance abroad, but it also subordinated the Greek lifeworld to an administrative system that complied with European surveillance, granting the Greek experience of modernity with dangerous nationalist overtones.

Negotiating identities, stigmatizing 'others'

Whether one chooses to see in Wyse a representative of the colonial mind or not, he was a sharp and insightful observer of Greek political reality. In one of his excursions in Attica, he came across an encampment of Vlachs, 'a wild, savage-looking race' the Greeks of the Kingdom regarded as the main cause of crime. According to Wyse's Greek friend, 'the Vlachs protected and harbored Davéli and Karabelíki and other brigands, and by their aid and sympathy kept up that state of things in the country' (Wyse, 1871, p. 70). But such fleeting impressions were part of the Greek cultural landscape. One of the things independence brought to the surface was the diversity of cultures and customs in the Greek peninsula, preserved throughout Ottoman rule. Constant migration of populations to mountainous areas, inaccessible to the Turks, had transformed the human geography of the Greek space. Thereafter, the demographic legacy of the Ottoman period had been handed down to the Greek state; but social fragmentation was never eliminated partially due to the existence of mountain peoples who spoke languages other than Greek and lived separately from the main body of the Greek metropolitan population and the towns of Attica and the Peloponnese (McGrew, 1985, pp. 17–18).

Among all these ethnic groups the Vlachs and the Sarakatsans were the ones most strongly linked to economic activities such as stock rearing that forced them to live in the countryside. In some territories of European Turkey the largest of these groups, who considered themselves Greek, was the Albanian, but there were also instances in which their ethnic designation was confused with that of the Vlachs. In so far as the Vlachs in Eastern Thrace and Western Macedonia were of Albanian origin, there is a historical basis for this correlation. However, a series of further associations plunged the origin of these groups into obscurity, often making the boundaries between them 'fluid' (Barth, 1969, 1994). The Vlachs and the Sarakatsans were constantly confused in Bulgarian records, while in those of the early modern Ottoman Empire it was the Greeks and the merchant Vlachs of the Balkans that became terminologically interchangeable. Within the framework of modern Greek identity, this blurring formed a historical *problématique*, because there was a direct correspondence between the eighteenth- and nineteenth-century Albanian activities at a time when the Ottoman Empire was losing its authority, and the collapse of Byzantine authority during the thirteenth and fourteenth centuries, which led to movements by both Vlachs and Albanians into the Greek peninsula (Winnifrith, 1987). Apart from the hint we have that the Albanians were of Illyrian origin (Winnifrith, 1992) and that the Vlachs spoke a Latin language, it would be difficult to trace the ethnic links of all those groups. The Greek state had serious difficulties as well: in 1836 the government had identified at least four such groups of 'tent-dwellers', in whose eyes the Greek state was only an intruder and the Greeks remained a shadowy urban people, scarcely know in their communities.

But the purpose of this study is not to restore some primal truth concerning the origin of the Vlachs and the Albanians of Greece *contra* the truth of the nineteenth-century Greek state. To adapt Bakhtin's reflections, categories 'are conditioned by specific historical destinies and by the task an ideological discourse assumes' (1981, p. 270). The 'real' of the origins of the Vlachs/Albanians itself has no place in this analysis, which will focus on what truly mattered for the spokesmen of the Greek conversational community: an effective symbolization of identity. Specialized researchers found it difficult to arrive at definite conclusions, and had recourse to further classification of regional identities (Dhima, 1994, pp. 127–58). There was a grain of truth in the Greek accusation that Vlachs harbored brigandage. The Vlach shepherds, being geographically cut off and socially marginal, lived close to brigand hideouts – hence, extortion as well as recruitment of them by brigands was a common phenomenon. In 1869, Andreas Moskonisios, a Greek second lieutenant, published a treatise under the title *The Mirror of Brigandage in Greece*, in which he argued that two thirds of a brigand band usually consisted of Vlach shepherds and only a third of peasants or deserters.

But identifying particular social circumstances that encourage or force a group to have recourse to crime is not the same as suggesting its complete identification with that crime. The 'question' of brigandage as an 'endemic national malady' had been discussed in the Greek Parliament (1856) long before Moskonisios' study. This on-going debate led to the appointment of a commission to examine the problem. The reports of the commission repeated the narrative recorded by Wyse: the Vlach shepherds, these '"illiterate" and "uncouth"' (Koliopoulos, 1987, pp. 172 cf., 173) tribes, were to be blamed for this 'scourge'. As for the rest of the Greek nation, it was innocent.

Hence, the argument that 'exorcized' the evil was ready at hand when the Dilessi episodes erupted in 1870. In this conjunction of circumstances the Greek state had to re-address and solve the question of brigandage to the satisfaction both of Greeks and a British government under internal pressure to occupy Greece. Additionally, Greek 'honor' had to be restored in the eyes of a European audience demanding nothing less than the regeneration of ancient Hellas. It is telling that a report on the episode sent by the Greek Ministry of the Interior to *Aión* included observations that most of the brigands 'belonged to the tribe of *Vlachopoimènes*', or Vlach-shepherds (9 April 1870). According to the nationalist *Palingenesía*, the Greek nation always denounced such crimes, as opposed to 'those nomads' who harbor them: 'but it is a fact that the Greek nation does not consist of this small race, which lives a primitive and savage life' (15 May 1870). The article was titled 'The English Press' and formed a response to the bellicose language of English journalists, who harped on associations of brigandage and Greek politics, showing no respect for 'the natural rights of nations (such as the Greek)... consolidated by treaties' (*ibid.*). This rhetorical practice aimed to discipline Greece's imagined European interlocutors, reminding them of the holy cause of the Greek Revolution and the subsequent treaties of liberation. Simultaneously, however, it generated a discourse in which brigandage was placed within the category of savagery, which, in its turn, was associated with Vlach identity.

The origin of brigandage was investigated after the Dilessi murders by the director of the French school at Athens, Émile Burnouf, in a treatise published in the *Revue des Deux Mondes*, a journal initially associated with the Orleanist regime, which had come by 1870 to occupy a generally open-minded position and display an attachment to middle-class French culture. The *Revue* was widely circulated and Burnouf's thesis hit the mark: for the Greeks this 'voice' came to (conveniently) represent French opinion. In addition, Burnouf was considered a well-informed observer when it came to Greek affairs. It was not just that his treatise supported the Greek journalistic argument, granting it with a much-needed *reliability* in Britain: Greek newspapers, anxious to attack those British commentators who found the Greek argument concerning the Vlachs unconvincing, were now able to present his reflections as the voice of 'France', another 'civilizing' protector of Greece. For Burnouf the brigands in Greece were not Greeks 'properly speaking', but 'Albanians or *Vlachopoiménes-Vlachs*' (*The Pall Mall Gazette*, 20 June 1870). *Palingenesía* translated Burnouf's work and added that the Greek nation is not guilty of those crimes, 'but a victim of villains'. Greeks may want to admit in their national community 'the good and virtuous Vlachs, but it is unfair to be charged with the crimes of the vicious ones!' (15 June 1870; *Aión*, 25 June 1870).

Not everyone was sympathetic to Burnouf's arguments, however. In *The Times* of 3 June 1870, George Finlay offered an analysis of how the Greek authorities and King Otho himself had occasionally cooperated with 'brigand Vlachs' for their own interests. It was unfortunate for the Greeks that Finlay was in a position to illustrate his point by reference to the example of Takos Arvanitakis, one of the brigand chiefs of the Dilessi band. Although a Vlach, Takos had participated in the anti-Ottoman revolution that King Otho instigated in Thessaly and Epirus during the Crimean War; thereafter, he was employed by the Government to pursue brigands. While Takos' biography offended the Greeks, it was the second part of Finlay's analysis that skillfully addressed the question of national identity. If, Finlay argued, one examined the processes that take place in the melting pot of Greek society after the Revolution, Greekness appears as an arbitrary category, inclusive rather than exclusive.

> It must be observed that many of the benefactors who enriched the Greek Kingdom and the city of Athens by their donations of money, by founding charitable and scientific societies, and by erecting some of the principal buildings that adorn Athens had been of Vallach [*sic*.] and not of Greek nationality. This non-Hellenic race furnished Greece with one of its most eminent statesmen in Colettes [*sic*.] and one of its best judges in Clonares [*sic*.]; and if I am not mistaken the first Greek press in Turkey out of Constantinople was established not by men of Greek race, but by these Vallachs [*sic*.] at Moschopoli (*The Times*, 3 June 1870).

The argument was not new, and it certainly did not apply to the Vlachs only: in the 1850s informed British observers were praising the 'self-denying race of Epirus' (Albanian-Vlachs) for its contribution to the foundation of the Greek Kingdom, and its excellence in the civil service and the Chambers of Greece (Roving Englishman, 1877, pp. 215–16). In both cases the Albanian-Vlachs were presented as Greeks, but categorized as 'non-Hellenic': Greek from *Graecus* was the word the Romans used to designate the Hellenes as imperial subjects – an effective twist which divested the latter of any claims to a glorious and admired past, the Hellenic cultural heritage, which was appropriated by their masters. For modern Greeks, *Grekós* was an ambiguous designation that signified the *heterochthone* (non-native) Greek, but also the 'orientalized' Ottoman subject. It is more likely that Finlay's comment is a reference to the pre-Hellenic historical background of the Vlachs that occupied European scholarly debates in the nineteenth century – something to be borne in mind for future reference. Yet, this point must be expanded upon, because it sheds light on the distressing reality of Greek cultural hegemonies. Significantly, Herzfeld (1987, pp. 57–8) recognized a similar hegemonization of the past in Campbell's (1964) comment that in Greek nationalist discourse the Sarakatsans 'lack of history'. Even today, to a Vlach-speaker *Grekós* is the Christian whose mother tongue is one of the Greek dialects that have been spoken in the Balkans down the ages. Nevertheless, as a designation, *Grekós* has always carried political overtones and been used during the nineteenth and twentieth centuries to describe social groups who, although their mother tongue was not Greek, considered themselves a part of the modern Greek nation. 'The term *Grecoman/Grikumánu* is an extension of those political ideas. It essentially meant a non-Greek-speaking but fanatical supporter of the "Hellenic idea", and was used as a term of abuse by the rival factions' (Koukoudis, 2003, p. 1). Looking at the politicization of ethnicity diachronically, enables us to comprehend the furore Finlay caused in 1870. Press responses to his commentary might have varied from moderate (*Clió*, 30/11 July 1870) to aggressive, but generally took issue with the British journalist for 'dishonoring' the names of Klonaris and Kolettis. 'Even if we presume that they were born Vlachs – something yet to be verified – we should not dismiss the fact that they were born in the bosom of Greek society, they were fed by its milk [...] while the brigands are born and nurtured as nomads and receive nothing from our society' (*Palingenesía*, 15 June 1870), was the response, which mobilized images of a loving family to describe the 'nation'. The nomadic, 'criminogenic' way of living characterized one category of Vlachs, the non-assimilated 'savages' of Greece. Those Vlachs who conformed to the Greek rules of citizenry and the European codes of civility were blameless.

Slowly, the Vlach/Albanian brigands were transformed in Greek political discourse into brigand invaders from the Ottoman Empire.

Fragments of this suggestion appeared in various pamphlets published after the Dilessi murders. A pamphlet by a certain Rikakis (*Aión*, 13 May 1870) invited the 'nation' and the 'Greek authorities' to reflect on the situation so as to avoid similar international humiliations in the future (Rikakis, 1870, pp. 3–4, 28). Simultaneously, Antonopoulos was observing that brigands are elusive criminals because they 'escape to Turkish territories, in which not only are they not pursued, but they are also harbored' (1870, p. 1). Although the Vlachs did not figure here, his analysis was symptomatic of the Greek nationalist monologue. The identity of the brigands became a secondary issue, thus giving way to the connection of brigandage with the historical enemy of the 'nation': Turkey (*Aión*, 11 June 1870). In his pamphlet Koronaios proceeded to show that the name Arvanitakis derives from *Arvanitóvlachoi* (Arvanite Vlachs) 'that is, nomads' (1870, p. 8), who invade the Greek Kingdom from Turkey, causing political havoc (*ibid.*, p. 11).

But it was Gennadios' ability to absorb and classify information from the English and Greek press that reconstructed the frame of Greek discourse concerning the social and ethnic identity of the Vlachs and the Albanians in Greece and their relationship with the essential qualities of the Greek 'nation' (Jenkins, 1998, p. 113). His argument was addressed to an English audience – which is why he published his work in English. His statement that the Albanian-Vlach-brigands were Turkish agents seeking to damage Greece's reputation was based on a brilliant combination of argumentative fragments: the first and most important was that because the collaborators of the Arvanitakis and their mysterious supporters had committed 'high treason', they no longer belonged to the Greek national community (see for comparisons *Méllon*, 21 April 1870; *Aión* 9 April 1870). The second fragment was that the Arvanitakis band consisted of Vlachs, and the third that the Ottoman Empire repeatedly refused to cooperate with Greek authorities in the suppression of border crimes. The alchemic outcome of this mixture was the golden theory of the immaculate nation: the murders had not been committed by Greek brigands, but by Vlach/Albanian brigands *in* Greece.

This logic provides us with an insight into Greek self-definitions predicated upon history, official discourses of self-presentation to outsiders, rather than 'custom', intimate knowledge of an intolerably heteroglot national 'self' (Herzfeld, 1987, 1997b, 2005; Sutton, 2000). Gennadios' point of departure was similar to that of *Aión*, which noted that most of the captured brigands were not 'natives of Greece and Greek subjects' but nomads of the Ottoman Empire.

> They belong to a class of nomadic shepherds [...] who exist both in Greece and Turkey, and who form a nationality of themselves. They are known by the name of Koutzo-Vallachs, a tribe who immigrated from the borders of Danube into Greece during the twelfth century. They have a dialect of their own, but most speak Greek. The brigand bands that infest Greece and Turkey are recruited almost exclusively from this tribe. [...] It would be evident to all who have glanced at the ghastly photograph of the heads of the seven brigands shot during the engagement that these men were not of Greek *but of Slav origin* [...]. Their names are also sure indications of their nationality. 'Arvanitaki' means 'little Albanian,' and is not a surname, properly so called, but a kind of distinct epithet, such as most of these men are known by, so as to contradistinguish them from others of the same Christian name (Gennadios, 1870, pp. 117–19, emphasis mine).

What is interesting in Gennadios' argument is the ambiguity concerning the identity of the brigands that 'infest' Greece: (a) the vast majority of the Dilessi band *is of Slav origin* – yet another statement that has to be borne in mind; (b) brigands in Greece often *come from Turkey*; and (c) sometimes they speak Greek. What is left outside Gennadios' argument is also important: not only is he unconcerned with his Albanians/Vlachs' self-designation, but also he avoids the question.

Gennadios went so far as to condemn Finlay's article, thereby following *Palingenesía's* policy. '*The Times* correspondent', he declared, 'has evidently confounded the Greeks of Epirus, who have undoubtedly shown themselves the greatest benefactors of our common fatherland, with these Vallach nomads, who, far from having ever produced anything but good soldiers, are proverbial for their inaptitude to intellectual culture and civilization' (*ibid.*, p. 118). He even claimed that the brigands appealed for amnesty both in Greece and in Turkey, because they were 'Turks-Albanians' (*Turkalvanoí*). 'Civilization' and 'intellectual culture', a combination now of Western European and Greek claims to progress, became intrinsic Greek qualities that the mountainous and nomadic Vlach tribes of Greece and Turkey do not possess.

Gennadios offered a fascinating narrative of Greek identity by using the principle of negation, that is, by defining what *was not* Greek. Later, Greek politicians used his argument to defend Greece against European criticisms (Milisis, 1871; Chadjiskos, 1871). Sadly, the whole argument was unfair: the Vlachs-Albanians, were, if not Greek-speaking, at least Orthodox Christians, 'who formed a part of exactly that persecuted population which Greece was claiming the right to "free" from Ottoman "oppression" and annex to herself' (Jenkins, 1998, p. 125). If we were to follow folk tradition, some of those Vlachs and Albanians (thoroughly 'Hellenized' at the time in Greek nationalist discourse) could claim the lion's share in the Greek struggle for independence (Herzfeld, 1982). Although many of these groups could communicate with the Ottoman Albanians, who were fighting against the Greeks, they called *themselves Arvanites* and had a sense of separate (Albanian-speaking Orthodox) identity (Tsingos, 1983). But this hardly mattered. It is not because the Greeks ignored the truth; it is rather that, in general, truth should not be thought as being in a consistent or identical relationship with the 'real' world (Žižek, 1991, pp. 234–44). Different societies have different regimes of truth, or what Foucault called 'general politics of truth, the types of discourse which they accept and make function as true' (Foucault, 1980, p. 131; van Dijk, 1993, p. 96). One wonders, however, not only how, but also *why* this particular 'truthful' discourse had come to have such a hold on Greek nationalist thought, contradicting folk memories of resistance to Ottoman 'tyranny'.

In the second half of the 1860s there was in Greece an anxious repetition of this association between Vlach shepherds and brigandage. The political pressure to respond to the Cretan Insurrection, and the unstable political situation during the Interregnum period of 1862–3 had allowed crime to flourish and led many political fugitives to join brigand bands. In order to sever the attachment of political fugitives to brigand bands, the Koumoundouros government of 1866 was left with no choice other than to grant them amnesty. The lack of Turkish cooperation in suppressing brigandage, and the role of the Vlachs in Greek identity were coupled and crystallized in political discourse: this situation was becoming a 'miasma' (*Palingenesía*, 1 June 1864; 11 June 1866; 22 July 1866; 26 June 1867; 30 April 1881) that must be eradicated at all costs. Brigands in Greece were (a) Albanians originally from Turkey; (b) Vlachs from Turkey; (c) 'uncivilized' Vlachs and Albanians resident in Greece; or (d) Albanian-Vlachs of Slav origin. The attempt to implicate Turkey and the suggestion of a Slavic element figured in the press almost mas much as the idea that 'these *Vlachopoiménes* live a semi-civilized life' that threatens 'the constitution and the laws of the country', which 'are grounded upon liberal and civilized principles' (Anonymous, 1867, pp. 16–19).

There were, of course, objections to this argument, which gestured towards a negotiation rather than definite conclusions regarding the story's credibility. A protest against this mythologization appears in *Thanos Vlekas*, Kallighas' novel on Greek brigandage, which was published as early as the mid 1850s. Kallighas was a jurist, Professor of Law at the University of Athens, MP and Minister of Justice in 1854 – therefore, he had considerable involvement in politics and public affairs during the Crimean War (Vitti, 1991, p. 29). In his novel the Greek brigand Tasos, who is pursued by Greek troops, escapes, crosses the Ottoman border, and together with some Albanians first works for 'the Turks', and then resigns his 'job' and devastates Greek villages (Kallighas, 1987, pp. 43–7). The audience for Kallighas' deconstruction of the Greek 'ethnic truth' was almost exclusively Greek. It is not surprising therefore that his 'anti-Greek' narrative did not find an imitator within the community of the Greek literati and sank into oblivion: no law-abiding Greek subject was prepared to accept that brigandage was a Greek problem.

The fact that Greek anxiety is directed against the Vlachs and the Albanians is significant: the chain of interchangeable terms (Albanian, Turk, Vlach, Slav, brigand, nomad) would often be followed by the fear that brigand disorder was a 'pest', a 'scourge' on Greece, a sin that had to be swept away, a 'miasma' imported from Turkey – metaphors that characterized other European discourses on crime over the same period (Blinkhorn, 2000, p. 343). The selfsame language of separation and exclusion accompanied the edicts issued by the Holy Synod for the excommunication of brigands from the Greek body social. The Holy Synod had taken similar action on the question of fraternization – a very common 'heathen' practice in brigand communities (Koliopoulos, 1987, p. 224). As early as in 1855 an encyclical directed Greek priests to preach against brigandage so as to unite the 'faithful' against brigands and their collaborators. The priests had to 'explain' that brigandage was 'both a "sin" and a "betrayal" of one's neighbor' (*ibid.*, p. 173). The action was drastic, given that Greek Orthodoxy imposed a series of practices that enable the operation of Greek communal life. On a symbolic level, these edicts might have been designed to stress the importance of religion as a purifying power. The edict issued after the Marathon Murders was along these lines, because it denied the brigands and their collaborators the right to belong to the Orthodox – that is Greek national – community (*Aión*, 2 and 4 May 1870). The measure was the outcome of British threats against the Greek government that, unless it managed to root out brigandage, Britain would take over in the Greek Kingdom. Additional threats concerning the future of Greek sovereignty (a temporary British occupation of Greece) and the general European 'outcry' provided the preconditions for Greek 'impression management'.

One must not disregard the profound connection between dirt and social disorder. Any structure, any 'order', is extremely vulnerable at its margins, when identity definition falters and cracks. Dirt is a by-product of systematic ordering and classification, which the Greeks had to present to their European interlocutors in order to be recognized as part of the civilized/ordered European world. To achieve this, they decided to act against those without a fixed place in the ordered Greek social system: the Vlach/Albanian nomads of Greece. Since the crimes of outlaws were likely not only to go unpunished but also to disgrace Greece abroad, the Greeks called in *metaphorically* 'pollution beliefs to supplement the lack of other sanctions' (Douglas, 1993, p. 132). The accompanying narrative of the Albanian/Vlachs' 'dishonoring' of Greek identity exposes the bipolarity of Greek self-presentation: a masculinized nation corresponds to 'a grandiose and dehistoricized Classical past', handy for external consumption, as opposed to a shameful feminized Greece (*Romiossíni*), which expresses 'an ideology of intimacy' (Herzfeld, 1987, p. 65; Herzfeld, 2005, p. 16). Unsurprisingly, correlations of shame, marginalization and crime were used extensively by the Greek state after Dilessi. State propaganda addressed to European, especially British readerships, was nicely reflected in press reports on massive arrests of Vlachs and the introduction of restrictions in their roving movements (*Aión*, 13 May 1870; *Palingenesía*, 26 May 1870). Shortly after the episode, a Greek parliamentary debate concluded with the decision to pass anti-brigand laws (Kofos, 1980, pp. 308–9).

It is suggestive that, although the Slav origin of the Vlachian/Albanian tribes in Greece figured in most sources, the main target of Greek discourse was the Ottoman Empire. While the Vlachs and the Albanians of Greece were by no means considered foreigners in the Greek Kingdom, their inferior social status was nonetheless indisputable. In official discourse at least the term *Vláchos* signified the Koutsovlach-speaking shepherd whose identity was Greek but whose primary mark of difference was language, or dialect. As opposed to state discourse, in everyday parlance 'the term [became] one of moral exclusion' (Herzfeld, 1987, p. 132). Even nowadays *Vláchos* signifies the illiterate or unintelligent, someone who is lacking civilized manners. My compatriots from Michaniona (a town southeast of Thessaloniki) insist that the original natives of the region are *áksestoi Vláchoi* (coarse Vlachs): is it a coincidence that their collective self-designation as *Mikrasiátes*, Asia Minor refugees from the last Greek-Turkish war (1919–22) has been associated with a 'high culture' of Hellenic (Ionian) origins (Tzanelli, 2007c, p. 7)? As Hirschon (1998, pp. 28–31) explains, proud of the cosmopolitan flair of Asia Minor town life, refugees constructed a positive self-image as carriers of a glorious socio-economic heritage *vis-à-vis* that of the 'less progressive' Greek relatives of the metropolis, who remained trapped in Western discourses of backwardness and incompetence. Despite their initial social exclusion, today, all three Anatolian generations pride themselves of their *Mikrasiátiki koultoúra* – a culture that has come to represent universally recognized aspects of modern Greek culture.

Stereotypes set groups apart from the dominant social order in the absence of visible markers of ethnic difference. They are the 'building materials for practical nationalism' (Herzfeld, 1992, p. 73), rhetorical devices that enable us to come to terms with distressing social realities (Theodossopoulos, 2003, p. 181; Brown and Theodossopoulos 2004, p. 4), masking the more embarrassing aspects of nation-building. The Greek state did not manage to stabilize Greek identity before the beginning of the twentieth century – and this only until the end of the twentieth century, when the national borders opened to labor immigrants from European countries and North Africa. To compensate for this frailty, the nineteenth-century Greeks defined their identity by social analogy and relativity: those who were designated as outsiders 'were the people [the Greeks] "knew less" – a clear relationship between social distance and knowledge' (Herzfeld, 1987, p. 154). A third pair (Greece and Turkey) accompanied binarisms predicated upon civilization and its lack, Greek society and the Vlach/Albanian communities of Greece. This move signified an initial internalization and eventual exorcism of a Western European discourse on Greek identity. In this discourse modern Greek culture appeared to be infected by 'Oriental barbarism' after the conquest of Byzantium by the Turks. Greek 'regeneration' was concomitant with the restoration of order, which in the modern state vocabulary signified public security and competent administration. When the Greek state was accused of uncivilized contact, brigandage, a defect criticized by European powers, was presented by Greeks as 'foreign'. Consequently, the Vlach and Albanian shepherds linked to it also became 'foreigners'.

The analogue of the nineteenth-century discourse can be witnessed in Greece nowadays. Recently, the idea of 'leaking (Greek-Albanian) borders' was reintroduced in the Greek media, after the massive migration of Albanians and Epirote Greeks to Greece (Tzanelli, 2006). These populations formed part of the Greek imagined community while they stood outside the Greek borderland, and during the nineteenth and the first quarter of the twentieth centuries were part of the 'unredeemed' Greek populations. The collapse of the old Albanian regime, and massive immigration to Greece reawoke fears of boundary transgression. Nowadays, those who cross the border to Greece, be they Albanians or Greek Epirotes, are presented in journalistic discourse as dirty, criminal and uncivilized aliens (see Seremetakis, 1996; Lazaridis and Wickens, 1999). Research reveals that similar xenophobic stereotyping of Albanian migrants as criminal, disorderly and of 'loose' sexual morals has become endemic in other receiving countries in the Mediterranean region (King and Mai, 2002, pp. 190–4; King and Mai, 2004, pp. 264–6). The structural sim-ilarities between the criminalization of contemporary immigrants and nineteenth-century Vlach/Albanian nomads should not be dismissed: we may draw parallels between them and the demonization of Gypsy/Roma populations – the 'traveling underworld' of European imaginations. McVeigh (1997) explains that because nomadism posits a threat to hege-monic 'sedentary' identities, it is scapegoated: moving across geographic borders becomes analogical to challenging the stability of social norms of the 'host'. Historically, this translated dangerousness into a quintessential Roma attribute, and sanctioned racist attitudes and policies of social exclusion across European countries that targeted a fictionally uniform gypsy identity (*ibid.*, p. 16; Gheorghe, 1997). Migration and nomadism are exposed thus as two faces of the same 'threat' for territorially bound national cultures.

Another foreign element attributed to the Vlachian and Albanian iden-tities was the Slav. In Greece, reflections on the role of the Vlachs and the Albanians in Greek national identity were the offshoot of the discussion concerning the 'Hellenic' identity of the modern Greeks. This debate was instigated by the Tyrolean historian Fallmerayer (1790–1861) – the figure who embodied *mishellenism* or hatred toward the Greeks in post-independence Greek culture. Although Fallmerayer was a classicist, his main interest became the continuity of Hellenic civilization in the Byzan-tine era. His work, a product of its age, marked the moment the Greeks were poisoned by the evolutionist controversy. Fallmerayer's reading of Byzantine sources led him to conclude that modern Greeks were a 'Slavonic race', emerging during the fifth and sixth centuries from a racial intermixing of the Slavs who settled in the Greek-Byzantine peninsula, and its 'Greek' inhabitants. Fallmerayer, who was seen by the Bulgarians as the agent of Panslavism, was not interested in producing anti-Greek propaganda. His theory was the result of the terror of degeneration the Panslavic elements – at the time stubbornly backed up by Russia – might have introduced in Germanic/European culture (Skopetea, 1999, p. 100). Historic associations of Slavic identities with the 'Orient' further con-tributed to the demonization of the Slavs in continental imaginations: the word 'Slav' was derived from the European practice of selling Eastern

Europeans as slaves to Islamic lands in exchange for oriental products (Lewis, 1993, p. 136). Evidently, Fallmerayer's argument rested on a confusion of 'continuity and origin, of race and culture' (Gourgouris, 1996, p. 144). But the unhappy coincidence of his theory with the institution of modern Greece in the 1830s, turned him into a 'Satanic figure' bent on destroying the nation. Ironically, the controversy that consigned this 'impostor' to the fires of hell made Fallmerayer a first-rate star in Europe (Tsoukalas, 2002, p. 33).

Hence, in nineteenth-century political discourse the Albanians and the Vlachs figured both as an *Ur-Hellenic* and an Oriental component of Greek identity. The discourse directed by Greeks to others and themselves after Dilessi correlated the Vlachs and Albanians of Greece, an internal limit, with an external border, the Turkish/Slav evil 'others', transforming them into a surplus of Greek identity. Not only were the Vlach/Albanian brigands symbolized as foreigners (Slavs), but they also became agents of Greece's national enemy, the Ottoman Turks. In this way political 'disorder', the Greek Kingdom's defect, ceased to be regarded as a domestic problem. The narrative fulfilled two functions in Greek self-narration: first, it enabled the Greek 'nation' to recognize itself as a *pure* unity, and second it allowed the Greek state to seek recognition from its European protectors.

Circuits of nationalist monologues: identity in historical perspective

The phenomenon of border crime in both Greece and Turkey continued to be discussed in British and American officialdom long after Dilessi. In 1872 and 1877, Tuckerman received praise from the Greek state for linking brigand crime to 'sloppy' Ottoman border regulation (Tuckerman, 1877, p. 206). The problem was debated in British Parliament in 1874, when fear was expressed that brigandage was going to flourish again on the Turkish, Greek and Albanian borders (*The Times*, 6 July 1875). 'At present', someone else was stating in 1876, 'this country is free from this scourge, partly in consequence of the severely repressive measures taken by the Government after the Dilessi massacre, and partly from the cordial understanding [...] between the Hellenic and Ottoman authorities [...] although the race of Albanian Wallachs (or Vlacks) [*sic*], amongst whom these bands are raised, still exist to the number of about 30,000 in Greece' (Young, 1876, xi). Even foreigners were not sure who these Albanian/Vlachs were. Greek racialized discourses of identity that originated in European racist outlooks were now being recycled abroad.

The anxiety about the Vlach/Albanian brigand threat intensified in the late 1870s, when the establishment of an independent Albanian state began to find support abroad. Because the Albanian nationalists' self-designation was different from that of the Albanian-Greeks of the Greek Kingdom, one should not dismiss the political setting: Albanian nationalism was recognized as an issue after the Berlin Conference in 1878. In 1879, when the Austrians and the Germans set the basis for the *Drang nach Osten* Germanic policy, Italy tried to create its own sphere of influence in the Balkans. When part of the Albanian elite proposed to King George of the Hellenes a plan for an Albanian-Greek Federation in Epirus, a region the Greek state wanted to annex, Italy incited Albanian nationalism in the region and cancelled further negotiations. Consequently, at the beginning of the 1880s the Greek press openly incited anti-Albanian hatred, associating the Albanian irredentists with Turkish anti-Greek propaganda, and baptizing them Vlachs and 'Turkalbanian brigands' (*Aión*, 10 and 14 July 1880; *Palingenesía*, 3 April 1881). The nationalist subtext of this definition became clearer: those 'Vlachs/ Albanians' wanted to plunder and de-Hellenize territories belonging to the Greek nation – even though the Greek state continued to use brigand bands as irredentist forces to claim European territories of Turkey. At the dawn of the 1880s, the Greek 'ethnic truth' began to support the reverse logic: non-Greek (Vlach/Albanian) national enemies were *represented* as brigands (*The Times*, 14 August and 7 September 1876).

Albanian identity retained an ambiguous relationship with Greekness throughout the twentieth century, because of the so-called 'Northern Epirote' Question. 'Northern Epirus' is today that part of Albania that the Greek state tried to incorporate before the foundation of the Albanian state in 1911 on the grounds that a substantial Greek minority existed in the region. On the eve of the Paris Peace Conference, Eleftherios Venizelos, then Greek Prime Minister, laid claims on 'Northern Epirus', arguing that a portion of its population, some 120,000 identified as Greeks, '[had] formed part of the Greek family for centuries, long before the foundation of the Kingdom of Greece' (Venizelos in Carabott, 2005a, p. 24). Venizelos' cunning use of an inclusive language of intimacy cannot be dismissed, given the exclusive practices of the Greek state already outlined. This language of intimacy corresponded to the religious and pedagogical-linguistic 'Hellenization' of the diverse populations in Macedonia by the Athenian center during the so-called 'Macedonian Struggle', which commenced at the beginning of the twentieth century as a Greek hegemonic project that countered Bulgarian and Serb influences in the region (Kitromilidis, 1989; Karakasidou, 2000). The Greek-Bulgarian

Convention of Neuilly (1919) would further polarize ethnic groups and lead to the classification of Slav-speakers as non-Greeks who had to move to Bulgaria. This found an unhappy continuation during the Metaxas regime in the 1930s, which also bracketed together Slav-speakers with communism (Carabott, 2005a, pp. 29–30, 47–50). During the Second World War, Muslim Albanian groups on the Greek-Albanian border (known as *Chámidhes*) were targeted by the Greek royalist and irredentist resistance group EDES, and by 1944 their communities had been destroyed (Mazower, 2000, pp. 25–6). In the post-communist Albanian order it was the Albanians' turn to terrorize the Greek communities of Northern Epirus. Undoubtedly, the term 'Northern Epirus' is not geographical, but political.

Much like the controversy over the name of the Former Republic of Macedonia (FYROM) in the 1990s, the 'Northern Epirote' Question is for Greeks an issue of national integrity: none in Greece would dare refute that 'Northern Epirote' populations are still Greek. When FYROM authorities began to propagandize for the liberation of their alleged 'brothers' in northern Greece that 'remained oppressed' since their migration in the middle ages, the Greek side responded with protestations that the 'Slavic' identity of their ancestors had been long assimilated into Greek culture (Karakasidou, 1997, p. 229). 'Northern Epirus' is still viewed by Greeks as a territory in which they can raise claims of historical continuity, reversing thus the game that FYROM played in the 1990s. If anything, there is a hidden 'hegemonic play' (Kearney 1995, p. 548) at work here, finding expression in the relationship between national centers as they vie for control over each other's political life. Human transnational flows (immigrants) become a useful tool in the hands of different nation-states.

With time, and due to the emergence of new nation-states in the Balkans, the differential treatment of Albanians within Greek society was explicated on the basis of differentiated identities: the Albanian populations of southern Greece (the so-called *Arvanites*) were deemed assimilated, 'Hellenized', ex-Slavs; the Albanian groups of the North, however (Muslims by religion and Albanian citizens after 1913), were regarded as enemies of Greek unity and 'purity'. Although during the Metaxas dictatorship (1936) Arvanite communities suffered persecutions by the authorities, they still participated in the Greek-Albanian conflict of 1940, fighting on the Greek side. Language criteria deteriorated their position in the Greek state again during the colonels' regime of 1967–74, as their dialect clashed with the junta's determination to promote a 'pure' form of Greek language (*Katharévousa*) – and by extension, Greek identity

(Gefou-Mandianou, 1999, pp. 420–1). Language competency worked as a prerequisite for gaining access to civic rights, promoting a disciplinary civic agenda that denied the recognition of internal cultural difference.

Contemporary Greek political discourse has adapted the nineteenth-century formula of Albanian exclusion hermeneutically. Like its antecedent, it is structured around conflations of physical boundaries with symbolic borders (criminality, deviance, dirt, disease) and promotes a fictional preservation of racial purity against 'alien contamination', feeding Greeks' desire to claim direct *racial and cultural* continuity from antiquity. This promotion of linear continuity circulates in all Greek institutions, including that of the school. In 1999 the Center for Social Research published a survey of 1,200 school students, who were asked about their identity. It was reported that 'over 70% [...] agreed that all Greeks descended from the same ancestors and belong to the same family' (Verney, 2002, p. 12). Such ethnocentric reasoning is complemented by a deep-seated xenophobia that native pupils and their parents display against the children of immigrants and immigration in general (Dimakos and Tasiopoulou, 2003). The study conducted by Frangoudaki and Dragonas (1997) on the reproduction and construction of national identity in the Greek educational system shows how Greek curricula consolidate exclusivist and xenophobic conceptions of Greekness. The narration of the Greek historical experience is characterized by antithetical and oppositional relations to other cultures and 'nations' and exaggerates the existence of historical 'enemies'. Greek historical continuity is re-asserted in Greek textbooks with the narration of a flowing, uninterrupted Greekness from Hellenic antiquity to the present (Avdela, 2000).

The Greek political uses of the past are exemplified in teaching resources and performances related to the so-called *Albanian Epos* of 1940–1941, the conflict between Greeks and Albanians (Italian allies) during the Second World War – a regrettable coincidence for the children of Albanian immigrants, who are expected to internalize Greek nationalist discourse. In all Greek schools pupils learn in their history classes to be proud of Greece's Second World War resistance against the 'evil' German, Italian and Albanian forces. Ideological infiltration is characteristic of nationalist pedagogy, and in Greece it finds its finest expression in the celebration of national days with school festivities of calendrical nature (Connerton, 1989; Theodossopoulos, 2004, p. 31). The indoctrination of youngsters (especially migrant pupils) through biased versions of history complements the demand for competency in modern Greek. As happened in previous periods, the two work together as institutionalized prerequisites for gaining access to civic rights, promoting a 'disciplinary' civic agenda that denies the recognition of cultural diversity of modern Greece. Of course, this phenomenon is not exclusively Greek: the revival of this agenda in other contemporary Western European contexts uncovers the autopoetic function educational systems perform in the modern nation-state. Moreover, the political fragmentation of the Balkan region after the break-up of Yugoslavia supported similar forms of memory reconstruction that reconfigured citizenships as exclusive national goods. Serb, Croatian and Bosnian schools promote different versions of the same ethnic conflicts: in Bosnian schoolbooks the Second World War Bosnian genocide is attributed to the Tchetniks whereas in the schools of Sarajevo young Serbs learn that the first 'Yugoslav' state of 1918 assisted in the Croatian and Slovenian oppression of the Serbs (Rosoux, 2001, p. 183). At the same time, Croatian pupils learn that Yugoslavia was a state controlled exclusively by the 'evil' Serbs. The historical indistinctness of these new national identities due to their previous cohabitation in mixed ethnic enclaves is eradicated. Such historical revisions followed, or are followed by ritualized remembrance that promotes violent forms of nationalism (Ray, 1999).

It is in this context of selective amnesias that Greeks learn about their Byzantine heritage first, without questioning the validity of claims over Byzantium's history. The ghost of Fallmerayer is still exorcized even in Greek academic production, especially in works published in Byzantine Studies circles. As Karakasidou (1994) has argued, the relationship between intellectual production and promotion of political discourse is very strong in Greece. Her own case is an excellent illustration of this phenomenon: her book *Fields of Wheat, Hills of Blood: Passages to Nationhood in Greek Macedonia (1870–1990)* (1997) was met with brutal criticism in Greek academic and intellectual circles, because it exposed practices of Greek assimilation of ill-defined ethnic groups in Macedonia from the late nineteenth century. The Greek response to Karakasidou was formulated on the selfsame nineteenth-century official counterblast to Fallmerayer's 'accusations'. She has summarized the critique in the following:

The population of Macedonia has been nothing but pure Greek since antiquity [...]; the Slavs who migrated into the area during the sixth and seventh centuries had been assimilated into Greek culture, although some Greeks in Macedonia picked up a Slavic 'idiom' of speech (Karakasidou 1997, p. 229).

Today, the degree of 'European-ness' that different states can claim is tied to different forms of 'symbolic capital' (Löfgren, 1989) that they can display: from political/economic power, to cultural value. Historic continuities are essential components of the self-image that peripheral countries, such as Greece, display abroad. Even two centuries after the birth of the Greek state, resolving cultural ambiguities functions as *sine qua non* for the achievement of global recognition.

Institutionalized narrations of identity develop defense mechanisms to attack centrifugal powers developed in the imagined-conversational community to prevent the components of the nation from acknowledging that there is in fact no center, no core of the 'nation' (Gourgouris, 1996; Laclau and Mouffe, 1985). It is the ritual of defense and constant re-selection of the nation's components that makes the nation 'real' – or rather, brings the nation into life. During the nineteenth century, the interests of the Greeks were represented by the Greek state, a not yet fully formed power apparatus, which sought ways to consolidate itself and achieve recognition from its subjects and its European protectors. The immediate problem the state had to overcome was the diversity and richness of cultural experience (the Greeks of Diaspora, the 'unredeemed' Greeks, the liberated Greeks). Even within the Kingdom, there were different scales of experience (the local, the social) that promoted fragmentation. And then, there was a series of problems that accompanied the very process of state-formation. Brigandage was the by-product of this process, but also a 'slur' on national honor abroad. In a period in which the Greeks were seeking ways to define themselves as a 'civilized European nation', brigandage made them the object of derision abroad. In the expression of anti-Greek sentiments Britain, one of the Great Powers and a 'civilized protector' of Greece, had a leading role. When Greece became the 'uncivilized' country of European political discourse, the 'nation's' spokesmen sought a way to redefine Greek national qualities. The defects European observers identified in the Greek nation had to be excluded from it – they had *to be identified as alien.*

The defect named brigandage was transferred to the Vlach nomads and the Albanians brigands who were in a marginal social position in the Greek Kingdom. These ethnic groups were symbolized as aliens, although they often regarded themselves as Greeks, and the state wanted to incorporate them. But in the imagined life trajectory of the Greek 'nation' their social difference became a threat, which had to be obliterated at all costs. Subsequently, the 'scourge of brigandage' despised abroad became a non-Greek quality that defined marginalized social groups in the Greek Kingdom. For the nineteenth-century Greeks, to act out the fear of contamination from alien elements became equivalent to what

Žižek called 'the future's primacy' (1991, p. 18): repetition of this ritual of re-selection of 'national qualities' testified to their collective engagement in the preservation of their identity. *A historical past* haunted this discourse on Greek identity that related brigandage to nation-building. *Klephtism* was a form of ethnic resistance in the close 'Oriental past' of the Greeks but after the institution of the Greek state it became a detested deficiency that was projected on to the 'enemy' against which it had been used: Turkey. An examination of this strategic move alongside representations of brigandage in relation to forms of Irish nationalist protest sheds light on internal systemic contradictions. Nationalist ideologies often comprise competing discourses. Such discourses may aspire to solidify into commonly accepted viewpoints, but almost always preserve their internal contradictions. The process of nation-building is replete with 'contention, struggle and displacement', making the study of nationalist discursive identifications 'a study of ambiguities [...] unstable moments of signification and the extrinsic forces which nurture such identifications' (Thongchai, 1994, p. 173). On a systemic level oblivion operates synchronically as well as diachronically: competing discourses coexist but occupy different domains (the colonial/ international, the national). This is how official discourse on brigandage became a discourse of separation and purification from the 'filthy' Ottoman and Slavic elements that allegedly adulterated the 'European-ness' of modern Greek identity. The weakening of memory protected the Greek community, as it always protects national communities from endogenous divisions, but it discarded those national 'autobiographies' that brought the 'nation' to life.

Part II
Disciplining Identity

4
Anthropological Encounters

Disciplinary archaeologies

Disciplinary scholarship is regulated by theoretical conventions by which we abide. We tend to disagree, revise and reconsider the arguments of its 'founding writers', but use them as valid starting points in our work, conforming thus to the monologues of science. Disciplinary monologism imposes an internal discursive order (Foucault, 1980) to manage intra-textual dialogues, grant scholarly voices with authority or strip them of their plausibility (Smith, 2007, p. 212). Scientists and scholars perceive the world in relation to the form of knowledge appropriate for the purposes of the interest group to which they belong. Inevitably, epistemological inquiry must come first in any inquiry into understanding – in other words, 'we delineate the objects of scientific enquiry before such an inquiry begins' (Bernard-Donals, 1994, p. 40). Disciplinary monologues are contextually bound. They are 'the matrix of ideological values, signifying practices, and creative impulses which constitute the living reality of language [but] are subordinated to the hegemony of a single, unified consciousness or perspective' (Gardiner, 1992, p. 26). For example, even though Durkheim's objectification of social phenomena led to a suppression of 'the presence of actual people' in his theory (Smith, 1989, 1998, p. 67), his rules became constitutive of a sociological discourse that did not always treat social realities with the required sensitivity. We need a Mannheimian voice to repeat how every ideological complex has a depth structure that constitutes its historical identity. It is naïve to excise the emergence of human sciences from the ideological structure in which they were born (Mannheim, [1936] 1968, pp. 292–309).

Anthropology, another discipline seduced by Durkheim's 'rules', was also born without sincere concern about its subject. Its first aspiration was to become the definite *logos* of the *anthropos*, the reasoning of the human *in abstracto*, rather than an interactive understanding of human beings in the socio-cultural world they build (Honneth and Joas, 1988). Abstractions grounded in historical discourse filled the empirical gap of the discipline, relegating people to a nebulous whole that an equally de-hypostacized scientific 'gaze' transformed into valuable knowledge. Very much like the communities of nations, anthropology 'imagined' humans in order to produce textual versions of a reified, unitary humanity. Much like the communities it imagined, however, it was caught in the momentum of internal and external dialogues it initiated with other cultures. These dialogues transformed it into a socio-culturally situated study of human beings. The conviction Herzfeld expressed that, as a discipline, anthropology 'is as much a symbolic system, and as concerned with the differentiation of identities, as any of the social groups it reifies and studies' (1987, ix) directs us to the source of its dialogic transformation. The drama of human interaction was bound to suggest to anthropologists that reflexivity is something they share with their subject (Herzfeld, 2005, p. 212). I am rushing here: this 'revolution' would not happen instantly and without any casualties. A much later (and more productive) manifestation of anthropology's attraction to universalisms can be traced in Harris' belief that his peers have wasted valuable time in pursuing the trivial and the superfluous and it is about time to 'assert the methodological priority of the search for the laws of history in the science of man' (Harris, 1969, cover page). Organized theory has been as important as clearly demarcated empirical materials in the anthropological revolution. The revolution was mediated through a particular form of anti-colonial resistance that occured on the epistemological domain. To reverse this: anti-colonial nationalism's split voice between the material world of Western domination and the nation's spiritual universe (Chatterjee, 1986, 1993) ended up mirroring postcolonial anthropology's oscillation between the materiality of culture and its active symbolization by its creators and users. The production of state-controlled scholarly knowledge was both the democratic pillar and the systemic-ideological outcome of this resistance – two types of 'knowledge-constitutive interests' early Habermasian epistemologies place in a dialectical relationship (Habermas, 1972, p. 211; Swindal, 1999, pp. 90–1). Dilthey's reflexive humanism, which regarded the acquisition of self-consciousness as the main prerequisite in struggles for emancipation from nature, still has much to teach us regarding the process of knowledge-production (Smith, 2007, pp. 55–6). While colonial anthropologists were imagining other cultures, the observed learned to imagine themselves through their observers.

Greece became one such site of proto-anthropological encounters: it had been more an imagined *topos* than an actual place for foreigners since the birth of classicism. Long before the War of Independence travelers with different agendas would visit regions burdened by a Hellenic past to compare surviving classical texts with the physical loci of Hellenic civilization (Leontis, 1995). This coupled reading of 'monumentalized' history with actual places gave meaning to the Grand Tour, a succession of visits to countries such as Italy, Greece, the Ottoman Empire or even the Holy Lands. This habit, widespread in upper middle class and aristocratic families, had a pedagogical impetus (Gourgouris, 1996, pp. 128–40). The tour familiarized young travelers with past civilizations, such as Athens and Rome (Towner, 1985), and brought them in contact with foreign customs and people (Cohen 1996, p. 102). 'Grand tourists' were not exclusively young students of aristocratic parentage broadening their intellectual horizons, or artists seeking inspiration in remote countries. Often, they were established diplomats on political missions that propelled them to produce lengthy accounts of their experiences and observations. Work, education and leisure were coexisting modes and motivations for travel, all equally important in the history of the Grand Tour. Indeed, it has been argued that this blending of work and leisure contributed to an increasing rationalization of travel that later provided the modern tourist system with a *raison d'etre* (Urry, 1996, p. 120). This socio-political exercise, never restricted to Greek regions, began in Italy and soon moved eastwards.

It is noteworthy that in late nineteenth-century travel accounts the notion of the Grand Tour is used progressively less to describe British observations in Greece: terms such as 'observation'; 'travel', or geographical reference, gradually replaced it. This is not simply a linguistic comment: the erasure of the term from travel diaries marks the shifting institutionalization of scholarly knowledge in Western Europe. Although difficult to encapsulate this process here, still in its infancy during the nineteenth century, there is a significant difference between eighteenth and late-nineteenth century visits to Greece. On the one hand, the role of visitors in the Grand Tour was to be acted upon, transformed by the experience of seeing and absorbing the knowledge engraved on the cultural landscape; they were the *object* of classicist pedagogy. By contrast, the role of later observers was to catalogue, classify and encapsulate this history in their writings. They were acting as *subjects* who studied the observed landscape, thus transforming it into an epistemological object.

Another change related to the thematic of travel accounts, and establishes a link between the nineteenth-century ethnographic and the twentieth-century travel 'gaze'. Early records focused more on the lifeless statues of the Parthenon, while the study of living Greeks remained largely a sideline, with passing comments squeezed into the marginalia of European writings. Gradually, however, their presence, though undesirable and almost always negatively colored, came to occupy more space. Even the remoteness of the Greek peninsula would cultivate unease that travelers recorded in their diaries. The geographical proximity of 'Greece' to the Ottoman 'Orient' was often translated into an essentialized 'dangerousness' of Greekness (Colbeck, 1887, pp. 36, 96; Mahaffy, 1876, pp. 1–8; Tozer, 1973, pp. 19–20, 196–7, 1890, pp. 1–2) that remained torn between 'Asiatic' and 'European types' (Jebb, 1880, p. 2). The modern Greeks' presence was deemed undesirable when they began to be viewed by European observers as a half-oriental 'breed' that hardly resembled their magnificent Hellenic ancestors. Being neither fully Western nor quite Oriental, they found themselves occupying the epistemological *and* political interstices of Europe.

After the institution of the Greek state, foreign readings of modern Greek culture 'for pre-established signs' (Urry, 1990, p. 12) based on history rather than interaction and experience were universalized, and even populations outside the Greek kingdom were placed under scrutiny. Thus the didactic element of the Grand Tour began to operate as a performative act communicated to future audiences through writing. As de Certeau argues, travel itineraries 'create and destroy the paths they take' (1986, p. 37): gazing upon other cultures, domesticating them, assists in the production of cognitive meaning. Travel book narratives became 'spatial trajectories' (de Certeau, 1988, p. 115) that clearly 'mapped' and arranged locations in imagined registers for readers and virtual travelers elsewhere in Europe. Travel writing on the sites of the Grand Tour, heavily influenced by classical literature, became a *poetic* endeavor: it produced and re-produced historical narratives (White, 1973) that mediated now indecipherable local custom and experience. The 'Greece' of proto-anthropology was tragically lost as a vision of historical antiquity only to be re-discovered as a European cabinet of curiosities that amused travelers and readerships at home.

These developments did not occur in a vacuum; rather, they define the crypto-colonial status of modern Greece, and of any culture that falls short of European standards prescribed from outside and above. Naturally, the political turbulence of the latter nineteenth century in the Balkan region brought Greece unwelcome attention. The Cretan Insurrection (1866–9), the establishment of the Bulgarian exarchate (1870) and the subsequent eruption of Balkan revolutions (1878–81) were destabilizing factors in the Southeastern Mediterranean region and an indication that the future of the Ottoman Empire was bleak. The so-called 'Eastern Question', the preservation of an Ottoman Empire by those who had economic interests there, increasingly implicated the Great Powers of Europe in Balkan affairs. This unhappy coincidence contributed further to the objectification of Greek culture, because it opened a gateway to British observers of different status and interests. In this respect British travel diaries and records of the period comprised practices we nowadays term 'anthropological', even if their creators were not adherents to an academic discipline. Significantly, most travelers had a background in classics, studied at Oxford and subsequently joined the imperial bureaucratic machine. Oxford graduates manned the imperial stronghold constantly, reproducing the credence that 'the study of the Greats was the best possible preparation for a political or administrative career because it taught good judgment' (Symonds, 1986, pp. 1, 31–46).

Unacknowledged biases in travel accounts often defined British reflections. The origin of such biases sheds light on the links between an emerging 'anthropological' interest in Greece, British political involvement in Balkan affairs and the very nature of European colonial projects. The flood and cataloguing of new information about this marginal territory of Europe paralleled ethnographic research and cataloguing of non-European colonized cultures for the purpose of maximizing control over indigenous populations. It has been acknowledged that the history of anthropology is also the history of colonization (Cohn, 1987; Kuklick, 1991; Stoler, 1989b, 1995; Thomas, 1994). Elsewhere in the world, colonial power sustained physical proximity between European colonizers and the colonized, creating preconditions for the human intimacy that enables anthropological fieldwork, but 'ensur[ing] that intimacy would be one-sided and provisional' (Asad, 1973, p. 17). This chapter forms an attempt to re-establish the link between European ethnographic observations on a culture still in search for self-recognition, and crypto-colonial agendas. I will, however, move beyond this line of inquiry, assessing the impact of informal cultural encounters on the formation of national modes of resistance to foreign intrusion. I aim to illuminate hidden ethnographic discourses we encounter later within European anthropological milieus. The distinction between 'ethnography' and 'anthropology' is not artificial and meaningless. Suffice it to say that constant redefinition of the boundaries between ethnography and anthropology partook in the political production of the discipline itself (Harris, 1969, pp. 2–4; Urry, 1992, p. 3). Instead of seeing the two as inseparable, we should place them in a dialectical schema: before becoming a scientific tool, ethnographic work (or fieldwork) enabled observers of other cultures to define their role and presuppositions. Simultaneously, however, their 'fieldwork' was informed by an unconsciously active, proto-anthropological discourse (Herzfeld, 2001, pp. 4–6). This dialectical relationship between action and theory, or theory in action, is examined in the next pages.

The emphasis on British encounters with Greek peasants is concomitant with my conviction that, although the latter's responses did not differ from those of the modern Greek 'highbrow' culture, they should not be seen as the products of hegemonic nationalism. Gellner's argument (1983, pp. 57, 72), which views national identities as products of integration of 'low' into 'high' culture, is modified. I will argue instead that peasant appropriation of foreign attitudes may establish a new archeology of Greek folklore as the product of counter-European hegemony. Henceforth I proffer that British travelers often *observed and recorded without always fully understanding* – without becoming intimate with their material. Social intimacy played a central role in anthropology's self-recognition as a discipline (Herzfeld, 2001, p. 23). As opposed to them – and, crucially, as opposed to the first Greek folklorists – Greek peasants comprehended their own responses in Anglo-Greek encounters, *granting them with a meaning and a context*. In this respect, they were the originary Greek folklorists: their interpretative actions were the product of a rationalized reflexivity that we find only much later in Greek and British academic milieus. If indeed reflexivity partakes in the humanization of nature within us (Smith, 2007, pp. 60–1), the actual 'civilizing process' of Europe started in the minds of its so-called 'primitives'.

The shifting hermeneutic understanding of other and self from the folk lifeworld to a systemic environment of 'Europeanized' academia echoes Foucault's (1997) thesis on the discursive establishment of disciplinary thinking. I prefer to term my analysis of this development 'archaeology' rather than 'genealogy' because there is nothing linear and fully organized in it: fragments of the discipline's method and theory lie scattered across the temporal plane of European imperial histories. Overlaps, discontinuities and conflict of theory and method coexist in travel accounts, confusing the tidy picture conventional historical narration may propagate. The state-sponsored development of academic disciplines is not presented here as the true champion of counter-hegemonic nationhood or the guardian of modernity. According to Delanty and O'Mahony nationalism 'gains credence as a meaning-generating response to a world that has lost its cosmological anchorage' but 'can also profit from the rise of cultural forms of modern traditionalism which are frequently also revolts of the cultural or geographical periphery against cultural and political centers' (2002, p. 35). They do not discuss the social peripheries that exist within state controlled cultural peripheries: do they not matter *at all* in the European history of nation-building? It is one thing to trace the disciplinary production of national identity in institutionalized responses to the European ethnographic gaze (for a critique see Herzfeld, 1987, pp. 16–18) – in other words, to track down for Greek folklore a straightforward line of descent in the European political centers of power. But ironically, this argument suffers from an epistemological lameness that postcolonial critics identified in anthropological discourse, because it demotes the observed peoples into amorphous and passive recipients. The folklorists of Greek academia lagged behind Greek peasants who had already devised ways to deconstruct and reconstruct, rationalize and re-enchant their cosmological orders for themselves *and* their significant others. Active engagement of Greek peasants with amateur British ethnographers has a special place in a history of European nation-building narrated from the viewpoint of ordinary socialization. This history suggests a dialogical *and* reciprocal fashioning of 'native' culture by the underdogs of a social science still in search of a sound political agenda.

The following section examines observations on Greek culture and customs recorded in diaries of British travelers in Greece. Such observations may remain dominated by classicist discourses that view modern Greek custom through westernized perceptions of ancient Greek civilization, but simultaneously one sees traces of theory and the promise of method that will emerge only later in British disciplinary milieus. The same travel diaries record responses of Greek rural populations to foreign observation and recording. In the third section of the chapter I treat these reactions as both rational and creative aspects of Greek nation-building: they are rational because they contributed to a 'social poetics' that granted Greek identity with meanings concealed to outsiders; and they are creative, because they produced versions of national culture from below. The cultural intimacies of peasantry are viewed as legitimate predecessors of folklore discourse, presenting nation-building as neither a 'top-down', nor a 'bottom-up' process, but a creative intersection of the two.

Anthropology in practice: before theory and method

Lévi-Strauss' metaphor for time keeping in ethnographic observation applies to British travel accounts. For Lévi-Strauss observers and observed resemble passengers who board two different trains. The vehicles' relative paths determine the span and angle of mutual observation, and a great deal is distorted by velocity and distance. Likewise, Lévi-Strauss concluded, the anthropological observers' perceptions of other cultures are often based on transitory observations, even though such observations determine the nature and quality of their data (Lévi-Strauss, 1971, p. 190). The point is not minor: British perceptions of anthropological time in Anglo-Greek encounters formed a conspicuous *problématique* that became constitutive of the thematic in British records. At times, British observations were overdetermined by an antiquarian historical discourse that placed Greece on the evolutionary ladder of European civilization. Yet the uniformity and linearity of time was also challenged by an epistemological relativism akin to that of nationalist discourse, which advocates the uniqueness of national culture. Not only did this oscillation promote nascent academic reflections 'at home' and abroad, but also encouraged a coexistence of Enlightenment and Romantic modes of thought.

Travel accounts already contain theoretical insights systematized in anthropological discourse only in the first half of the twentieth century. Take for example the obsession of British travelers with varieties of the Greek national dress. The costume for women is discussed as an aspect of function and structure: perhaps their complicated 'toilet' is seen as a sign of vanity, a trait only attributable to 'ignorant races' (Roving Englishman, 1877, pp. 170–1), but the coins tied around their foreheads are regarded both as an oriental exhibition of wealth and an object that signifies their dowry (Van Lennep, 1870, p. 237csf). Although this discourse locates Greek culture in the Ottoman Orient, because it revolves around the typical oriental themes of exhibition and colorfulness (Gallant, 2002, p. 70), it also accounts for the structural inevitability of custom.

Comments on women's dress were less negative when the recorder was female. Women travelers gave detailed accounts of Greek female national costume, and praised Greek women for their charm and cleanliness (Poole, 1878, pp. 40–1; Walker, 1864, p. 257). In male travelers' descriptions of the Albanian kilt adopted by Greek men post-Independence there is deliberate emphasis on the national costume as something giving Greeks 'a comical appearance' but which does not detract from their manly 'dangerousness' and 'dignity' (Colbeck, 1887, p. 92). Such commentary appears also in the Ionian postcolonial context, the first site of long-term Anglo-Greek encounters. On this occasion, history is dropped in favor of ritual processes and the 'white-kilted, splendid and savage Albanians' figure mainly as part of carnival celebrations on Corfu (Farrer, 1882, p. 8). The description mobilizes two conflicting ideas, as the Albanian dress simultaneously 'disguises' and exaggerates masculinity. The context of the carnival operates in British travel discourse as the 'anti-structure' of symbolic anthropology (Turner, 1969; Gallant, 2002, pp. 70–1): the comic ambiguity inherent in the participants' appearance empowers them *vis-à-vis* their observers. The man in the Albanian dress is both masculine and comically *carnivalesque*.

This ambivalence was integral to the romantic debate on Greek tradition, which transformed the Albanian dress and its wearers into symbols of pure, primordial, Greekness. Respect for Greek ethnic specificity is expressed when travelers commend Greeks in Albanian costume for not exchanging it for the stiff and artificial fashions of Paris (Bagdon, 1869, pp. 7, 47; Murray, 1872, p. 43; Young, 1876, pp. 48–9). Their dress is even compared to ancient Greek armory of the Periclean age (Benjamin, 1867, p. 208). Prefiguring later academic debates in Scottish and Oxford classicist circles (Jebb, 1880, pp. 85–7; Tozer, 1890, pp. 76–7), nineteenth-century travelers proffer a romantic conception of Greekness, even when they question the peasant's 'civilized' nature (Young, 1876, p. 47). The discourse on authenticity is prominent: only those Greeks who preserve vanishing ways of life were valuable scientific objects. This was part of a widespread discourse concerning the safeguarding of cultural frontiers and the demarcation of the occidental realm that some European empires shared (van Lennep, 1862, p. 7). Within the Greek kingdom there existed a hierarchy even for the peasantry itself, which was built on custom and varieties of dress: so, according to the traveler and academic Henry Tozer and the British Minister at Athens, Wyse, the peasants of some regions were superior to those of others (Tozer, 1873; Wyse, 1871, p. 88). The ambivalence adduces the first British attempts to establish a genealogy of Greek national dress, generating thus a discourse of Greek origins. In this discourse the War of Greek Independence becomes a rupture point in Greek history.

The primordial and masculine, dangerous and comic, character of the Greek in Albanian dress was also connected to Victorian constructions of masculinity, creating relationships of analogy between Greek men in Albanian dress and dandy performance (Young, 1876, p. 47). The phenomenon of dandyism, which originated in Georgian England, presented Victorians with an ambiguous masculine identity (Garelick, 1999). Dandy performance was equally ambiguous: the effete appearance often clashed with exaggerated gentlemanly mannerisms. Victorian Puritanism certainly faced a challenge in dandyism exemplified by the self-presentation of Oscar Wilde, when contemporary aesthetes recognized a disturbing female element in him. Not only do images of the comic Greek savage-dandy allude to historical changes in the production of British masculinity, but they also comprise proto-anthropological comments on ritual and form.

Comparative discourse on the national costume oscillated between universalism and particularism: firstly, the Albanian character and appearance figured as an *Ur-Hellenic* element, a comment that would re-appear in Greek observations of the period (Tuckerman, 1877, pp. 213–14). Often, the costume would also be declared the first garment of humanity (van Lennep, 1862, p. 57). But relational structural analogies were not excluded, and the man in the Albanian dress would be compared to Highlanders (*ibid.*, p. 31). The kilt symbolized primordial, pre-British, Scottish-ness, *just as* the Albanian-Greek costume stood for the past of pre-Hellenic European humanity. From the mid-eighteenth century the Scottish Highlands came to represent in British culture a form of civilized, tamed and 'controlled wilderness' (Mackenzie, 1997, p. 70). Part of the stereotypical Highland image was the kilt, a Quaker invention, which eventually attained value as a survival of universal medieval dress (Trevor-Roper, 1986). Associations between Greek and Scottish costumes disclose an evolution-based approach to tradition.

British descriptions of the nationalization of Albanian costume activated evolutionary time: the observer witnessed a process that had taken place in British culture *a long time before* (Fabian, 1983; Harris, 1969, p. 9). The idea that history is written twice appeared in other contexts too: the culture of regions not yet part of the Greek Kingdom, and which had a history of ferocious resistance to Ottoman rule, was also likened to Highland civilization. Crete, struggling for unification with Greece, was repeatedly selected for this purpose: Cretans were deemed to resemble the Highland warriors (Skinner, 1868, p. 70; Spratt, 1865, pp. 53–4). This valorized the Cretan 'type', a form of marginal Greek identity, by association with the masculine image of the Highlander, a form of romantic British otherness whose role in the production of British identity was central. It is worth noting that Europe's suspension of Cretan identity 'between East and West' became a *leitmotif* in the following decades. Apart from (or perhaps because of) the indeterminacy of the island's political identity (perpetrated by its numerous insurrections and intense ethno-communal strife), Crete was also going to figure as an 'archaeological el Dorado', with the British leading the competition for the excavation of the great Minoan civilization (Carabott, 2006). The politics of another 'sister discipline', archaeology, were coinciding with European colonial agendas (McEnroe, 2002).

Comparative evolutionism, contemporary anthropology's enemy, applied to Greek peasantry as a whole: Greek peasants would often be compared with the subjected 'races' of the great European empires or non-European peoples. Sir George Campbell, a colonial administrator in India and a traveler to Greece in the 1870s, praised the rural Greeks for their 'considerable capacity for self-government', but compared their villages with Indian villages 'of a good class *plus* a church' (Campbell, 1876, p. 70, emphasis in the text). The in-betweenness of the Greek rural character alludes again to the protean, semi-European nature of modern Greek identity (Herzfeld, 1987; Todorova, 1997). Campbell's thoughts re-emerge in the writings of other travelers who had little to do with colonial administration but identified in peasant 'simplicity' traits only subjected 'races' display (Young, 1876, p. 58). On such occasions Greek peasants would become romantic 'noble savages': the contrast between their 'natural', childlike qualities and those of the townspeople, who are corrupted by urbanism (Newton, 1865, vol. I, pp. 209–10), was in accordance with the ethnological interest in primordial forms of culture (Herzfeld, 2001, pp. 171–2). The underlying binary opposition nature vs. culture is both romantic and evolutionary (Harris, 1969, pp. 36–40, 65–6), and delineates a comparative positivist agenda reminiscent of Oxford scholars (Symonds, 1986, pp. 83–7).

During the nineteenth century the rural world came to occupy a special place in European imaginations. The Romantic movement expressed nostalgia for a rapidly disappearing country life (Stocking, 1987) and espoused positive attitudes toward the 'folk'. In Britain, which was peculiar among industrialized nations in having both a flourishing intellectual culture and an underdeveloped university system, anthropological endeavors found their scholarly expression in the experience of travel. Because the British folklore movement grew out of an antiquarian tradition, amateur anthropologists were obsessed with traces of the past that survived in the present lives of the 'uneducated'. But Romanticism in the version advocated by the German philosopher Herder (1744–1803) questioned this linear time, in which everything could fit into the same hierarchy (Todorova, 1997, p. 129). The *Volksgeist* or 'spirit of the people' was viewed not as part of a uniform human experience but as a unique entity with its own role in the world (Hutchinson, 2005, p. 47). This double history, in which a single linear, and a multiple time coexist, is mirrored in British observations on Greek culture. The Greek in his national costume could be gallant and degenerate, comic and noble simultaneously because the traveler made a compromise between Enlightenment (evolutionary) and Romantic ideas (*Geist*, 'uniqueness') (McClintock, 1995, p. 187). While nuances of both times can be found in British accounts, evolutionary ideas seem to triumph. Rural Greek culture is moving in progressive time when compared with Scottish and colonial cultures, and Greek urban culture is described in terms of degeneration, a negative aspect of social evolution.

The 'occidentalized' metropolitan Greek was rejected as an object of study because the peasantry better fit into British observations. British social pathologies found their safety valve in observations on Greek rural life. The Greek peasant, carelessly enjoying his *retsína*, was praised for his sobriety, in contrast to the drunkenness of the British 'besotted lower orders' (Young, 1876, p. 43). Alcoholism, a well-known social problem of industrialized Britain, troubled British observers whenever they visited wine shops to inspect peasant customers (Colbeck, 1887, p. 93; Murray, 1872, p. 44; Poole, 1878, pp. 26–7). Comparative observations were codified in terms of class structures: for example, the absence of class distinctions in Greece was regarded as a unique phenomenon worth recording (Wyse, 1871, p. 38; Bagdon, 1868, p. 251). Britons generally conceived themselves as belonging to an unequal society, 'characterized by a seamless web of gradations' (Cannadine, 2002, p. 4): class mattered in domestic and colonial contexts alike, providing the British with a ready-made formula to understand alien socio-cultural formations. At the beginning of the nineteenth century a discussion of British civilization that centered on economic, moral, political and class issues resulted in a thorough transformation of the notion itself. This concept's meaning 'was strongly conditioned by what was going on in British society – especially with regards to the lower, poor classes' (Stocking, 1987, pp. 30–6). This process almost coincided with the discovery of the oppressed nationalities in the East, rendering English working-class and Balkan ethnic problems interchangeable terms. Ultimately 'the East offered easy possibilities of translating in simple terms the complex issues that the English colonial metropolis was facing at the time' (Skopetea, 1992, pp. 91, 136). We have evidence that the 'rivalry' between Greeks and Turks was also translated into conflict between classes – those of ruled and rulers (Benjamin, 1867, p. 34). Only when Greek peasantry would be compared directly to British upper classes would issues of social rank be translated into questions of purity, cleanliness and decency (Bagdon, 1868, pp. 261–2; Leech, 1869, p. 19). In the fashion of 1960s structuralist symbolic anthropology, discourses of hygiene would be mobilized to naturalize social demarcation and civilized manners (Lévi-Strauss, 1974).

The subjection of Greek rural culture to scrutiny, recording and interpretation did not go unnoticed by the observed peasants. Perhaps we should not call the peasants 'objects', since they responded to foreign interest in meaningful ways, making ethnographic observation of, and meticulous note-taking on Greek social life an eventful business. If the British observer was conscious of his task, so was the observed peasant. In practice, the British 'occulocentric' technique of 'domination' (Fabian, 1990, 1991) could provoke a reaction prompting a discursive reversal of role making. In this symbolic reversal the anthropological subject (the British traveler) would be transformed into an anthropological object (the observed). Simultaneously, however, some British travelers read this counter-scrutiny as 'intrusiveness' (Farrer, 1882, pp. 67, 87–8), a Greek attribute of Ottoman origin. Historical reading of behavior would prevail again, and counter-observation would be demoted into an irrational, oriental vice: the observer's epistemological privilege would be reserved for the traveler. Embedding Greek behavior in history and acknowledging its role in the Greek present brings to the fore an engagement with structural conditions and values in society (Kelly and Kaplan, 1990, pp. 120–2) – questions that occupied Radcliffe-Brown and Malinowski decades later.

Remarkably, travelers refused to acknowledge that *their* presence and labors introduced both suspicion and curiosity into the encounter. We encounter this phenomenon in the Ionian colonial context a year before Britain ceded the islands to Greece (Ansted, 1863, pp. 64–5). Generally, the fact that the Greek 'type' 'did not like to be inspected' but wanted to inspect the stranger is commonsensical: the traveler was, after all, the real intruder who disrupted the mode of everyday life. The presupposition that Greek peasants are entrapped in an anthropological 'Panopticon' (Foucault, 1991) disregards the micro-practices of everyday life that subvert the omniscient and omnipotent gaze (Jay, 1993, p. 415; de Certeau, 1986, pp. 185–92). According to Foucault, imprisonment and constant observation within a Benthamite semicircular prison result in the internalization of the practice of observation: the prisoners (peasants) begin to monitor themselves. By contrast in our case, the traveler and his diary are accessible to the peasants, who occasionally inspect the observer's tools and challenge their omniscient gaze (Young, 1876, p. 146). The collapse in traditional divisions between observer and observed, subject and object, is an issue that today flies in the face of the familiarity anthropologists try to establish with the communities they study (Geertz, 1963, pp. 16, 115; Just, 1995, pp. 285–6;

Rapport, 2002, p. 17; Herzfeld, 2005, p. 214). The transition from native knowledge to social intimacy in fieldwork rests at the core of anthropological epistemology, and dates back to the ethnographic project of Malinowski (1948, 1967), who saw in local self-knowledge the practice of ethnography itself. Although nineteenth-century British travel accounts often reproduce forms of native culture instead of advocating its understanding (Thomas, 1996; Lévi-Strauss, 1953; Turner, 1986, p. 35), a basic understanding of Greek counter-reflexivity is not totally absent from British observations.

Travelers were aware that access to the sphere of female socialization was severely restricted. It is worth noting the postcolonial context of the Ionian Islands, which, again, may suggest the origins of British observations. Ansted, who was acquainted with Greek Ionian culture, deemed it impossible to gather any information on women because Greek men 'guarded' them zealously, forbidding their interaction with the 'Lords' (1863, p. 58). No more information is provided by this account, yet we encounter the same comment in another travel diary by an anonymous expert on the Eastern Question. In this narrative, foreigners cannot approach women, who flee to find refuge in domestic spaces:

> I am lightly shod and I do not make much noise, nor am I a very fearful apparition… but I have no sooner entered the street than a change comes over it. When I first turned the corner, young women were gossiping and laughing together in the doorways, and from the windows: now I hear the click of many doors closing stealthily; and the lattices are shut everywhere. A Frank is a rare sight in this obscure quarter, and the women are wild as young fawns. They are watching me from all sorts of places; but if I stayed there for hours, not one would come out till I was gone. I know why the Greek girls are as shy as young fawns, and it pains me to think of it: a thousand tales are fresh in my memory of harmless young women who, by chance, caught the eye of some terrible Turk, and soon after disappeared mysteriously (Murray, 1872, pp. 235–6).

These women's curiosity parallels the observer's gaze upon them. Their withdrawal blocks the observer's gaze, while permitting *them* to become privileged observers: to see without being seen. Again, women treat the narrator as an intruder in a 'forbidden' world. The doors are barred for him, because he cannot access a rigid code of native conduct, which holds that interaction of women with men is allowed only as part of ritual matchmaking – a formalized process of arranged marriage called *proksenió* (literally, 'acting for an outsider') (Herzfeld, 1991, p. 89). The British nineteenth-century narrator lacked the necessary mediator and he is also a *ksénos*, a foreigner in the Greek national community. It is noteworthy that in the writings of female Victorian travelers, Greek women appear as friendly and communicative (Poole, 1878, p. 50). Again, therefore, the significance of ritual is vaguely acknowledged in travel writing (see Greenberg on Evans-Pritchard [1993: 117]). It may be significant then that the actual intruder is male *and* a foreigner.

The rationale of this gendered exclusion is encapsulated in the writings of Wyse and Finlay through use of the antiquated term *xenelasía* (from *ksénos* and the verb *elávno*, meaning 'to persecute'), or 'the disgusting of foreigners' (*The Times*, 15 December 1871; Wyse, 1871, p. 281). This exclusion is perceived by Wyse and Finlay as disgust, an allusion to Greek 'aversion' to strangers. Mahaffy similarly discusses the 'jealousy' of the nation towards foreign political interference (Mahaffy, 1876, xii). In Greek culture women symbolize the private sphere that must be rendered impenetrable from the 'outside' (Herzfeld, 1987, p. 117, 2001, p. 217; Gallant, 2002, p. 64). From the British observer's standpoint this barring is already perceived as a discourse of 'sterilization' (Douglas, 1993, pp. 125–6). The way the traveler discusses the 'mysterious disappearance' of women who 'catch the eye' of the Turk fits the same pattern of anthropological understanding. The Greek women's exposure to the Ottoman outsider, who is the site of 'pollution' in Greek culture, reveals that the British see in their exclusion from the women's world a discourse of symbolic purification. In such British reflections we already have a conceptualization of what Herzfeld (1997b, 2005) termed more than a century later 'cultural intimacy'.

The British urgency to find a gateway to Greek peasant culture might have been dictated by an unexpressed fear: if industrialization ever reached the peninsula, Greek peasantry and its Hellenic remnants would disappear. Britons thus assigned themselves the mission of immortalizing in their writings 'primitive' Greek attributes. It is unfortunate that the presence of the 'Lords' was enough to change everything. Ansted was convinced that the Greek peasant who expected from the British traveler a *bakshish*, or 'payment for annoyance', illustrated the adverse effects of travel in Greek culture.

> It must be acknowledged that our country people have brought this upon themselves. Nothing of this kind is observable in country villages out of the way of tourists... Experience has taught the natives

of the frequented spots what they may expect as the reward of clamour (Ansted, 1863, p. 57)

Note that the Ionian Islands, on which Ansted writes, constitute a unique case of Greek marginal identity because they were briefly under British rule. They were a popular and familiar destination for British travelers. However, the same merging of function with strategy occurs when observation concerns Greek-speaking territories of the Ottoman Empire (Walker, 1864, p. 230). References to structure, strategy and history permeated accounts of British travellers who constantly complained that the Greeks are 'untrustworthy' (MacKenzie and Irby, 1877, p. 69; 'Roving Englishman', 1877, p. 355; Young, 1876, p. 65), 'thieves' (Farrer, 1882, p. 128) and 'unable to observe the principle of truth' (*Letters of Mr Frank Noël*, 1871, p. 87). Some observers attributed these vices to self-protection against the cruel Turkish ruler (Poole, 1878, pp. 58–9), constructing thus an orientalist genealogy. It is important however that in these observations deception is also read as a strategy against foreign rule that belongs to the cosmological order of Greek culture. The allusion to Greek deception formed a controversy in historiography also, with some historians simply recording it (Angelomatis-Tsougarakis, 1990, p. 103) and others connecting it to the notorious oriental silence (Tozer, 1869, vol. I, pp. 7–8, 72), which allows the occidental observer to speak on behalf of the subaltern (Skopetea, 1992, p. 95). Oriental silence *and* incapability of accuracy, which some Britons traced in the 'Greek character', may easily have been connected to lying and deception. Even the most acute contemporary analysis of the Greek *poniriá* (low cunningness), this 'attitude of insubordination' to the oppressor (Herzfeld, 1985, p. 25, 1987, p. 29), mainly refines nineteenth-century British observations. This debate should not be dissociated from comments on the 'Greek entrepreneurial spirit' (Van Lennep, 1862, p. 73), its 'Odyssean mercantile essence' (Campbell, 1876, p. 41; Tozer, 1869, vol. I, p. 17; Wyse, 1871, p. 15) and its 'versatility' (Mahaffy, 1876, p. 21; Tozer, 1869, vol. I, pp. 115, 153, vol. II, p. 257; Young, 1876, p. 116). The double image of the Greeks figuring in these descriptions was based on the twofold reading of a 'commercial character' that the British and the Greeks shared. Comparative observations are repressed by British travellers who criticized Greek manners for good reasons: lying/deception affects the distribution of power. Lies 'add to the power of the liar, and diminish that of the deceived, altering the choices of the deceived at different levels' (Bok, 1978, pp. 19–28). The 'crafty' Greeks continuously undermined the

British scientific Panopticon by distorting the information British observers aspired to collect.

Greek deception would soon be associated with actual stage performance. Again, this insight, articulating the principles of Goffmanesque self-presentation, echoes the writings of contemporary cultural anthropologists, who distinguish between a private and a public collective self (Geertz, 1980, p. 121; Herzfeld, 1997b, 2005). The ritualistic aspects of the Goffmanesque 'frame' replace historicism in travel narratives, but also allude to a hidden cultural whole. According to a traveler, the Greeks were 'born actors'.

> Self-consciousness, which brings with it the usual train of mannerisms and affectations, is said to be the curse of the English stage, if not of English society. On the stage and off the stage it is apparently unknown to the Greeks, who, bumptious and boastful though they often are, do not *look* conscious or self-absorbed; never seem, when in public, to trouble themselves the least in the world whether or no people are looking at them, admiring them, or criticizing them, and, consequently, never appear nervous or ill-at-ease among themselves, as is the case with so many of our countrymen. Their habit of gesticulation, which we may call forced and exaggerated, is in reality as much part of their nature, as it is part of an Englishman's nature to carry an umbrella! (Young, 1876, p. 201)

Note that the initial demarcation between rural and urban Greekness is now dropped. Here the traveler's analysis moves away from Goffman's by presenting Greek performative mannerisms as 'instinctual' (Farley, 1876, ix). Like Bourdieu's wavering between the unconscious performances of *doxa* and strategic mobilizations of *habitus* in the social field, Greek mannerisms comprise a set of *inculcated* rules that cannot be renounced or replaced (Bourdieu, 1999). Like later anthropologists, Young sought ways to organize his data in relation to the unconscious conditions of social life (Lévi-Strauss, 1967, p. 25; de Certeau, 1986). Of course, history remains hidden behind his narrative: gesticulation, the bodily language of the 'savage', had been dropped by the British who were perhaps 'poorer in gesture', but 'more civilized' in manners. This discourse, which was articulated by Tylor, automatically placed Greek inculcated values (theatricality) in the lower stages of civilization (Herzfeld, 1987, p. 137). The passage beautifully demonstrates how anthropology assembles its theory in British travel writing by selecting what was ignored in historical discourse: gestures, posture and mannerism – *Greek habitus as hexis*.

Greek *habitus* troubles Westerners, who find the combination of truth and art evidently disquieting. The fact that the ethnography of our travellers brings into play an 'equivocation with the truth' (Metcalf, 2002, p. 3; Herzfeld, 1991a, 2005, p. 24) is dismissed. Theatricality is occasionally linked to Greeks' 'duplicitous' dealings with foreigners and the rivalry that characterizes Greek society (Wyse, 1871, p. 149). The observation alludes to entrepreneurialism: like any kind of 'performance' for the foreign 'Lord', and like the peasant's expectation of remuneration, jealousy signifies the shift 'from an agro-town and guild economy to one penetrated by [...] the tourist trade' (Herzfeld, 1991b, p. 99). The jealousy Wyse identifies in 'things Greek' has its root in the market-oriented relationship between Greeks and foreign visitors. The very notion of 'professionalism' in Greek–European exchange was based on the expectation that the more experienced party will 'cheat' the other (*ibid.*, p. 52). This series of Greek virtues, skills and 'vices' (entrepreneurial spirit, lying to foreigners, performance and jealousy) comprise components of the theoretical apparatus that British observers constructed to comprehend Greek culture.

> *jealousy:* a desire for what the rival/other has
> *entrepreneurial spirit:* acting on this desire
> *performance of mannerisms:* the means for acquisition of what
>   is desired
> *Greek lying:* the deceived 'other's' feeling of exploitation
> *English self-consciousness:* because jealous Greeks lack this they
>   might succeed in deceiving the British

The schema frames a critical anthropological question: what is authentic and what is performative? How much of what we see is fabricated *for us*? For this reason, Britons mobilized self-perceptions so as to understand Greek character through comparison (both Greeks and English are commercial people) and contrast (English self-consciousness vs. Greek natural performance). Ironically, their discourse was predicated upon the notion of lack of Greek self-consciousness, which makes Greek mannerisms 'natural properties'. As natural properties, however, they are not easily recognizable and make the Greeks powerful deceivers. Hospitality as a constituent of Greek character (Wyse, 1871, p. 88; Young, 1876, p. 192) was discussed as part of the same logic. The hospitality of the poor peasant was a pattern of 'social investment' analogous to the cultural capital of the rich. In intercultural exchange it also served to exercise control and assert superiority over the 'hosted'. By controlling the right to treat, 'locals maintain moral advantage over strangers who may represent offices and countries of much greater political power' (Herzfeld, 1991b, p. 84). Unsurprisingly, Greeks describe their hospitality as 'disinterested', the most 'sacred' and 'ancient' of Greek institutions (Gennadios, 1870, pp. 175–6), thus concealing its strategic function in social poetics. As Clifford argued, 'ethnographies often present themselves as fictions of learning, the acquisition of knowledge, and finally the authority to understand and represent another culture' (1986, p. 108). British travel accounts figure as 'ethnographic allegories' that allude to the interchangeability of power and deception: those who can 'cheat' hold the power.

Evidently, the primary aim in the inspection of the modern Greek character was the detection of continuities and discontinuities in Greek history. As the project of British ethnography was mainly antiquarian, observations on the urban population also had a historical resonance: could, for example, modern Athenian custom be preserving ancient Greek values (Campbell, 1877, p. 28)? Undoubtedly, curiosity about urban life never replaced the fascination with rural Greece. Even British commentators whose stay in Greece fulfilled purposes other than traveling displayed interest in Greek character and beliefs. Newspaper political commentary of the 1860s and 1870s was 'flavored' by observations on Greek regional character: in 1868, *The Morning Post* correspondent in Crete published a series of letters in which, alongside political developments, he recorded Cretan Greek customs and beliefs (24 September and 11 November 1868). Interest in the 'Cretan character' just when Crete threatened Ottoman stability, provides yet another link between anthropological remarks and administrative control. The same practice was applied in editorials during the Eastern Question crisis in 1878 (*The Morning Post*, 29 July 1878). Some British travellers even managed to devise areas of research: religious ceremonies such as weddings, funerals and baptisms (Grey, 1870, p. 197; Colbeck, 1887, p. 57; Newton, 1865, vol. I, p. 66; Bagdon, 1868, vol. I, pp. 180–3) social contracts such as dowry arrangements (Roving Englishman, 1877, p. 233; Newton, 1865, vol. II, p. 9; Spratt, 1865, pp. 170–1) popular beliefs in nereids and vampires (Newton, 1865, vol. I, pp. 211–12; Spratt, 1865, p. 364; Walker, 1864, pp. 227, 231) and traditions for the siege and re-conquest of Constantinople (Benjamin, 1867, p. 7; Campbell, 1877, p. 29; Van Lennep, 1862, p. 9) were treated as shortcuts to Greek history. Not only did these efforts prioritize history, they also concentrated on taxonomy rather than interpretation. It seemed that in the nineteenth century battle for anthropological reflexivity, form and order was winning over content.

Antiquarian requiems *qua* anthropological beginnings

These proto-anthropological efforts emerged in the milieu that produced Tylor's *Primitive Culture* (1871). In this work, Tylor discussed ideas and customs that fulfilled no function in modern societies and were regarded as 'irrational' because they had survived from previous periods. The focus of Tylorian research became peasant societies in Europe, although the work was based on second-hand knowledge of reports from abroad. The so-called 'doctrine of survivals' helped Tylor and his contemporaries to endorse a happy marriage between modern civilization and primitive man, allegedly preserved intact in 'backward' peasant cultures of Europe (Stocking, 1996, p. 10). Despite the theory's evident Eurocentrism, Tylor advanced anthropological knowledge: because in his theory savage customs were viewed in an evolutionary framework, they gained a rational quality previously denied to them. Even 'backwardness' was becoming the object of scientific investigation. If we relate Tylor's antiquarianism to the European debate upon Greek history, we can understand the challenge that the Greeks posed to British observers. The motion of time in Greek culture is double, because of the divide between urban and rural life. Urban time emulated western progressive time unsuccessfully, whereas rural time was almost static. Greek rural culture was burdened by a famous past, which was preserved *unconsciously* in popular beliefs. Contrariwise, there was a historical disruption in urban modes of thought. British observers' merging of Enlightenment (evolutionist) and Romantic notions of culture suggests that they were caught between evolutionist history and Herder's romantic ethnography, Greek degeneration and national *Geist*, in the interstices of ethnohistory. I explore this question at length in the next chapter.

For much of the period before the 1880s we cannot talk about anthropology as a self-contained field of knowledge. In Britain proto-anthropological endeavors were just beginning to find shelter in the *Anthropological Institute* and the *British Association for the Advancement of Science* (BAAS). Amateur anthropologists were almost exclusively middle-class Victorians, often serving the interests of the British Empire abroad as administrators and missionaries rather than scholars. The establishment of anthropology as a field resulted from Pitt Rivers' ponderings on the comparative value of armory as an indicator of human progress (Symonds, 1986, p. 147). Tylor, the first to secure a post at Oxford and publish work that named the discipline-to-be (*Anthropology*, 1881), was welcomed by professionals such as W.H. Flower, Director of the Natural Science Museum. The development of museums as shrines of 'scientific' research on alien species imported from the colonies was closely associated with anthropological research, especially in the British colonies (van Kreuren, 1989).

Scientific positivism, which dictated the physiological, rather than sociological study of human beings, prevailed until the 1890s, when A.C. Haddon favored ethnographic survey as opposed to physical anthropology. In the dawn of the new century, W.H.R. Rivers, President of the BAAS, battled against the presuppositions of physical anthropology, ultimately replacing them with ideas of historical diffusionism. The idea that Europe could rely on the study of 'savages' to recover its past was vigorously contested, and a divorce was issued between natural sciences and humanities-based research, especially classicism. Paradoxically then, the interest in historical research, so closely tied to the justification of colonial projects, was now serving to sanction the ontological difference between natural and social worlds. Still, history, philosophy and classics were fully formed, professionalized disciplines when geography and anthropology were introduced in University curricula. The ancient world continued to form part of anthropological enquiry: as Ridgeway at Cambridge, Myers at Oxford, Lang and Frazer's enquiries in the *Golden Bough* betray, comparisons between recorded savage custom and ancient sources did not disappear, ensuring the preservation of evolutionism in the theories of the forefathers of social anthropology, Malinowski and Radcliffe-Brown. Both Frazer and Tylor contributed to editions of collective volumes on folklore studies. In 1907 Frazer was ready to admit that anthropology was 'not so much a science as a pleasant hobby' (Urry, 1992, p. 24): academic research was still a pastime for amateur anthropologists.

Rivers, however, a psychologist by training, was keen to introduce questions of method and research. 'Facts' themselves were not sufficient, what truly mattered was *how* they were collected. The question of 'fieldwork' figured in Rivers' work repeatedly (associated with the 'Cambridge Method' of research), questioning the reliability of data collected by untrained missionaries and colonial administrators. Rivers' efforts almost replicated Haddon's preceding attempts to produce 'pure' factual accounts of the essential 'wholeness' of other cultures, unspoiled by researchers (Slobodin, 1978, p. 105). Although Rivers' late diffusionism swayed him back to comparative evolutionism, at various points in his career he contented that observed societies exist outside the familiar territory of the fieldworker. Rivers also suggested that fieldwork was a scholarly skill and therefore data ought to be collected in native language and terminology. He opposed the practice of guiding natives by questions and contended that the fieldworker should act just as an observer. For Rivers, other social worlds ought to be researched sociologically. Most importantly, however, he maintained that the specifics of social life point to wider social interrelationships. Functionalism was taking its first clumsy steps.

When Malinowski published his first accounts of the Trobriands in 1916, the field was on its way to a revolution. Malinowski attacked the 'sacralization' of facts propagated by Rivers' ethnographic obsession, and claimed that no data exist outside the realm of observation and recording. In his own words: '*only laws and generalizations are scientific facts*' (1916, p. 419, emphasis in the text). The firm belief that data are the product of inductive reasoning and selection was adumbrated in Rivers' distinction between *intensive fieldwork* and bureaucratic *survey work* (Urry, 1992, pp. 32–3), only Malinowski systematized the argument. Malinowski embodied the discontinuities and regressions of anthropological theory: on the one hand, *The Argonauts of the Western Pacific* (1922) refined 'fieldwork' on the social life of other peoples (in part and in whole, in native language and cosmology) and resolved Rivers' functionalist predicaments. On the other hand, Malinowski's fixation upon colorful narrative and historical reference (exemplified in the title of his groundbreaking *Argonauts* that mirrored Frazer's *Golden Bough*) exposes the persistence of antiquarian fascination in his research (Stocking, 1983, p. 106; Stocking, 1996, p. 270).

Despite its colonial roots, the split between descriptive and comparative ethnography was not new in Malinowski's time. Distinctions between recorders and interpreters date back to Tylor and Frazer's confused attempts to separate fact from speculation and socio-cultural context (Stocking, 1987) – although their belief that savage custom is an unconscious record of human history today sounds naïve. Malinowski set out to uncover the subtle links between 'the laws of science and the Gatling gun' (*ibid.*, p. 247), articulating thus the dangers hidden in the historical convergence of power with knowledge long before Foucault. His most significant contribution was the humanization of the observed: living as 'a native among the natives', and 'conversing with them in their native tongue' introduced exotic others into the field of anthropological vision (Stocking, 1996, p. 233). Physical proximity and social intimacy in fieldwork were beginning to converge.

Haddon's student, Radcliffe-Brown, changed the face of the discipline. Haddon's meticulous collecting techniques and Rivers' scientific approach to fieldwork impacted on Radcliffe-Brown. His interest in genealogy and ritual, two emergent issues in British travel accounts of the latter nineteenth century, was combined with a re-working of classical sources alongside Durkheimian and Bergsonian theory, making *The Andaman Islanders* (1922) an ethnographic synthesis of secondary sources rather than first-hand accounts. Radcliffe-Brown eventually renounced survivalist and diffusionist arguments, suggesting that social forms can be better understood in relation to their function – a Durkheimian thesis that nineteenth-century British travelers were working towards. The distinction between *social statics* and *social dynamics* articulated the need to examine social structure and function (in order to interpret fieldwork research), and synchronicity and diachronicity (in order to understand other cultures). Following Radcliffe-Brown's theoretical elaborations, Evans-Pritchard's *Witchcraft Oracles and Magic Among the Azande* (1937) and *The Nuer* (1940) infused data with interpretation and theoretical synthesis, thus resolving some tensions between theory and method that occupied his predecessors. Both Radcliffe-Brown and Evans-Pritchard's interest in providing an analytic, holistic account of other societies through localized studies, separated history (particularized and descriptive) from social anthropology (generalized and analytic) (Stocking, 1996, pp. 304–8; Urry, 1992, p. 130). The anthropologist's job was to shed light on the resonance of other cosmologies while retaining some respect for their specificity.

And so, the 'natives' were given back their voice – even though this voice continued to be mediated through the observer's account. Malinowski's inheritance often troubles anthropologists, especially after the emergence of post-colonial critiques of the discipline, which explain that even pioneers such as Radcliffe-Brown and Evans-Pritchard had strong ties with colonial administration (McCall, 1980, p. 98; Stocking, 1996, pp. 339–40) and read Mods and Greats (Symonds, 1986, pp. 155–7). When the anthropologist 'relinquish[ed] his [*sic*.] comfortable position on the veranda of the missionary compound, Government station, or planter's bungalow, where, armed with a pencil and notebook [...] he [*sic*.] has been accustomed to collect statements from informants' (Malinowski in Metcalf, 2002, p. 55), other cultures revealed themselves as vast universes. Naturally, to analyze and interpret them while retaining some respect for their specificity clashed with the need to be selective and synthetic – in Metcalf's (2002) metaphor, a liar by default. Nineteenth-century British travelers stumbled upon this anthropological 'dishonesty' that would wrack the brains of generations of scholars. Their oversight was to project this dishonesty exclusively onto Greek peasants, presenting them inadvertently as what they truly were: proto-anthropological performers.

The 'price' of knowledge: cultural intimacy as anthropological intimacy

The fact that British travelers acknowledged their exclusion from the cherished aspects of Greek life did not stop them from trying to penetrate the protective shield under which one finds what only insiders can enjoy. Ironically, the shield protected the observers more than the Greek peasants. British travelers were just not sufficiently prepared to respond to what they would find underneath it: a collection of what we may call (cautiously) 'pseudo-authentic' events. Most travelers discovered that they were denied access to social events, such as weddings, without a generous financial 'contribution'. Soon it became evident that access to the private sphere of peasant communities was enough to destroy the spontaneity of social interaction: the peasantry would respond to British curiosity by inventing a 'front social stage' for foreign spectators (McCannell, 1973). All those aspects of Greek everyday life that supposedly encapsulated the 'Greek character' were rearranged to produce a new 'social-symbolic order' (Gourgouris, 1996), a new mode of communication with European visitors.

Nowhere is this reaction more pronounced than in the context of dance and music. Wyse's initiation into such Greek practices at Achmetaga in Euboia is noteworthy. His participation in a local festival, in which the Greeks danced something that reminded him of the 'Irish jig or Scotch reel [...] with a customary marvellous solemnity', was followed by a symbolic action:

> On the dance relaxing, I went up with a dollar to the clarionet-player [*sic*.], which he accepted with a dignified air, and then struck up the old tune with renewed energy, placing the dollar on his fez over his forehead, for he was dressed in the usual foustanella style. The clarionet did its outmost, and I soon perceived not without result (Wyse, 1871, pp. 219–20).

As Achmetaga was the property of the English family of Noëls, we cannot be sure how far back the staged event can be traced and whether its performance related to the hosts' practices. Yet, there is an oscillation between the economic nature of exchange and the symbolic function of reciprocity in this particular context (Mauss, 1954; Ardener, 1989) requiring further analysis: the observer emphasizes the former when the Greek performer primarily *reciprocates* British observation. Wyse's reference to the 'dignified air' of the clarinet-player may be a perceptive comment on this oscillation between modern economic notions of exchange and symbolic reciprocation of interest. This indeterminacy betrays how Greeks attempt to open the space of cultural intimacy to British 'others' in search of cultural recognition. Dancing and music, something outsiders enjoy as an authentic experience, was accompanied by accepting money, a version of the *bakshish*, whose meaning (performance and symbolic reciprocation) only Greeks seem to fully comprehend. The Ottoman practice of *bakshish* is an embarrassing stereotyping the Greek clarinet-player performs nevertheless. Whereas 'staging' tradition could be viewed as a native attempt to shut the observer outside the realm of native culture, an *ordinary* weapon 'of relatively powerless groups' in encounters with others (Scott, 1986, p. 6), the *process* itself produced 'truthful' accounts of tradition. The issue of theatricality that British travelers recognized in Greek mannerisms ought to be re-addressed as the core of ethnographic knowledge: for those Greeks, the notion of truth is dialogic in the strictest Bakhtinian sense, because 'it exists only as a succession of mutually constructing speech events' (Metcalf, 2002, p. 9).

It must be stressed that the consequence of the observer's 'intrusion' was not corruption, *but rearrangement* of the Greek symbolic universe. Dancing and social events that previously serviced the Greek community, now assumed a twin value. Firstly, they established a channel of communication with the European other: their staged authenticity signified their plausible appropriation to the needs of a foreign audience/ readership of signs ('the Lords want to learn about our culture') (Urry, 1990, p. 9). Secondly, they helped the rural Greeks select for concentrated attention experiences whose ritualistic aspect enlivened memory and linked the present with the relevant past, but simultaneously modified it (Douglas, 1993, pp. 63–4). As elsewhere in Europe and beyond (Pemberton, 1994), Greek ritualism attained an 'exegetic' stance: it began to mediate between the habitual and the interpretative, producing native forms of self-knowledge (Turner, 1967, p. 20). In 'the struggle for possession of the sign' (Comaroff, 1985, p. 196), the Greeks managed to produce their own form of cultural hegemony.

We have established an archaeology of modern Greek tradition, noting that once 'custom' lost its spontaneous character, it was both incorporated into national culture and also became part of institutionalized knowledge: the discipline of folklore (de Certeau, 1986; Herzfeld, 1987, 2001, p. 48; Kyriakidou-Nestoros, 1975, pp. 92–3). Interaction with the 'civilized foreigners' made the rural Greeks conscious of what tradition is, or rather *how it is to be performed* (Cowan, 1988). A note is needed here to avoid confusing scholarly and peasant responses:

reflection on these processes by Greek academics was crucial in the development of folklore into an autonomous discipline. But peasant responses must understood as an independent form of *carnivalesque*, a *conscious* resistance mechanism that deconstructs the observer's pretensions to omniscience (Bakhtin, 1968, pp. 255–7). Their logic is the rational counterpart of formalized folklore discourses. Every time the peasants would recognize and perform the 'disreputable' aspects of their culture for foreigners, they would not simply reciprocate the observer's interest, but also attribute meaning to the British observers' interest in Greek culture, performing a counter-analysis of British 'conduct'. Peasant reciprocation of British interest is not simply *homologous to*, but *constitutive of*, contemporary anthropological practices. At the same time, the peasants would self-narrate, explain to themselves what constitutes their own culture, an enterprise in which Greek folklorists were involved only later. Hence, peasant cultural intimacies activated aspects of a proto-anthropological intimacy until the Greek folklore *qua* anthropology movement emerged and established itself as an academic discipline. The dual aim of folklore studies as both the subject matter of the *lore* of the people and the study of the people presents the two facets of cultural-as-anthropological intimacy in the best possible way (Ben-Amos, 1998, p. 270).

The negotiation concerning preservation of rural customs was not an exclusively British concern but a common European one (Kurti, 1996, p. 14), suggesting that traditions of Hellenic genealogy in danger of extinction must cease to exist unconsciously and become institutionalized (de Certeau, 1986, pp. 78–9, 216). The Greeks themselves displayed this urgency, echoing Haddon's anxiety to preserve antique forms of culture. In the late 1860s there were Greek societies inside and outside the Greek kingdom dedicated to collecting 'survivals' of ancient Hellenic civilization in Greek culture. The Greek Philological Society of Constantinople, an important institution for Greek studies, was recognized as one of the leading institutions in this subject (*Palingenesía*, 20 September 1878). Inside Greece, the Philological Society of Parnassos established in 1870 a journal dedicated to identifying Hellenic survivals (*Parnassos*, 1870, vol. I, pamphlet 1, p. 4). Ultimately, European anthropology was complemented by Greek folklore: the gaze on the other became the gaze upon the internal other, the rural 'people' whose dialogically produced discourses were slowly 'vanishing' (Ivy, 1995). This movement – not exclusively Greek or European, as Handler (1988) points out in his study of Québecois nationalism – originated in the Greek urban center of Athens.

Some of my remarks rely excessively on 'archaeological' hindsight: although the debate about 'survivals' appears in Greece in the 1830s as an offshoot of the Fallmerayer controversy (Skopetea, 1999, p. 99; Gourgouris, 1996, p. 143), the institutionalization of this scientific interest is detected in the early 1880s. The Greek Historical and Ethnological Society, a national institution for the development of folklore studies, was founded in 1882, and it was not until 1884 (and again in 1909) that Nikolaos Politis gave the first institutional definition of Greek folklore (Kyriakidou-Nestoros, 1976). Politis, the first folklore scholar, published his first work in 1871, the date most associated with Tylor's *Primitive Culture*. In this work he reiterated how important ancient survivals in Greek peasant culture are for folklore discourse. Indeed, upon reading Politis' later definition of folklore (1909), one realizes that the institution of Greek *laografía* was marked by a combination of the *totality and synchronicity* of anthropology with the *specificity and diachronicity* of history (Kyriakidou-Nestoros, 1981, p. 277). Politis retained the dualism of high–low culture, regarding peasants as objects to be observed, not as subjects to interact with and understand. A typical 'armchair academic', Politis replicated Tylor's habit of *imaginatively* placing himself in the place of 'primitive' people in order to comprehend them (Burrow, 1966; Tylor, 1964 [1878]). The idea of peasant irrationality (by analogy to the irrationality of the colonized) was adumbrated in the nineteenth-century Anglo-Greek anthropological encounters, although the outcome of such encounters was not exclusively the result of Anglo-Greek exchange: other Europeans had performed the same role during their Greek tours.

Notably then, in its inception, even Greek folklore lacked any 'intimacy' with Greek peasant culture, because it happily replaced an intense engagement with its material with historical discourse. Only Politis' student, Stilpon Kyriakidis, managed to escape survivalist discourses by stressing the dramaturgical aspects of peasant culture. In his *Hellenikí Laografía: Mnimeía Lógou* ('Greek Folklore: Speech Monuments'), published at Politis' initiative, Kyriakidis was more inclined to challenge the subject–object, highbrow–lowbrow approach. In *Ti Eínai Laografía?* ('What is Folklore?') he explicitly renounced Tylor, explaining that his 'survivals' were in fact old *practices* coexisting (*symbiómata*) with new ones (Kyriakidis, 1948, p. 139). The emphasis on understanding peasant practice instead of superimposing history on it successfully combined cultural and anthropological intimacies into an epistemologically conscious and methodologically sound thesis. By extension, Kyriakidis symbolically denied Tylorian outsiders the right to intrude in, and domesticate aspects of modern Greek identity and culture. Nevertheless, the nineteenth-century peasants had been there before Kyriakidis: while safeguarding their culture from outsiders, they had granted it an explicit context. This context was conditioned by a dialogue between what British (and other European) survivalists traced (pure, Hellenic Greekness), and what modern cross-cultural exchange demanded (performance of Greek culture as resistance to its appropriation).

We can trace nineteenth-century peasant responses to foreign intrusion in extra-academic circles. Take for example folk ballads, allegedly representative of the *Neohellenic Volksgeist*: not only did amateur Greek folklorists collect and classify them in different typological systems, but they also *(re)produced* them. This practice, which resembles the *Ossianic Lays* amongst other movements (Hutchinson, 2005, p. 51), and betrays an awareness of their importance *as oral history*, configured repeated Greek attempts at stimulating British philhellenic feelings during international crises. The Greek press published a series of such ballads entitled 'products of the popular Muse', which were in fact written by contemporary Greek poets in a 'traditional fashion'. An inspired 'traditional' polemic against European intervention, which reads as a brigand ballad, appeared in *Palingenesía*, a Greek newspaper with an explicit nationalist agenda, during the Cretan insurrection (3 April 1867). A second example is found in *Palingenesía* in 1881: a 'folk song' written by the obscure Marietta Bitsu and dedicated to 'the famous philhellene and British Prime Minister Mr. Gladstone' (16 March 1881). Greek cheating, once again: apparently, Greeks had managed to take the European cues.

The formalization of anthropological and folklore discourse – the acquisition of an institutional 'home' for these disciplines – came much later. But I was more interested in capturing the moment that this discourse was still not fully recognized as anthropology or folklore. Nineteenth-century British accounts of Greek culture can be read as the ideological *and* epistemological counterpart of institutionalized anthropological discourse. The boundaries between critical and uncritical British observation were already becoming blurred, something that invites a serious reappraisal of what today we discard as mere colonial prejudice (Herzfeld, 1987; Smith, 2007, p. 216). Travel accounts of peripheral European cultures have a place in the history of anthropology as they complemented the efforts of 'armchair academics' to create a new discursive space. Equally important, however, has been the appropriation of proto-anthropological practices in modern Greek culture, especially in rural responses to European outsiders. In this chapter, I shifted focus from scholars' concern with native cultures of the 'intellectual periphery' (Bauman, 1995, p. 229; Bakalaki, 1997; Faubion, 1993; Gefou-Madianou, 1993; Seremetakis, 1994) to the very object of scholarly analysis: the peasants. Peasant reflections on encounters with European 'others' are constitutive of contemporary anthropological discourses. We encounter this peasant reflexivity only much later in Greek academic or literary contexts. The role of peasant response is twofold: it must be recognized as both an inspiration for Greek academics and the origins of the modern nationalist project of folklore. Greek peasant responses to European-Greek encounters constitute a willfully forgotten counterpart of 'highbrow' academic discourse and ought to be accommodated within debates on national resistance to foreign hegemony.

5
Crimes of Ethnohistory

A manual for bloodless murders

Chapter 4 suggested that the production of proto-anthropological knowledge must be related to other macro-social changes taking place in Europe during the nineteenth century. The uneven development of academic 'disciplines' in non-academic environments betrays an increasing differentiation of social organization (Alexander, 1982) through which imagined-conversational communities aimed to transcend the archaic conditions of social life. As in the case of the bureaucratic centralization of violence explored in Part I, the production of knowledge would eventually secure the systemic attempt to rescue 'imagined' forms of collective identity. Weber (1985) first explained that capitalist modes of action are followed by a conceptual rearrangement of the known world that reaches its 'perfection' in the rationalization of human experience. Bypassing the classical Marxist thesis, he argued that different spheres of human experience are rationalized (and compartmentalized) in different directions. Consequently, what bureaucratic machines present as dangerous or redundant for efficient governance may become a valuable tool in other social spheres. Nationalist thought can idealize forms of social organization and action that do not fit contemporary conditions, ultimately transforming them into cultural myths that have political currency. These myths acquire the status of lost values that continue to preserve pre-modern 'irrationality' in the modern world. Ultimately, idealization provides 'a *compensation* on the symbolic level for the political and economic processes that have destroyed the traditional fabric of [...] societies' (Spurr, 1993, p. 132; Elias, 1996, p. 231; White, 1978, p. 153). Modernity creates traditions from the cultural resources of the past, but it does so without disclosing its subtle interventions in the making of new social realities.

Consider nineteenth-century Greek brigandage, which was incorporated into the language of political aphorism by Greek state actors and Greece's European protectors. This move revealed how such crimes partook in the production of political centers of power constitutive of empires and nations alike. Yet, memories of this contribution survived in folk memory and often granted the discourse on 'disorder' and brigandage the status of a transcendental idea. This chapter will follow the re-working of such memories and traditions into some rationalized modes of national self-narration that differed significantly from the ones produced in European (including Greek) officialdoms. Such types of rationalization informed the production of *Völkische* discourse – a phenomenon we find scattered across different British and Greek genres (travel and novel writing, political commentary and journalism) on brigandage-banditry. The analysis of brigandage took place at two overlapping temporal levels: at the synchronic level, it was studied as a 'picturesque' but socially interesting subject in a controlled, scientific environment. At the diachronic level, its connections with banditry granted the phenomenon with historical depth. This method of analysis, which, drawing on Smith's (2002, p. 30) recognition of cultural artifacts as national symbols, I will term *ethnohistorical*, consolidated the heroic image of national rebels, but divested it of its contemporaneous political shortcomings. Melosi's otherwise narrow-mindedly Marxist claim that 'since the inception of modernity and criminological thought in the nineteenth century, representations of crime and criminals have been oscillating between a sympathetic and an antipathetic attitude' (2000, p. 296) certainly finds some application in this chapter. Unlike Melosi, however, I do not believe that such sympathies and antipathies can be explained on the basis of good or bad socio-economic conditions respectively. We need only observe how proto-anthropology's re-enchanting of Greek brigandage as banditry removed the main obstacle in the 'civilized' nationalist struggle for recognition – bloody violence (Gallant, 2002, p. 143; Hobsbawm, 2000) – *even though* over the same period brigandage was politically condemned across Europe. During their unintentional contribution to this process, the brigands fully regained their social identity but symbolically lost their life in order to join the textual museums of proto-anthropology. Even this observation may fall short of explaining the complexities of such 'scholarly' endeavors – not least because some of its pioneers were British writers. The taxonomic systems produced for brigandage in relation to social phenomena as varied as English and Scottish banditry and anti-Ottoman resistance, tied national and imperial histories in a competitive game for the 'possession of the sign' (Comaroff, 1985, p. 196), but did so in a 'sterilized' scientific environment that used ethnic strife in the articulation of ethnic identities. The paradox of British and Greek *ethnohistorical* discourses was that, despite their attempts to establish themselves as 'monochronic' and hierarchical, they ended up disclosing precisely what they tried to conceal: the irreducible *relativity* of national and imperial pasts (see also Bakhtin, 1981, pp. 19–28).

In the following section I explore how the history of *klephtism* was related to Scottish and Irish myths of social protest, producing a bloodless picture of nationalist outlawry and associating it with particular forms of masculinity. Further associations of this phenomenon with ancient Greek history defined a survivalist methodology that characterizes folklore studies, while the production of taxonomies on Greek folk myths and ballads also sustained the synchronic study of *klephtism*. In the final section I concentrate specifically on visual depictions of *klephts-listés* to examine the re-creation of criminal types in 'safe' scientific environments that adumbrated the rise of museum cultures in Europe. The coexistence of evolutionist and romantic modes of Greek and British research might have endorsed the crypto-colonial status of Greece further, but also remained complicit with the project of Greek nation-building.

Imperial pasts as national histories

The association of Greek brigandage with Scottish and English outlawry summoned up the intricacies of British identity formation. *The Handbook for Travellers in Greece* (1872) stated that being a *klepht* under the Turkish regime was similar to being 'an outlaw in the time of Robin Hood, or a gentleman-cateran in the Highlands of Scotland a hundred and seventy years ago'. The *klephts* were immortalized by Greeks through ballads as much as Robin Hood-style outlaws were by English peasants, because 'these robbers of Greece were no vulgar plunderers' but defenders of their country. Two complementary narratives coexist in the *Handbook*: on the one hand, Greek *klephtism* is discussed as the outcome of modern national history. On the other hand, the *klephts* are presented as the degenerate relics of an ancient Greek past that survived during Ottoman rule (Murray, 1872, p. 27). The narrative, which replicates Greek nationalist thought's dialogicity, is formulated around a crude reference to the body of classical literature. At the same time, the persona of Robin Hood 'who stole from the rich to give to the poor' is associated with the Greek *klepht*, this glorious 'relic of antiquity' who fought for Greek independence. In the next page of the *Handbook* the reader is informed that the *armatoles*, brigands employed by the Ottomans to persecute other brigands, were called '*Palicars* or common soldiers' – another relic of Greek antiquity for Murray whose function resembled that of the *Black Watch* of Scotland. It is also claimed that the Irish 'boys' (*ibid.*, p. 28) can be classified into the same category as the *Klephts* and the *Black Watch*. Unlike political references to Fenianism we encountered in Chapter 2, travel speculations on the Irish political past are not negatively colored. A comparison of Greek banditry with alleged Irish fusions of Celtic pagan and Christian cultures persists (see also Hutchinson, 2005, p. 52), re-asserting the interplay of history and structure. *Like* Celtic-Christian, Hellenic-Christian fusions symbolically operate as evidence of ethnic unity and historical coherence. More correctly, the metamorphosis of these incompatible cultures becomes 'a mythological sheath for the idea of development – but one that unfolds not so much in a straight line as spasmodically, a line with "knots" in it, one that therefore constitutes a distinctive type of *temporal sequence*' (Bakhtin, 1981, p. 113, emphasis in the text).

Just as Murray, who compares the Irish 'boys' to Greek-Hellenic bandits, another traveler describes how Greek 'rogues' preserve in their mannerisms the behavioral patterns of the 'ancient outlaw'. This type of Greek '*pallikári* is an adventurer, a bully, who can strut around like a turkey-cock, rob his neighbor, shoot his brother' (Benjamin, 1867, pp. 160, 166) and not the noble *klepht* of Murray's *Handbook*. The methodology encompasses synchronic observation of past phenomena that survive in the present, while establishing the primordial form of those phenomena. The comparisons resemble Lang's researches into Scottish history, and his collection *Highways and Byways of the Border* (published in 1913). An amateur folklorist and declared 'authentic' Highlander, Lang both excelled in classics and promoted the study of folklore 'survivals' in literary forms in the 1880s (Montenyohl, 1988; Stocking, 1996, pp. 50–3). Simultaneously, the survivalist agenda of British travel writing conceals the double-edged nature of 'social poetics' (Herzfeld, 2005, p. 187): *Palikári* is a term of historical gravity, because it refers to the dramaturgical projection of Greek masculine 'excellence' as resistance to the Ottoman rulers. It embodies ideas of ethnic respectability and honor – two *stereotypical* components of the poetics of manhood in Mediterranean societies. There are hardly any anthropological studies today of 'Mediterranean societies' that do not touch upon questions of 'honor' and 'shame' (e.g. Gilmore, 1987; Abu-Lughod, 1993; Dubisch, 1995) – although the idea that these phenomena are not consistent throughout the Mediterranean has been debated (Davis, 1987; Marcus, 1987). In such nineteenth-century reflections the expression of anti-colonial bravery retains stronger connections to self-presentation (the display of honorable bravery) than to outright 'violence'. Greek masculinity, exemplified in *eghoismós* (egoism as self-presentation) is always at public display (Herzfeld, 1985, p. 11): 'saving face', restoring one's honor in 'public' (in front of peers or in the eyes of the state) may require the use of violence. But even when violence enters our writers' narratives, it is presented as a noble ('civilized' and therefore permissible) form of anti-colonial resistance.

Evolutionist comparisons between Greek, Scottish or Irish 'rogues' appeared in British journalism too. Skinner, *The Daily News* correspondent and a philhellene who joined the Cretan rebels in 1867, also saw in the Greek warriors of the island the 'ancient chieftains of Scotland'. On this note however, he returned to the question of the English conquest as a 'civilizing' project to compare it to the actions of the 'Turks and the Arabs [who] neither construct roads, not disseminate letters, on the contrary, they devastate and destroy' (Skinner, 1868, p. 4; *Palingenesía*, 15 June 1867). Similar comments appeared in Finlay's journalism over the same period (*The Times*, 19 April 1869). Political upheaval in the Ottoman Empire had given birth to anthropological observation, promoting a crypto-colonial classification of phenomena through analogy, tautology and opposition. In Skinner's writings, contemporary Greek brigands-*klephts* are identified with past Scottish or medieval English outcasts and the civilized 'Englishman' is compared to the Scottish semi-civilized chieftains who replace the Greek brigand-*Klepht* in the classificatory system. Finally, the Arabs and the Turks are unfavorably compared with the English. The discourse works through substitution of one or both of the terms of the binary couples. The whole system operates on the assumption that the observer belongs to a higher stage in the cultural ladder when they analyze phenomena that for them may belong to history, but are identified with, and are believed to constitute the present of the observed. The standpoint of British observers is always higher *vis-à-vis* the observed culture.

It is noteworthy that some of the commentators are of Scottish origin: Hilary Skinner and George Finlay who regard themselves as Englishmen 'proper', endorse a narrative of English 'civilizing process' for Scotland, asserting thus their colonial identity. Let us examine

Finlay's observations on the Greek inability to meet European political prerequisites:

> Our own history in the last century, not only in the Highlands but in the neighbourhood of London, may convince us of the possibility of an honest nation tolerating a system of organized robbery, and we might refer for a parallel with the state of Greece to the earlier annals of England and of Germany, showing honest and laborious burghers and peasants oppressed and harried by robbers claiming to be heroes (*The Times*, 6 May 1870).

This comment comes right after the Dilessi Murders, when the whole Greek nation was considered 'a race of *Klephts*' that represented the unhappy, degenerate survivors of a splendid *Ur*-European history (*The Times*, 3 May 1870). In this climate some journalists even searched for specific passages in Gibbon's *Decline and Fall of the Roman Empire*, in which the author claimed that the Homeric heroes were robbers, in order to denigrate Greek banditry-as-brigandage (*The Daily Telegraph*, 4 June 1870). Gibbon had been part of the circle of scholars who reflected on recurring phenomena in history (Bowler, 1989, pp. 193–5) and his survivalist methodology was a convenient political tool. In the same vein, in his analyses on brigandage, Finlay built up a system of labeling by comparing the career of the Dilessi brigands with that of Scottish cattle-dealers and outcasts of the eighteenth century (*The Times*, 3 June 1870). Despite his Scottish origin, Finlay saw English and Scottish history as a unity and obliterated past Scottish struggles against England from his narrative. Thus the past is romanticized and internal British conflicts are written out of history. Even Finlay however oscillates between idealization and condemnation. His inclination to romanticize Greek brigandage while subjecting it to evolutionist comparison is traced in his *History of the Greek Revolution* where he recognizes how the oppressed 'were always attracted by independent life, even when it was lawless'. He uses the example of the Greeks, who 'heroicised their chieftains and transformed them into a sort of "Robin Hood". They exaggerated their deeds and extended their life span as myths in ancient years. The patriotic Klephts in demotic poetry though are recent artefacts' (1973, vol. I, p. 37). The Greek mythologization of brigandage is a *recent* phenomenon for Finlay, a kind of deliberate folk enchantment in a disenchanted world.

The same discursive logic permeated British journalism, promoting an analysis and assessment of the *mythistorical* aspects of Greek brigandage:

mythical because it belonged to the peasant world, the domain of the illiterate 'other', and historical because peasant myths would enter the domain of written (recorded) memory. Robin Hood and Rob Roy, the most important legendary outlaws, would constantly be exhumed and used in metonymic or metaphoric processes to illustrate the 'graces' of the Greek brigand *par excellence* (*The Pall Mall Gazette*, 16 May 1870; *The Daily News*, 26 April and 16 May 1870), 'a personage whom time has left to his generation to remind us, amid the strange mutations of our day, of Robin Hood and his merry men [...] a link between our own and former ages. To trace his origin we must look back twelve hundred years to the rise of Mahomet, the camel driver of the desert' (Benjamin, 1867, p. 222). Such comparative reflections create a complex schema of evolution that outlines the problematic of exchange between 'occidental' and 'oriental' civilizations. In the survivalist discourse, contemporary Greek crime and past British forms of outlawry were classified into the same category.

Rob Roy and Robin Hood were *mythistorical* constructs, mythical narratives of socio-historical processes. Although Robin Hood had been remodeled through the centuries, one important element engraved onto British popular recollection was his supposed struggle against Norman invaders (Holt, 1989, pp. 7–13, 183–4). Rob Roy's story was more ambiguous but equally interesting. His introduction into literature, especially in Walter Scott's romantic novels, produced a well-rounded character (Scott, 1890, vol. I), who owed his fame to his resemblance to Robin Hood. He was allegedly a cattle dealer for a period and later on, as an outlaw, had his own protector, the Duke of Argyll. Analogical thinking constructs a discourse that expands geometrically: the triptych Rob Roy-Greek brigands-Robin Hood is a substitute for the three-faced nature that Greek brigandage possesses, the gallant/romantic aura, the political networking of brigand crime and social rebellion (as national resistance). However, if we combine spatial representation with the presence of evolutionist time then we should ask why Greek brigandage was seen through the lens of *a* British past. The way the analysis of brigandage is pursued corresponds to a common historical practice that involves the introduction of a series of continuities and discontinuities in history's 'linear sequence' (Fabian, 1983, 1991). By introducing various events as a rupture or an important moment in the history of outlawry (Rob Roy and Robin Hood's stories) the British *are in a position to make history*. And the history they make is impregnated by what truly matters for them. The driving force behind the interest in the history of *klephtism* is a British urgency to idealize Scottish outlawry. Reflecting back to comparisons between Greek brigandage and Irish Fenianism, we could also regard this need for idealization as a resistance mechanism to the discourse on Irish-Greek disorder. These two conflicting narratives are symptomatic of British modernity: what in the present is homologous to Greek brigandage (Irish Fenianism) is rationalized and denigrated, but its past equivalent (Robin Hood, Rob Roy) is romanticized and praised. What we have here is a critical reversal of 'the figure, which organizes the practices of a society' (de Certeau, 1986, p. 24): bandits cease to be regarded as unwelcome scoundrels and re-emerge in textual narratives as the champions of anti-statist colonial resistance.

Greek reflections are symmetrical to the British, but glorify the Greek *Klephti* or *Palicari,* who 'have been mistranslated into English "brigand"; in the original the words signified the "hero"' (Xenos, 1865, p. 104). Other Greek observers stressed that even in eighteenth-century England there were brigands (Sotiropoulos, 1866, pp. 116–18), or that 'in all these [English] ruffians, there is nothing of that patriotic feeling which excused formerly the Greek klepht, and absolutely no redeeming trait as may be found in the more degenerate [Greek] brigands of today...' (Gennadios, 1870, p. 132). Rob Roy is compared not with the post-Independence brigands but with his 'nobler' Greek equivalent, the *klepht* of Greek Independence. Thus, Rob Roy, a mythical and historical persona, is used as raw material for the transformation of a historical persona, the *klepht,* into a national myth of rebellion and resistance to foreign rulers. The re-enchantment of brigandage betrays a reciprocal refashioning of the Greek history of resistance to Ottoman domination: the social nature of 'Greek' anti-colonial rebellion is reinstated through a quintessentially English myth of popular revolt.

Non-British observers also romanticized the brigand-*klepht.* For example, the American Minister in Athens, Tuckerman, supported the idea that brigandage in Greece was an exceptional phenomenon, because it was 'born in the Turkish oppression' (Stevens, 1989, p. 126). It was unfortunate that Tuckerman had used Robin Hood in his analysis of the development of *klephtism* into a corrupt political system, in which blackmail, intrigues and murder prevail. The corruption of Greek resistance was denied by Tuckerman's Greek translator, a clerk at the Ministry of Foreign Affairs, who saw blackmail as part of the 'English and Scottish traditions' that preserve in their language 'the proper word to describe the process of blackmail' – as opposed to the Greek language, 'in which the term does not exist, and there is no fear or reason for it to be invented' (Tuckerman, 1877, pp. 197–8). Language stands metonymically for culture – indeed, it embodies the virtues and drawbacks of national cultures, challenging the commonplace survivalist inclination to dismiss folk etymologies as 'unconscious error' (Herzfeld, 1997b, p. 60, 2005) while studying them. The translator referred to the tribute extracted on the Scottish border by freebooting chiefs who offered immunity from pillage – a practice that did not differ from the protection Greek brigands 'offered' to villagers. However, the way he posited the question of 'blackmail' suggested a re-organization of the British scale of civilization: now Greek culture appeared to be morally superior to that of its European protectors.

Tuckerman's views simply mediated his Greek translator's attack of 'English' and Scottish history. But his *mythistoricization* of the *klepht* was predicated upon the work of Cornelius Felton, one of the foremost Greek scholars of America whose interest in modern Greek brigandage was literary. Felton, an eminent Professor and later President of Harvard, left a detailed record of his time in Greece during the early part of 1853 in a posthumously published series of lectures on *Greece: Ancient and Modern* (1862) that he had delivered before the Lowell Institute of Boston (Stearns, 1905). In his University course on Greek poetry, Felton investigated the nature of ancient and modern Greek composition, concluding that the original modern Greek compositions were those of the mountaineers, especially of the 'semi-barbaric heroes' known as *klephts*. These warriors who 'retain[ed] many of the customs, superstitions and traditions of the ancient times, were the most formidable assailants of the Turks during the war of the Revolution. [...] But the point of significant reference to them is their strong sensibility to poetry, and their facility in composition [...]' (Felton, 1867, vol. I, pp. 261–2). Felton's historical ethnology invited an analysis of folk memory and tradition through peasant poetic sensitivity – an analysis that Tuckerman later filtered through politics. Not only do Felton and Tuckerman present us with the two facets of rationalization, they also suggest their theoretical coexistence beyond.

The survivalist methodology, which established a relationship between ancient and contemporary forms of social organization, was a *leitmotif* of emergent European nationalisms. It was characterized by internal, dialogical contradictions, manifest in nineteenth-century Greek and British reflections: while scholars constantly asserted the historical continuity of their national culture, their relationship with the selfsame past could also become a relationship with the 'other'. In the discipline of folklore, which places greater emphasis on diachrony, this attitude is a prerequisite for scientific investigation. As other historians noted, the folklorist occupies a vantage point, and predicates his scholarly identity upon a division of the nation into 'high' and 'low' cultures (Dickie, 1999, pp. 90–2). Greek proto-folklore investigations, which present us with the equivalent of foreign elaborations on Greek culture, are nicely reflected in scholarly reactions to the Dilessi Murders. After the murders, the Greek Society of Parnassos in Athens organized a forum in which its distinguished member Dimitris Pantazis delivered a talk. Pantazis' argument was constructed upon the hypothesis that Dilessi and Oropos, the locations where the group of noblemen was murdered, present the Greeks with two cases of dangerous historical *topoi*, which 'were always atrocious and sites of crimes' (*Palingenesía*, 13 May 1870). Pantazis voiced the Greek 'nation's' defense against European accusations of decline through Herodotus, Thucydides and Strabo, whose writings allegedly testified to the relationship of the inhabitants of these two sites with pirates and the Athenians. Thus, brigand crime was historically constructed in terms of an unequal relationship between core and periphery, capital and countryside. Pantazis realized the pitfalls of his analysis, since the Arvanitakis were Greek-Vlachian mountaineers, but he was not disheartened. Instead, he tried to prove that the inhabitants of Oropos, who allegedly had an ambivalent relationship with piracy, moved to the interior of the country in order to protect themselves from the ancient pirates, 'the Arvanitakis of the sea'. It is not necessary to linger on details: Pantazis' narrative established a genealogy of Greek brigandage, which asserted the argument of Greek historical continuity. In this genealogy, the Hellenic past's otherness successfully stood in metonymically for the anthropological otherness of modern Greek 'low culture'. The argument managed to integrate ethnographic and historical observations, and use them to exclude the 'otherness' of brigandage from 'civilized' Greek qualities: the brigands were the 'savages' of the Greek nation.

The anthropological discourses both the Greeks and the British mobilized to analyze crime operated on certain principles. Their respective methods, more historical than anthropological, converged when the category of brigandage was mobilized to interpret practices employed by Greeks and Britons in different historical periods. Hellenic, modern Greek, Scottish and Irish histories and myths occupied the same discursive space and intermingled. Foucault called this *heterotopias* (*heteron* = other, *topos* = place), the result of conscious and intentional misplacement of time-levels, which enables human actors to rearrange experience and reconceptualize phenomena (Foucault, 1986, pp. 16–17). Greek and British intentions differed: the principal 'authorities' in the debate on Scottish civilization were Scots. Their attempts to restructure their ethnic history as a romantic form of savagery therefore bespoke a desire to affirm their participation in a British imagined community, that of the Empire. Contrariwise, Greek commentators were keen to establish a continuum of national histories allegedly written 'from below' and sanitized from any embarrassing, 'uncivilized' – hence, non-European – elements.

We can also account for some investigative work on modern Greek brigandage by British travelers, which involved the collection of legends about the Greek brigand-*klepht* – an exercise resembling early anthropological scientific taxonomies. For example, we find in the travel diaries of two women travelers to Greece an extraordinary gamut of incidents concerning 'folk prejudices' about the Greek brigands-*Klephts*. In recorded peasant stories, the Greek brigand was presented as a *Vrykólakas* or vampire in the region of Olympus, which 'was believed to be haunted by the restless spirits of dead Klephts, who roam about in the silence of night, bemoaning their fate, and crying vengeance on the oppressors of their race' (Poole, 1878, pp. 222–3; Tozer, 1869, vol. II, p. 51). The vampire myth, which had strong anti-Turkish elements, was spread across the Balkans and Eastern Europe during the eighteenth century. Precise genealogies of the myth, however, are of less importance here: as a political metaphor, the 'vampire' signified the burden of tyranny, an allusion already present in the remarks of the two travelers. Again, therefore, we are faced with an amalgamation of historical causality and folk 'prejudice' that characterizes other British collections of the period. Similarly, the Albanian brigand appeared in British travel narratives to possess uncontrolled powers and to exercise sorcery on Greek women (Tozer, 1869, vol. I, pp. 230–3, 251–4). These stories resemble the Greek discourse on Albanian identity and its relationship to brigandage as a type of crime (Mill, 1876, pp. 136–9). As in Pantazis' analysis, the backward 'low culture' that was recorded and analyzed was also deemed to possess an evil power, which can symbolically contaminate the experience of modernity.

Thus, the British romantic approach to brigandage was closely related to perceptions of *klephtism* in Greek rural communities (*The Times*, 26 December 1866). Campbell, whose lectures on brigandage attracted much attention in London, identified a serious obstacle in the 'extirpation of this crime' in the recognition by the 'lower classes' of a revolutionary epigone in brigands (Campbell, 1877, p. 96). This is the period over which *klephtic* ballads created by the popular Muse would become the object of study by European amateur ethnographers. Notably, Murray's description of rural customs (1872, p. 27) was accompanied by references to Claude Fauriel's collection *Chants Populaires de la Grèce*, the first attempt at gathering and classifying Greek folk songs. Modern Greek folklorists may argue that Fauriel fabricated ballads or bastardized them in the same fashion that Macpherson 'invented' the *Ossianic Lays* (Hutchinson, 2004, pp. 114–15). The 'rediscovery' of 'epic literature' that allegedly preserved the *Völkische* peasant past was a widespread phenomenon in Europe, exemplified in the Irish 'exhumation' of the Celtic Red Branch and Finn Cycles, the Norwegian *Edda* and the German *Niebelungenlied* (Hutchinson, 2005, p. 55; O'Mahony and Delanty, 2001, pp. 84–5). Lang's *Custom and Myth* (1884), a Tylorian study of mythology and folklore, promoted the comparative study of survivals in Britain at about the same period (Stocking, 1996, p. 53). Fauriel's collection of ballads was the first serious work on Greek folk culture and the only one that embraced a 'scientific' (taxonomic) approach until the emergence of Greek folklore as a social science in the 1880s. Fauriel's work influenced Murray, but did not eradicate his overwhelmingly negative comments on the production of *klephtic* ballads. The songs composed about Kitsos and Davelis, two of the infamous Greek brigands of the 1850s, were also criticized by Finlay and Wyse as harmful pieces of literature that promoted the 'sanctification of the Klepht' (Wyse, 1871, pp. 18–19, 74–5; *The Times,* 19 April 1869 and 29 April 1870).

Despite the condemnation, British interest in Greek ballad collection did not subside. The survivalist mission was not always easy: attempts to record *klephtic* ballads could fail, because the 'honest Greek fellows' repudiated attempts to connect them with the 'rovers of the hills'. So, a traveler notes, 'we have to be content with spontaneous ebullitions which take the form of a Tupper-like Proverbial Philosophy – as for instance, "When Zeus rains from heaven, 'tis well to have an umbrella for the head"; and other equally incontrovertible, and under the circumstances, impressive myths' (Farrer, 1882, p. 105). The dissemination of brigand *mythistories* might have been discouraged even by the peasantry and the brigands themselves then, forcing European collectors to improvise from the image of the 'romanticised Cleft [sic]' and to conclude that 'pathetic brigand songs' were inferior to those of the 'noble' *klephts* (Tozer, 1969, vol. II, p. 54). Greek cultural intimacies had to be guarded from such foreigners at all costs.

There were good reasons for this defensive attitude, which relate to the ways British commentators perceived the function of *klephtic* songs in Greek tradition: while they retained the privilege to romanticize past forms of crime, they denied Greeks rights to the same practice. There was, however, an analogous reaction within Greece, especially amongst emerging urban elites. It was even suggested by Antonopoulos that pedagogically it is better if 'the so-called *Klephtic* songs, in which any *listis* is praised like a hero [are] banned from the syllabus' (Antonopoulos, 1870, pp. 12–13). Likewise, the deputy for Ermionis, Milisis, delivered a public speech in 1871 where he attacked the interest displayed by academic circles and novelists in the 'demotic philology of crime' (Milisis, 1871, pp. 7–8). Such suggestions followed the Dilessi Murders, which damaged Greece's national image in Europe – therefore they might have been context-bound rather than generalized reactions. Evidently, *klephtic* ballads had made their way into the Greek educational system from an earlier period, reproducing nationalist ideologies and preserving a particular *mentalité* auxiliary to the project of nation-building.

Over the nineteenth century, the European *Raum* became inundated with cult heroes similar to the *klepht*. Such heroes were invariably set against 'key historical moments in exploring the struggle of national progress against tradition' (Hutchinson, 2005, p. 56; Hobsbawm, 2000, p. 58). Much like Scott's romantic figure of Rob Roy, the English story of Robin Hood and Cervantes' bandit Rocaguinarda in *Don Quixote* (Hobsbawm, 2000, p. 153), Greek novelists would create a voice for the universally condemned *lestric klephts*. As explained previously, the first amateur contributors to the process of nation-building were novelists and artists, not self-designated 'scientists' (Leoussi, 2004). Frazerian folklore, free of participant observation, was called in to bridge the gap between artistic creation and scientific method (Stocking, 1996, p. 127). In the early phases of nation-building literary *personae* acquired the function of *a-historical* social actors, becoming thus embodiments of the nation's perenniality. Such attempts at *mythologizing* ethnic rebellion did not go unanswered abroad: we have an acid analysis of Greek popular beliefs concerning brigandage in About's *The King of the Mountains* (1990), a novel considered by British and other European readers a *tour de force* during the 1850s. Unfortunately, this kind of literature started looking less fictional and more real post-Dilessi. Even earlier British travelers used the novel as fact, rather than fiction (Benjamin, 1867, p. 223; *The Times*, 8 February 1868; Wyse, 1871, p. 23).

It is said that it was About's disappointment with Greek 'political behavior' that gave birth to Chadji-Stavros, the Greek brigand chief with the peculiar Turkish name, the bank accounts in England and the various *protégés* in the Greek National Assembly (Vournas, 1990, pp. 30, 46–7). The novel narrates the abduction of two English ladies and the botanist Schultz. It is a witty French satire of nineteenth-century Greek politics presented through the eyes of Schultz who functions in novelistic discourse as About's fictional *alter ego*. We must not lose perspective here: the deviant Chadji-Stavros embodies both the petty tyrant of Greek politics who blackmails peasants and negotiates with political forces for his own interest, and the Rabelaisian giant of Greek folklore who displays the usual human weaknesses Greeks would attribute to their historical others – namely, an 'oriental' sort of greed and vulgarity (Bakhtin, 1981, p. 241). The ambivalence is constitutive of a Greek cosmology that views humans as fundamentally flawed (Herzfeld, 2005, p. 164). It corresponds to the negative of a fictionally decent 'I' that displays the virtues of a unified outer face – the 'abstract principle of individualism' – so that it conceals the fragmentation of the intimate Self – the multiple levels of [Greek] social reality' (Herzfeld, 1987, p. 160). The image of a Turk-Greek brigand, who runs dirty political campaigns from his Athenian headquarters while organizing attacks on 'innocent' travelers from his hideout painfully exposed Greek socio-cultural insecurities, because it issued a harsh reminder of some cultural hetroglossias meticulously erased by an amnesiac Greek officialdom (see also Chapter 3). *Ex post facto* (after 1870), such covert critiques began to rate equal to those unwittingly played out in Fallmerayer's Byzantinist endeavors. It is rumored that hatred for About ran so deep in the Greek Kingdom, that the novelist suffered considerable public defamation by his contemporaries (Stevens, 1989, p. 173).

The way that fascination with brigand crime affected Greek literary production was not unrelated to Greek reactions against About's 'anti-Greek' satire. Greek Romanticism, in which the Greek bandit-brigand genre emerged, combined French revolutionary and German *Völkische* ideas in suggestive ways: repetition, pessimism and resignation, the *leitmotifs* of nineteenth-century novelistic production in Greece, served to ideologically compensate for harsh political realities in which Greece remained a powerless country, disciplined by Europeans and mocked by the Ottoman 'enemy' (Vitti, 1991, pp. 16–18). In the latter nineteenth century most of the 'second-rank' works on brigandage follow the same model. *The Son of the Executioner* by Kantakouzinos (1857) and the *Insane Hermit* by Enyalis (1868) tell of young men, who, frustrated by 'society's inequalities and evilness', decide to become outlaws in the Robin Hood fashion or join Greek irregular troops against an imaginary Turkish invader. The core of the plot is usually an illicit or forbidden love affair that becomes conflated with an abstract perception of social unfairness, and not crime itself (Vournas, 1990, pp. 28–9; Koliopoulos, 1988, pp. 173–5). Periods of high tension between Greece and Turkey would revive the Greek irredentist dream and Greek aspirations would be reflected in literary works (Koliopoulos, 1987, p. 210). Thus, the failed reciprocity that sustained brigand crime against the state was forced into the costume of the Greek noble bandit who rebelled against Greece's former 'masters'. Perhaps only *Thanos Vlekas* (1987) deviated from this empowering norm, exploring perceptions of the *lestric klepht* in Greek rural communities in a more dispassionate way. The rudimentary polarization of 'good' and 'evil' was also present in the Greek theatre of the period, as British travelers noted (Young, 1876, p. 199). Even the Dilessi Murders inspired plays that supported narratives of national victimization by Ottoman and Europeans alike (Iatridis, 1870). The personification of evil, which also accompanied political accounts of kidnapping (Sotiropoulos, 1866, p. 24), became a social safety valve, a *myth* that could appease domestic audiences. Mythical narratives of brigandage-as-banditry overlaid historical experience, transforming the objectified brigand into the 'metanarrator' of his own development (Bennett, 1995, p. 44).

National histories, textual museums

Visual representations of the brigand-*Klepht* would eventually add an evolutionist dimension to the *ethnohistorical* project. A Greek cartoon of the period (Figure 5.1) depicts a fat shabby butcher holding a knife and the traditional Greek *kokorétsi*, a Greek delicacy made of animal entrails. The butcher wears a scarf *à la* Robin Hood, but seems unwashed, just like the so-called *leroménoi* or dirty brigands; given his scruffy beard and vicious look, he also seems to have a rather ambiguous relationship with the razor. The subtitle is a pun and a rhyme in Greek: 'Kebab-maker, and occasionally a brigand.' The dirt of the butcher's profession is metaphorically linked to that of the brigand 'profession.' This is not unlike comments found in the diaries of British travelers, claiming that in Greek markets butchers 'look like brigands, with a whole magazine of weapons thrust into the leather pouch attached to their scarf' (Colbeck, 1887, p. 95). Greek butchers were also associated with non-European indigenous populations (Young, 1876, p. 158) and brigand culture was repeatedly described as meat culture. This promoted associations between crime and cannibalism, echoing Tylor's comparative evolutionism and transforming Greek brigandage into the 'other' of European civilization. Such criticism was unexpectedly resurrected in the recent EU directive that banned *kokorétsi* from the permissible

Figure 5.1 Kebab-Maker (And Occasionally a Brigand)
T.A. (1974) *Cartoon Album*. Athens.

gamut of Greek delicacies. Should we read in this a rational decision that addresses health risks (e.g. the association of animal entrails with outbreaks of 'mad cow' disease) or a forceful homogenization of national cultures that conceals European abhorrence at such 'savage' dietary particularities? Indeed, underneath the modern discourse of health risk we may find a familiar version of the discourse of (cultural) pollution that excludes (peasant) Greek culinary traditions from the sphere of European modernity (Douglas, 1993; Douglas and Wildavsky, 1982). The resistances this has produced are masked as practices of cultural commodification: a quick Internet search shows that the lovers of *kokorétsi* have a virtual home that has launched a campaign for the global dissemination of this product (Kokoretsi.org). The website displays all the signs of exoticization we now relate to tourist simulacra (Tzanelli, 2007b): sunny verandas, good wine and food and adverts for holidays to Crete. On their part, Greeks protest that they have to 'go illegal' to enjoy the food they were brought up on (CNN, 28 September 1997) – a comment that bears telling similarities to the image of nineteenth-century *klephtic* meat eaters.

The Brigands of the Morea (1868), the British translation of a Greek official's diary of captivity in Greece, provides another excellent example of this marriage of evolutionism with history in the form of folklore. The first volume of Bagdon's work was more a description of rural and brigand custom than a political analysis – although the latter was not absent. As in other cases of brigandage, Bagdon outlined a code of 'rough chivalry' (Hobsbawm, 2000, p. 52): so, for example, Greek brigands might have been 'uncivilized', but refused to kill women and children. Women were also excluded from this 'criminal' world – indeed, like other 'outsiders', they were seen as the source of bad luck and pollution. It was often rumored that women brew rivalry and competition within the band, leading to its demise. The same brigands however, would become violent against their peers and state representatives when vendettas ensued. In Bagdon's account, brigandage becomes paradigmatic of an 'honor culture' (Gallant, 2002, p. 118), but is not necessarily disconnected from violence (Campbell, 1964, p. 151). Bagdon's translation maintained internal contradictions, evident where he extends an invitation to his readers to speculate on *klephtism* as a survival of a heroic age. The frontispiece of his book (Figure 5.2) suggested a romantic preconception of the phenomenon: the man in the picture is a contemporaneous *klepht* with a dreamy look. He appears to hold a scroll, echoing Byron's early nineteenth-century portraits. He is impressive in his Albanian costume, which is terribly clean for a *leroménos*. According

Figure 5.2   A Noble Brigand
Reverend J.O. Bagdon (1868) *The Brigands of Morea.* London: Saunders, Otley
and Co.

to nineteenth-century accounts, brigands had to wear dirty *foustanélles* or kilts, because the snowy color could betray them at night. The dirtier a brigand was, the more experienced he seemed to be. And yet, this noble *klepht* wears immaculate 'Western European' attire. The clash between visual and textual depiction in Bagdon's work corresponds to the ambivalence of the folklore project, whose evolutionist aims ran against its romantic pretensions. Van Lennep's *Oriental Album* (1862), the 'visual' account of Oriental civilization that the British found so authentic, cultivated the same ambivalence. Van Lennep painted in one of his drawings (Figure 5.3) an imaginative gentleman. Like Bagdon's, this 'species' looks rather harmless and retains all the characteristics of the idyllic country life. In fact, more emphasis is placed on the depiction of the rural background than the 'bandit' figure itself. All the same, in Van Lennep's textual analysis, Greek bands were presented as 'ferocious and religiously fanatical' (1862, p. 81). Both commentators de- and re-historicize brigandage to make it serve their own objectives – they 'naturalize' it in other words (Lévi-Strauss, 1972 [1962], 1964; Barthes, 1993).

The engravings in Cochran's travel book also partake in this taming of social banditry-brigandage. The Ziebec (Figure 5.4), struggling to retain a masculine posture, armed to the teeth, is placed in an uncertain but civilized environment – probably the corridor of a house. Although 'Captain Andreas', who is described as a fearful rogue by Cochran, happily displays his warlike prowess, his masculinity is strangely sanitized in the staged drawing (Figure 5.5). The 'brigand in Albanian Holiday Costume' resembles more a posed gentleman than a murderous villain (Figure 5.6). These pictures should not be examined separately from the text, in which Cochran discusses the background of Greek and Turkish brigandage, the tactics of the bands, and many stories of kidnapping (Cochran, 1887, pp. 347–57). 'The student of physiognomy', Cochran concludes, should dwell on 'the specimens of rascaldom displayed in the ponderous tome of criminal faces' (*ibid.*, pp. 355–6). As Cochran confesses in his diary, the head of 'Captain Andreas', a fine Greek brigand, was singled-out to be inserted into his album. Andreas is a 'specimen', a sample of an invisible whole that the reader has to imagine. As in the previous pictures of brigands, Andreas appears proud of his aggressive self-display and polished armory, and enjoys the cameraman's attention to the full. The brigand's performance of masculine *eghoismós* is relationally constructed.

Pictures of the Dilessi band before and after their execution also circulated widely over the 1870s. We even have a photo from Lord Muncaster's (the sole survivor of the crime) unpublished diaries that presents

Figure 5.3   Bandit-Gentleman
Reverend H.J. Van Lennep (1862[1962]) *The Oriental Album*. New York: Anson
D. Randolph.

Figure 5.4   A Ziebec
W. Cochran (1887) *Pen and Pencil in Asia Minor*. London: Sampson Law.

Figure 5.5   Captain Andrea and his 'Lieutenant'
W. Cochran (1887) *Pen and Pencil in Asia Minor*. London: Sampson Law.

Figure 5.6   Brigand in Albanian Holiday Costume
G.M.M. MacKenzie and A.P. Irby (1877) *Travels in the Slavonic Provinces of Turkey in Europe*. London: Daldy, Ibister.

the heads of the decapitated brigands in a hierarchical order (Stevens, 1989, pp. 32–3). Despite its gruesome nature, the photo became a souvenir that Greek and British audiences rushed to buy. The advertisement for the purchase of such phtotos, a sample of Greek entrepreneurial black humor, was published in the Greek newspapers *Palingenesía, Méllon* and *Aión* (21 April 1870), inviting readers to open their wallets and pay the artistic phtographer, a certain 'Mr Vathis'. The mock mourning tone of the advertisement becomes thought provoking when one discovers that in the absence of any photgraphs, Greek and British newspapers expended much ink drawing or describing the captured brigands. Comments such as 'his look betrayed audacity and savage confidence' (*Aión, Palingenesía* and *The Morning Post,* 15 May 1870) betray an interest in 'brigand physiognomy'. The Dilessi brigands joined a 'tourist' market that demanded new and exciting material to stimulate its imagination (Urry, 1990, pp. 136–9). *The Illustrated London News* copied the famous photograph of the captured brigands at trial, providing the British readership with a cheaper version of the unsavoury, yet 'scientifically interesting' spectacle.

It appears that in visual 'narratives' the brigands cease to be human beings and become a 'species' (Crawshaw and Urry, 1997, pp. 176–95). The result was their symbolic death through the distorting lens of the 'artist' and their treatment as objects of inspection and scrutiny, a 'relic of the past'. The severed heads of the Dilessi brigands, the head of Captain Andreas, become 'Darwinian fossils', objects of science. It is not only their heads, but *their whole being* that is severed from the environment in which they live and act: the uncertainty of the landscape-background contributes to the erasure of their social identity. Cochran's drawing of 'types' of 'Turkish irregular forces' (Figure 5.7) – a telling generic representation of banditry-brigandage, Turkish and Greek – is also placed in a cultural and natural void. The brigand 'types' retain a highly stylized ('oriental') pose that does not communicate violence. This process of symbolic 'embalming' enabled the 'civilized' observers to perform their role as students of science – in their own terms and not in the wild headquarters of the observed. When Wyse's niece and editor of his diary noted 'how much fitter' the heads of powerful brigand leaders, such as Krieziotis and Theodoros Grivas, 'would have been in Madam Tussaud's Chamber of Horrors than in the halls of a royal palace' (Wyse, 1871, p. 22), she effectively conveyed the same idea of de- and re-contextualization. The same logic governs Gennadios' diatribe, who views the Dilessi brigands 'like all the lower orders of creation' that can only flourish in their 'native fastness' (1870, p. 61).

Figure 5.7 Types of Turkish Irregular Forces
W. Cochran (1887) *Pen and Pencil in Asia Minor*. London: Sampson Law.

The subtext of such comments must be juxtaposed against practices of photography and the emergence of museum cultures. As Clifford (1988) notes, assumptions about cultural 'authenticity' are produced in a range of media and sites of representation, including popular writing and artistic production. The urge to collect and display various artifacts in galleries and museums must be seen as part of an 'art-culture' system that over the nineteenth century essentialized other worlds producing simultaneously 'knowledge'. British observers' interest in visual collections of brigands presents their taxonomical project as one operating on the principle of *representativeness* rather than *rarity* of the brigand 'class'. Winifred Wyse captured the spirit of such representations when she suggested the design of a *sample* of the brigand 'species' for the famous museum of Tussaud. We do indeed deal with the need for fabrication of a compensatory totality in the face of fragmented social experience of brigandage. There is no doubt that the Dilessi photos and sketches initially addressed the observer's curiosity, but their presence ultimately served in collective imaginations as an example of a wider (Greek) whole, which retained, and bore witness to, an essential difference *vis-à-vis* the humanity of the observer. Even today the creation of notions of a collective European cultural heritage come from 'high' culture, a game that impedes any definition on what cultural heritage actually is (Bugge, 2003, p. 63). It is disconcerting to acknowledge that likewise, nineteenth-century European observers achieved humanity through a sterilized relationship with the 'uncivilized' representatives of 'low culture'. Even the Greek apologist, Gennadios, argued that the brigand species needs its 'own' environment to survive, thus replicating the Darwinian thesis. This evolutionist pattern propelled self-discipline: the observers related to the observed as beings in 'incessant need of progressive development' (Bennett, 1995, p. 46).

The *ethnohistorical* project of nation-building was marked by multiple contradictions: while it used contemporaneous social phenomena to support nationalist discourse, it also replicated European narratives that deconstructed – though never truly discredited – such discourses. Analogies however between nationalist and colonial discourse were prominent, as the simultaneous romanticization and de-valorization of brigandage in Greece and in Britain suggests. Like *lestric kephtism*, which flagged its historical glory in the face of its contemporaneous criminalization, folklore used historical analysis to compensate for the absence of immediate engagement with its multifaceted subject. Subduing the complexities of ethnic crime to a single discourse produced knowledge that never fully emancipated itself from internal ideological negotiations (Mannheim, [1936] 1968, pp. 132–6).

Part III
Ideas of Greatness

6
Unpaid Debts and Duties

Moral obligations and nationalist discourse

Exploring myths of ethnic selection, Smith (1999, p. 125) stressed the historic survival of *ethnies* through any community's ability to '*identify with some persisting memories, symbols, myths and traditions*' (*ibid.*, p. 128, emphasis in the text). Smith alludes to the national community's self-election, without clarifying how this takes place – a question closely related to the disagreement between modernists and theorists who locate the nation in long-term historical processes. Although a sociologist with an appreciation for historical change, Smith seems caught between the two arguments. This tension is addressed in *History and National Destiny* (Guibernaeu and Hutchinson [eds], 2004), a debate on Smith's contribution to nationalism studies. Smith himself has corrected any conflations of historical evolution with political manipulation of myths by nations. As he claims, 'while most nations are formed and crystallize on the basis of a dominant *ethnie*, they may, and often do, expand and "develop away" from that original base and to some extent from its ancestry myth' (Smith, 2004, 1999, pp. 57–95; Hutchinson, 2004, 2005, chapter 1). In fact, most of Smith's empirical examples came from periods when nations did not exist as cultural (and political) units. If indeed 'other myths, memories, symbols and traditions (many of them admittedly pertaining to the dominant *ethnie*)' (Smith, 2004, p. 200) become important components of nation-building, should we not explicitly talk about *dialogical* interpretations of available pasts instead of affinities between *ethnies* and nations? Hutchinson already observes how in the social transformation of communities into nations we distinguish two strategies of cultural survival: the first involves an 'inner' activist change of the accepted concept of the past, and the second promotes the 'external' creation of a cult of sacrifice 'by a revolutionary elite' (Hutchinson, 2004, p. 109).

This chapter focuses on the interactive emergence of myths of self-election in the contemporary world, examining the *interpretive* potential of the narrative of 'the chosen' in national encounters with significant others. Dialogism produces the nation's 'integral ideational position' (Bakhtin, 1984, p. 252), modifying its *Weltanschauung* and inflecting native cosmologies through communication. I retain Smith's insightful comment that 'to be chosen is to be placed under moral obligations' (*ibid.*, p. 130) to the those who chose you to discharge your mission – a comment Hutchinson re-works creatively in a 'dialogical' manner. 'Debts' in geopolitics are never truly godly, nor are they seen as such by the nation's spokesmen, except if the 'elected' community finds it useful to grant them with a metaphysical aura. To follow the Weberian rationale (Weber, 2002, p. 185), religious narratives of election may be subjected to rationalization by the weak when addressed to powerful others for both value-oriented and strategic purposes. Nations have to both retain their moral principles and respond to challenges that come *from without* in an efficient manner. Again we look centuries back to examine specific Greek-European encounters. Although nineteenth-century myths of the chosen seem irrelevant in the age of European integration, readers may change their minds before the end of the chapter. Any community's responsibility to discharge its cultural-as-political debts exposes an inalienable facet of sociality: the moral urgency to give, receive and reciprocate to significant others. Debts both sanctify a secular community and consolidate its belonging to a human whole.

Even before the institution of the Greek state, Britain's relationship with Greece was burdened by the history of philhellenic support for the Greek cause. The cause's practical dimension (the political liberation of Greeks) was nevertheless overdetermined by the ideal of classicism. Unfortunately, the love of 'things Hellenic' was coupled in the post-liberation period with a fully articulated dislike for things *Neo*hellenic. This was aggravated by a rigid Greek nationalism, which soon after liberation acquired meaning as a 'Great Idea' of Greek expansion at the expense of the Ottoman Empire. The 'dead Greeks' Britons aspired to resurrect through political support, remained after Independence in every sense dead; worse, they had been replaced by living Greeks. This new 'debased race' could not philosophize like Aristotle nor orate like Demosthenes, but definitely could produce first-class brigands and the best political agitators in Europe. This, together with empirical research conducted in Greece, convinced British observers that the Muses had fled Greece for hyperborean countries, where they could fulfill their 'educational mission'; the gap left in Greek culture from this loss had been filled by Ottoman 'filth' and prejudice. Greek irredentism, which sought the acquisition of territories from the Ottoman Empire, was regarded by British governments as a 'nuisance' for Europe when they should remain content with what they had.

Alvin Gouldner (1960, 1973) points out that relationships of equality are based on mutual recognition and reciprocation. Yet, the Greek Kingdom was economically dependent on its European protectors, and not recognized as their equal. The love for things Hellenic (but not *Neo*-hellenic) could not be fully reciprocated by Greeks with an unconditional respect for the European contribution to Greek Independence from the moment Europeans were not prepared to express respect for modern Greece. Although late British philhellenism and Greek gratitude for the British contribution to liberation were intertwined, British demands that Greece discharge the financial and moral debt of Navarino (1827) generated the preconditions for an asymmetrical relationship of 'complementarity' (Gouldner, 1960, p. 162), in which Britain had rights and Greece only debts. The Greeks' expectation of British support for their irredentist dream went unanswered by Britons. In attempt to secure a reciprocal relationship Greeks created a different genealogy of this debt, in which they appeared as the first donors of Europe.

The enduring idea of cultural debts in Europe leads to an engagement with Bernal's controversial *Black Athena* (1991). Following Said (1978), Bernal argued that the contemporary historiographical imagination was plagued by a dilemma of political significance: did Hellenic civilization *owe* anything to non-European cultures (Bernal, 1991, vol. I, 1995, pp. 3–11)? If this was the case, the Western European colonial projects were based on a double myth of European-Hellenic superiority with catastrophic consequences for colonized others; the least we can do now is to admit academic complicity. For decades Bernal's infamy in Orientalist circles prevented scholars of nationalism from engaging with the changing, contextual, nature of debt in European imaginations (Herzfeld, 2005, p. 144). In the Anglo-Greek relationship, the idea that each side was a debtor to the other may cast light on the role of philhellenic criticism in the construction of a Greek counter-hegemonic nationalism. The Greek impression that with the War of Independence European philhellenes were discharging a debt to Hellenic civilization appeared in modern Greek studies as a metaphor (St Clair, 1977, p. 273; Dimaras, 1973, p. 201) rather than a point deserving systematic analysis. Since such myth-making deals a blow to academic integrity, it is not surprising that it was sealed into vault-like oblivion.

The theoretical disjunction between the 'Great Idea' and philhellenism manifested itself variously in academic literature on modern Greece. The exceptions are few: echoing Hutchinson's inner-outer divide, Gourgouris (1996, p. 13n) uses Castoriadis' (1987) distinction between the institutional and the radical imaginary (or state and society) to present the Greek narrative of 'the chosen' as a social-imaginary function. Re-working Balibar's (1990) speculations on nationalism, he argues that to be God's elected – an important aspect of the Great Idea – enables the nation to constantly select its participants (1996, p. 18). The narrative of self-election figures in other analyses of Greek nationalism that do not directly engage with this issue. It guides Tsoukalas (2002), who argues that in Greek meanings of 'Europe' we find a strategic interpretation of the historical meaning of Greece *by* other Europeans. Tsoukalas examines the process of Greek self-election in Europe diachronically. Others follow different routes: for example, the idea of self-election defines Jusdanis' (2001) defense of nationalism as a 'necessary' contemporary force. Ironically, Jusdanis' attack on an all-consuming Western modernity covertly complements the teleological character of his argument. What he fails to acknowledge is that the selfsame teleology both drives modern Greek cosmology (and any nationalist cosmology!) and gives soul to the predicament of a European modernity grounded on Aristotelian notions of perfection.

Analyzing the introversive function that mythical narratives of national formation may acquire, would not fully acknowledge that 'it is always through [a] process of interpretation' that cultures 'are kept alive' (Kearney, 1984, p. 38; Bleicher, 1980, p. 225). From the outset, in the European geopolitical arena the Greek 'audience' was split between external and internal interlocutors, imagined or real. Gourgouris' brief theorization of the 'chosen people' alludes to the symbolic function that imaginary constructs perform in political relationships. Gourgouris escapes the trap of pre-symbolic solipsism a blind Lacanian analysis might have dictated, and proceeds to acknowledge that the birth of 'Hellenism' in the European Enlightenment imagination became central to Greek self-narration. Like Tsoukalas, Gourgouris argues that Greece was, and remains, colonized by European politics in that it has internalized the European narrative of ancient Greece's 'civilizing mission'.

In this chapter I examine the enduring narrative of Greek election both synchronically and diachronically, to capture its shift from a pre-Independence lifeworld to a post-Independence systemic environment, that of European politics in which the Greek state was invited to operate. As noted by others (Hutchinson, 2004, 2005; O'Mahony and Delanty, 2001, pp. 18–21), national identity is the product of a symbolic mobilization of ideas with widespread appeal. Although the origins of such ideas may be found in radical-activist environments, their mobilization in institutional contexts can consolidate monocultural, exclusionist visions of society. Because I discuss the various historical transmutations that some ideas of Greek election may present, I do not pretend to dismiss Smith's prioritization of history in the development of nationalist discourse over the centuries.

The Weberian oscillation between value-ridden and instrumental reason in nationalist discourse returns me to Herzfeld's conception of *poniriá* or low cunning. Greeks applied this 'attitude of insubordination [...] furnishing an appropriate response to oppression' (1985, p. 25, 1991b, p. 52) to Britons to secure their moral *and* financial support. Herzfeld's argument that classicist orientalism did not go unanswered by Greeks (1987, 1997b, 2005), finds extensive use. Herzfeld's observation that for the philhellenes Greek self-interest was the 'very hallmark of their otherness', a characteristic that stood in striking contrast to the patriotic self-sacrifice of the philhellenes, is useful in that Greek self-interestedness originated in European accusations of uncivilized behavior (Herzfeld, 1987, p. 161). It requires us to examine in detail *why* British and Greek understandings of entrepreneurialism appeared to our historical actors to stand poles apart, generating mutual indignation and resentment.

Indignation has a magical power to reproduce in political discourse, sowing seeds in fertile ground and feeding on cultural insecurities. There is no better way to begin than by quoting Viscount Kirkwall's infamous missive to Gladstonian philhellenes that 'to love "not wisely, but too well" is a dangerous quality' (Kirkwall, 1864, p. 243) that the 'fallen' Greeks could only exploit. I will juxtapose this remark to a 'letter' an anonymous Cretan peasant wrote to his nephew following the outbreak of Bulgarian nationalism in 1878. In this letter, he vehemently curses the 'treacherous Franks of Europe' who offer – and then withdraw – their support as they feel, and 'their Navarino' that 'cannot be paid back', given the Greek state's decrepit economy (Anonymous, 1978, pp. 25–6). In a contemporary Europe shaken by wars morally grounded on the principle of ethnic uniqueness and financially sponsored by international political agents, the old man's accusations become a reminder of the power nationalist resentment has to shape dystopian futures.

(Self)blaming in treacherous partnerships

Although in the surviving list of philhellenes Balkan and German names predominate (Todorova, 1997, pp. 70–1), we remain attached to nineteenth-century discourses in which philhellenism was presented as a Western European contribution. The logic parallels that of nineteenth-century British observers, who were convinced that the Greeks owed eternal gratitude for the aid provided during their Revolution. The philo-Byronian societies that operated in Greece further misled British travelers, who were convinced that the Kingdom was replete with Britain's admirers (Campbell, 1877, pp. 107–8; Jebb, 1880, p. 144; Young, 1876, pp. 193–4). Such self-delusion could be followed by critical commentary on the 'inexplicable dumb and show noise' (*The Times*, 6 August 1864) of Greek expansionism, which compromised British political and economic interests in the Mediterranean region (Bagdon, 1869, p. 48; Strickland, 1863, pp. 3–4, 6; Wyse, 1871, pp. 8, 15). There was constant reference to the help Britain had offered the Greeks, who were obligated to 'please the Empire'. Palmerston's (1784–1865) ghost was, for example, a vigilant observer during a Cretan insurrection against Turkish rule (*The Times*, 23 October 1869). In Britain the battle of Navarino, the finest expression of European philhellenism, became incorporated in an imperialist rhetoric that served to increase Greek guilt every time Greece allegedly disturbed the peace of 'Europe' (*The Morning Post*, 11 November 1867). For example, British journalists, trying to emotionally blackmail the Greek government after the Dilessi affair, concluded that Britain should regret her past philhellenic kindness and withdraw further political support (*The Times*, 26 April 1870; *The Daily Telegraph*, 25 April 1870). Greeks retorted that the philhellenic contribution to Greek independence 'justified' Greek irredentism (*Aión*, 27 April 1870). The resonance of British indignation would draw upon the period of Ottoman rule. It was repeatedly claimed that, like other 'Christians in Turkey', Greeks had suffered so many wrongs, that they had developed a 'pride of sorrow: they were not averse to displaying their woes as a sort of marketable commodity [...] they had a very good assortment, and they sold very well' (Roving Englishman, 1877, p. 367). Suspicions were expressed in *The Times* during the Cretan Insurrection that the Greeks, 'remembering the history of Greek Independence [...] rely on the repugnance which the Christendom feels on hearing that a Christian people, seeking their freedom, are perishing by the sword of the Turk' (*The Times*, 8 April 1867).

Many British observers found Greek attempts to use Europeans' philhellenic past hurtful, and began to question Greek attitudes to repayment of the European loans that had supported Greek resurgence against the Ottomans. When in September 1868 the Greek government voted a Bill for appropriating a million drachmas annually towards payment of the interest on the loans of 1824–5 for the on-going Cretan Struggle, the British government immediately instructed the British Minister at the Court of Athens to deliver a note of protest, which compelled the Greeks to withdraw the Bill (*The Times*, 16 September 1868). Such reactions were the rule, rather than the exception. When in the aftermath of the Dilessi Murders Sir Henry Bulwer asked the Gladstone cabinet to restore Britain's honor with an occupation of Greece, the Greek politician Deliyannis sent him a letter demanding an apology. Bulwer replied in the same tone that he employed in his speech, accusing the Greek government of dishonesty in its dealings with Britain. The following quote shows where Bulwer's bitterness originated:

> I, myself, in early years, carried out and gave into the hands of those who, by universal assent, then represented the Greek people, the first instalment of a loan confided to Greek honour, and without which it would have been impossible for the Greek nation to maintain the struggle for its independence; and when I am told that national independence has produced such great results for the national resources, and know that not one farthing of the loan which so opportunely aided the achievement of such independence has been paid, I can only, I am sorry to say, feel confirmed in my conviction of the injustice and the incapacity of the successive Administrations which have paid so little attention to so sacred an obligation (*The Times*, 30 June 1870).

The gap between *credit* and *credo* or belief in one's integrity to reciprocate is obvious. *Credo's* function may be part of one's economic obligations, but in *credo* there is a sequence linking a donation to remuneration. This means that the one who credits abandons a present advantage in their relationship with the debtor allowing trust in the 'honesty' of the receiver to fill up the temporal gap left by the loan (Bourdieu, 1977, p. 6). To quote de Certeau, the believer 'hollows out a void in himself [*sic*.] relative to the time of the other, and, in the interests he [*sic*.] calculates, he creates a deficit whereby a future is introduced into the present' (de Certeau, 1985, p. 193). In the eyes of the British, *credo* in Greek honesty and payment of the *credit* granted to the Greek nation fail to come to an agreement.

And yet, Greek habits did not change. Throughout this period, British travelers notice an inclination 'the Greeks' have to try to make converts to philhellenic views, while reminding Britain of Canning's philehellenic policies (*Palingenesía,* 3 December 1876; *Aión,* 14 March 1866. 'They are particularly prone to "try it on" with Englishmen, whose influence on the affairs of Europe, they, as a commercial people, are disposed to overrate' (Farrer, 1882, p. 52; Campbell, 1877, pp. 124–6), concluded frustrated British travelers in Greece. Attempts at proselytism tested the limits of British patience. Knowledge that the Greeks were endeavoring to gain the ear of Europe 'by a constant repetition of boasts about themselves and their achievements, addressed to men who are prepared by education to sympathize with the name of Greece' (Anonymous, 1867, p. 5) began to annoy some Britons. 'The Protecting Powers are urged to employ the money of their subjects to deliver Crete, and Philhellenes are invited to pour out their blood and die gloriously [so] that the Greek Government may annex the island', stated Finlay (*The Times,* 6 October 1866). British suspicion that the Greeks were taking advantage of philhellenic sentiments in the Cretan venture did not prevent Greek journalists from exploiting the past. In August 1866, the Athenian press invented a scenario of a battle in Crete, in which unspeakable Turkish atrocities took place. 'It would require an Epimenides, one of themselves, even a prophet of their own, to separate the truth from the falsehood' exclaimed Finlay.

> This horrid massacre occurred in the year 1822, and a description of it, with an engraving from a sketch of the grotto, will be found in *Pashley's Travels in Crete*. Greek writers, talkers, and politicians, not repudiating their character in St. Paul's Epistle to Titus, appear to consider the massacre of 1822 a means of rousing the sympathy of Europe against the Sultan's government as effectual in 1866 as they were in 1822 (*The Times,* 20 October 1866).

If anything, the British side was acutely aware that *poniriá* was at play in Greek dealings with Europeans. The accusation leveled at Greeks is professional-as-moral deviance: not only do they not reciprocate British philehellenic kindness, but they also exploit it. The close-knit relationship between the economic significance of philhellenism and the Greek duty to reciprocate invoked in British reflections is undeniable and we do indeed find it in Greek attitudes of the period. Perhaps moral and market economies are regulated by different laws: the 'marketization' of Hellenic Greekness could be regarded as the *functionalization – de-symbolization,* to follow Berking's terminology (1999, p. 127) – of the West-East system of reciprocity promoted in the Greek nationalist cause. Mauss' study of the gift (1954) already presents the de-symbolization of gift giving as the symptom of modernity. We may remember Herzfeld's elaboration of 'structural nostalgia' (2005, p. 150), a call for the return of a long-lost social solidarity both the state and its subjects invoke in the face of modern fragmentation. However, we must recall the moral-cultural dimension of organized exchange: divorcing market and moral econ-omies reflects scholarly attempts to keep Marxist and Maussian theory apart, when global social realities point in the opposite direction (Appa-durai, 1986, p. 11; Sayer, 1999, p. 65). As Honneth alerts us, material dis-tribution is affected by value systems; when participants in distribution struggles aim at a redistribution of material resources, 'cultural inter-pretations play a constitutive role' (Fraser and Honneth, 2003, p. 158). Greeks would constantly use the 'situational value' (Appadurai, 1986 p. 5; Sahlins, 1965, p. 153) of Hellenic culture, because its emotional appeal to the 'civilized world' would transform it into a valuable commodity. The Hellenic ideal on which Europe based its self-image was a 'scarce resource' (Appadurai, 1981): it could only be used in so many ways, and it had to be used well.

Interestingly, the Greeks' response to European humiliations oscillated between resentment and self-guilt. My use of 'resentment' almost coin-cides with the meaning of Nietzsche's (1996, p. 55) *ressentiment*, this long-term, generalized feeling that is directed against powerful agents and involves both awareness of powerlessness and compensation by an imag-inary vengeance. Note for example the misgivings expressed by Gennadios, who was convinced that British 'calumnies' aim to obstruct Greek progress, keeping the Greek state under forced European 'tutelage' (Gennadios, 1870, pp. 160, 172–3); the fear vocalized by the MP for Ermionis, Milisis, who was sure that any compensation from the Greek state to a British subject is not philanthropy, because it is imposed by Britain as a 'debt' (Milisis, 1871, p. 71); or the fear that the election of the first Ionian plenipotentiaries for the Greek National Assembly would be sabotaged by shadowy *mishellenes* (Greek haters) who are unhappy about the Ionian unification with Greece (*Palingenesía*, 25 April 1864). These comments are always accompanied by an imagined revenge the Greek nation might take in the future, articulated in the language of 'progress' and solidarity against a 'common enemy'. Theorists stress the impact status insecurity has on the production of resentful nationalist discourse. Historically, nations that were positioned as the weak party in a relation-ship involv-ing economic and political control or stayed in contact with powerful external others (nations, empires) during and/or after their formative period, began at some point to display a feeling of injured self-respect and political impotence. Such occasions were often followed by the production of narratives supporting the idea of an immaculate 'nation' martyred at the hands of its political enemies (Pešić, 1995; Dimitrijević, 1999). Although the theoretical mobilization of Nietzschean *ressentiment* (Nietzsche, 1996; Scheler, 1961) sheds ample light on the modality of nationalist emotion, it facilitates less understanding of its political *uses* by the national community. Rather than taking for granted that nationalist *ressentiment* encourages passivity and submission to given and/or self-assigned inferior roles, we should examine its potential to metamorphose into affirmative action in the domestic (Greenfeld, 1990) and international arena, where the nation enters into dialogues with its significant others. In order to examine *ressentiment* as an essential component of national self-recognition it is necessary to consider the systemic environment in which resentment discourse functions. Unlike Greenfeld (1990), I do not limit this function to the constitution of national elites: although social centres control national systems, the system also has to assert its autonomy in the geopolitical environment it shares with rival national systems. I claim instead that the internal function of *ressentiment* sustains 'non-communicative action': a type of political action that prioritizes national interests and excludes any 'hostile' voices without negotiation. European accusations of Greek inefficiency were bound to figure as a uniform 'hostile voice' that, ironically, would assist the production of an equally monologic nationalist *Weltsanschauung*. I will examine the internal function of *ressentiment* extensively in the following chapter.

It is incorrect to attach nationalist resentment to Anglo-Greek encounters exclusively: in Greek political commentary France's relationship with Greece is not always presented as any less adversarial than the Anglo-Greek relationship (Rhighopoulos, 1979 [1881], p. 233). For example, rumors circulated at this time in Greece that the French encouraged the Cretans to revolt without offering any aid to their cause (*The Times*, 8 January 1869). Greeks would also view Russia as a malicious *mishellenic* power supporting *Panslavism* in the East. Historically, nineteenth-century Greeks located the origins of the Russian threat either in the Crimean war or the Peloponnesian revolution incited by Orlov in 1869–70 (*Palingenesía*, 20 September 1868; Pekios, 1880, pp. 16–17; Rhighopoulos, 1979 [1881], p. 220; Wyse, 1871, p. 8). The very same suggestion found its way into Greek historiography, suggesting that an external force is responsible for such 'national disasters' (Svoronos, 1991, p. 59).

Of course, there were also different opinions. As early as in 1864, remorse was expressed as British refusal to lend further to Greece became apparent. After the cession of the Ionian Islands, a Greek journalist acknowledged the gratitude Greece ought to feel toward Britain (*Palingenesía*, 25 April 1864). 'Those who do not recognize their debts are called *chreokòpoi* [fraudulently bankrupt], men [*sic*.] of bad faith, commercially speaking, untrustworthy' (*Palingenesía*, 21 March 1864; see also 14 October 1878) claimed another journalist who kept recording any progress on the philhellenic loans for the Greek struggle for Independence (1824–5). This paranoia had little to do with money, and everything with the moral debt of philhellenism that burdened Greece. As a contemporaneous Greek commentator remarked, 'England' had good reasons to 'hold bad feelings for the Greek nation' because of Greece's failure to meet British demands for remuneration. 'The Greek nation owes to the homeland of Byron and Canning, to that Great Island on which the first philhellenic organizations were born (Ialemos, 1877, p. 51). The complaint that the root of decay is internal translates self-blaming into self-exclusion from Europe – a self-styled 'oriental'. fatalism that has haunted Greeks ever since. Guilt and remorse follow the recognition that Greece is helpless in Europe and surrounded by states that covet its dominions.

And yet, the resentment Greeks expressed towards their Protectors never quite disappeared. The defensive conviction that Greece has a 'national mission' that its contribution to European civilization renders 'necessary' (Pantazidis, 1876, pp. 26–7) is analogous to Jusdanis' argument that the nation is a historical necessity due to its community-making essence. This logic is predicated upon a notion of 'lack' (Laclau and Mouffe, 1985, pp. 48–54, p. 128; Žižek, 1988, p. 112): the Greeks become the new 'necessary' element that makes the European structure complete and represents European civilization. The idea that Hellenic heritage belonged to Greece, not Europe, inspired Aristotle Valaoritis, the Ionian scholar who stood as MP for Lefkas in 1867, to explain in Parliament that, in spite of European accusations, the Hellenic past should now be mobilized in the making of a modern Greek future (*Palingenesía*, 19 January 1867). Bolder was the statement of the Greek Enlightenment scholar, Stefanos Koumanoudis, who insisted that the modern European lovers of ancient Hellas were not the first admirers of Hellenic civilization (*Palingenesía*, 18 April 1866.). Philhellenism proper is Greek heritage, because the first philhellenes were the Athenians.

From all those words similar to 'Philhellene' that were in use, only the 'Philathenian' has the same meaning, because Athens was the benefactor of humanity. [...] It is another matter if some times the ancient Greeks abused, or rather overindulged in the widespread beneficent action of philhellenism by naming some peoples 'phil-hellenes' even if they were not in fact. Catachresis is a common practice and it would not be odd if the conceited Athenians [...] imagined that there were philhellenes everywhere [...] Therefore, modern philhellenism is only a survival of past practices (*Palin-genesía*, 11 April 1866).

Koumanoudis refers to ancient allies' obligations to pay taxes to the Athenian League. This 'duty' is identified with the practice of modern Europeans to contribute to the Greek cause. Koumanoudis justified this ancient-modern practice on the grounds of an Athenian-Greek civiliz-ing mission. By right of heritage the *Neo*hellenes replace the ancient Athenians, as if the 'Greek nation' is a perennial form. The modern European nations are forced thus into the position of a morally obliged debtor to modern Greek culture.

The 'necessity' of Greek nationalism in nineteenth-century European politics would constantly be justified by a historical memory carefully manipulated so as to serve nationalist needs. Thus, for an anonymous Greek pedagogue, modern Greece 'the black sheep of the European family' *ought* to be recognized by Europe as the nation that will 'fill the gap left behind by the absence of its ancestor, this glorious Hellenic antiquity' (Anonymous, 1867, p. 41; *Palingenesía*, 5 April 1875). For Gennadios, Greece, 'the unfortunate Prometheus of nations' that brought the light of knowledge to Europe can look 'upon its ugly shores' and say to the British 'nation' without fear:

There is not one of you who may take up a stone and throw it at us. You began from worse, you are thoroughly sickly and immoral now; it is only your rich attire that hides your gaping wounds, and the vantage ground you occupy that lends respectability to your hypo-crisy. We, therefore, who are no worse, but whose sin is poverty and weakness, will not despair, for, with the help of our God, we will accomplish our great task (Gennadios, 1871, p. 145; see also *The Morning Post*, 15 September 1866).

The moralization of Greek nationalist discourse resembles Arendt's (1973) claim that unbearable suffering erodes not only one's humanity, but also one's ability to relate to the pain of others. In Greek national-ist discourse this de-moralization takes place only from the standpoint of the disempowered 'nation'. Whereas the other's thinking and action are judged to be morally incomplete, the Greek nation appears to struggle for survival in a hostile political environment. The Greek nation assumes form as a collective 'spectator' (Habermas, 1983, pp. 171–2; Yar, 2000, pp. 16–17), who vigilantly guards its right to morally act on the world, helping rid humanity of evil imperial presence. The teleological mechanics of this discourse resemble Benjamin's 'Angelus Novus'. The angel of progress, claimed Benjamin, cannot decide whether to look back, to the past, gather the pieces of debris around him and 'make whole what has been smashed' (1992, p. 249), or follow the Edenic storm propelling him toward the future. This metaphor beautifully captures modern Greek associations of 'progress' with Hellenic history. The European attachment to Hellenic civilization and the undeniable reality of Western dependence were pieced together to re-define the future of Greek-European relations in terms of an outstanding debt. In the following pages I examine the *redemptive* potential of this Greek narrative, for its religious façade nicely camouflaged its political content.

Choosing to be 'the chosen': sacrifice as redemption

The adversarial character of European-Greek encounters indicates a damaged reciprocity at play. Gouldner (1960, pp. 164–5) attributed reciprocal damage to the disruptive potential of power imbalance in relationships and Bourdieu related it to the 'dissymmetry of ostentatious redistribution which is the base of political authority' (1998, p. 210). Power necessitates the consolidation of symbolic testimonies of gratitude and moral indebtedness, legitimizing thus relationships of economic dependence, if not exploitation (*ibid.* pp. 191–2). It is no coincidence that Greek nationalist discourse constantly equates philhellenic economic and Greek cultural capital (Bourdieu, 1984): the two are by no means equal, but their exchange bears potential to rectify the 'damage' of Greece's political dependence. This cunning equation would eventually tip the symbolic scales on the other side. The manipulation of reciprocity aimed to secure the moral superiority of the weak side, reproducing thus an inverted relationship of complementarity: now the Greeks could demand from Europe.

This manipulation was rife with historical meaning. A *leitmotif* in Greek nineteenth-century sources was the image of a crucified Greece, a new 'philhellenic' martyr that raised the European West from cultural darkness – a gesture that Europe reciprocated by displaying a gross negligence in repaying some long-forgotten debts to the modern 'heirs' of

Hellas. On such occasions, the accusation directed against Europeans was that they behaved like 'Hebrews of the sea' who 'buy and sell nations as if they were flocks' (P., 1878, p. 17) with no concern about the damage done to humanity. The attribution of 'Jewish' and 'Jesuit' behavior to Disraeli (Ialemos, 1877) and even to liberal Gladstone (Rhighopoulos, 1979 [1881], pp. 228–9, 234; Xenos, 1881; *Palingenesía*, 13 October 1875 and 5 August 1876) during the revolutions of the 1870s in the Balkans, uncovers the profoundly racist religious façade of Greek cosmology. Both the images of the Jesuit and the Jew symbolize the religious foes of Greek Orthodoxy. The relationship of Orthodox religion with Greek identity made them time-resistant. Even today, *Ovriòs* (corrupt Hebrew) and *Iesouitikòs/Iesouìtis* (Jesuit) signify meanness, corruption, lying and subversion attributed to an evil, 'exotic' source.

Alternatively, European, especially British, politicians would appear in Greek nationalist discourse as 'Frankish pseudochristians' who have no respect for the cradle of arts and letters', and let Greece 'be tortured' and 'murdered by the Turks' (*Palingenesía*, 3 April 1867). Like the 'Jewish/Jesuitic' image of Europe, the 'Frankish' one was dubious and devilish (*The Times*, 8 December 1869). *Koutófraghos* or 'silly Frank' denotes in modern Greek someone who either can be deceived easily or displays a transparent, and therefore socially useless, type of cunning – unlike those who possess *poniriá*, a necessary skill for social survival (du Boulay, 1994, pp. 116–17). In Greek folk culture the 'Frank' could also become a synonym for the 'Antichrist' and the Devil, as the unknown old man of the introduction claims (Anonymous, 1878, p. 11). The image of the Devil as an envious (*fthonerós* in ecclesiastical language) angel who was exiled from heaven because of his arrogance (*alazoneía*) (Stewart, 1991, p. 141) presents the European as conspirator, jealous of the glorious Greek past and its modern heirs. Complementary to this image is the notion of *ponirós* that in Orthodox tradition designates both evil and the Devil, the deceiver of the faithful. Thus the 'Frank' is the envious outsider who wants to corrode the national community's bonds. The term becomes the carrier of *disemia* (Herzfeld, 1997a, p. 14), the pairing of two conflicting moral codes corresponding to the two facets of Greek culture: self-knowledge (anger stemming from European complaints about Greek moral deficiency) and self-presentation (cunningness akin to Greek *poniriá*). The term 'Frank' was linked historically to the twin commercial and moral character of the medieval Crusades that Byzantium regarded with suspicion (Hay, 1968, p. 54; Le Goff, 1993, pp. 100–1). Gradually, however, it became the vehicle of Christian identity and was used in Western European regions to designate the agents of the Pan-Christian (that is, Western Christian) mission against the 'infidels' (Bull, 1997). Modern Greek uses of the term allude to Western self-designations but invert Western discourses of the Greek 'Fall' from the European civilizational heaven. In this inversion 'Greece' takes the place of 'Edenic Europe' and the 'Frankish', 'Jesuit' and 'Jewish' Europeans become the 'fallen angels' of humanity.

Europe betrayed Greece then, just as Christ was betrayed by one of his disciples so that he suffers for the sins of humanity. This narrative inundated nineteenth-century Greek reflections on the country's relationship with Europe: the sufferings of the Christian 'Saviour' concur with those 'of Hellas [...] to make the Holy Week sorrowful', claim some Greek journalists after Dilessi (*The Times*, 20 May 1870; *Clió*, 30/11 July 1870); humanity must mourn the loss of Greece, just as Greece itself mourns its political state, claimed an MP the following year (Chadjiskos, 1871). The idea of 'sacrifice' is an important *topos* in other nationalist contexts, such as the Polish, the Spanish and the Irish. Sheridan's (1987) study of Irish culture reveals that the identification of the Irish people with Jesus as the suffering Christ of nations martyred by the British ran deep into nineteenth- and twentieth-century Irish Catholic culture. Pearse's discourse on the Easter Rising of 1912 sanctified the rebellion as a national redemption from Irish sins, 'drawing parallels both with Christ's crucifixion and Cúchulainn's triumphant death facing his enemies' (Hutchinson, 2005, pp. 69–72). This 'mythic overlaying' emerges in other contexts, European and non-European. Narratives of national suffering and redemption through a 'special mission' to civilize appear in Chinese culture: Liang Qichao presented 'the West' as a corrupt and decadent place, as opposed to China, the cradle of civilization and the pedagogical future of humanity (*ibid.*, p. 67). Italian self-presentations during the Risorgimento and throughout the Fascist era propagated an Italian primacy in ethics and civilization too, despite the feeling that Italy distanced itself from Europe after the decline of the Renaissance spirit. The sense of loss translates political oppressions into collective martyrdom in Latvian narratives of suffering, connected to the experience of Soviet rule (Skultans, 1998). Similarly, Czech visions of the nation as democratic, responsible and self-reliant served to re-integrate Czech history into Western European traditions, simultaneously obliterating memories of foreign rule and dependence (Williams, 1997, p. 134). Polish self-perceptions as the 'Bulwark of Christendom' against Turkish invasion reinforced ideas of sacrifice and responsibility in modern Polish political life (Davies, 1997). Ideas of sacrifice also permeate Serb nationalist discourse, which draws on the martyrdom and death of Prince Lazar in the battle of Kosovo against the Ottomans (1389). Lazar's choice of a sacrificial death for the Serb people over an earthly kingdom *ex post facto* epitomized the sufferings of the Serb nation in the hands of the Ottomans, Habsburgs, Nazis, communists and recently NATO (Duijzins, 2000). Current depictions of the Serbs as 'the Jews of the Balkans' who nevertheless rest at the heart of 'Europe proper' share with Greek nationalist discourse this sense of collective victimization at the hands of powerful others, as well as the conviction that national identity is 'a gift from God [...] exclusively granted to [the people]' (Šuber, 2006, p. 4).

Greece's sacrificial suffering becomes synonymous with the sacrificial offering of its inherited Hellenic culture and resembles what Georges Bataille termed 'general economy of exchange' (1988, vol. I, p. 97, p. 120) – an economy of excessive giving that translates the donor's generosity into autonomy and power. Greek 'loss' is not definite, however: because Greek commentators constantly remind their financial donors of this 'other debt' that Europeans have forgotten to discharge, they implicitly try to equate scarce economic aid, with Greek cultural offering (given in plenty to Europe by their Hellenic forefathers). Nationalist sacrificial giving belongs to the moral economy of exchange and can only be considered as an intersubjective construct (Gudeman, 1986; O'Neill, 1999). Greek *unconditional* offering idealizes political exchange by translating it into Christian *agápe*, God's love for humans and, by extension, the brotherly love for humanity (Herzfeld, 2005, p. 152). The Christian norm of *agápe* is exemplified in the biblical idea 'good to give first, don't expect return'. But, of course, Christian *agápe* contrasts with conventional ego-based Greek attitudes towards *philía* or friendship, the idea that love and appreciation of the other presupposes love of the self (Aristotle, 1976). The connection between friendship and self-interest is a prominent feature of Greek society. Friendships resolve tensions between familial solidarity and the hostility of an outside world: 'the central element in such relationships is not the deep personal significance of the one or the other but [...] a fortuitous union of self-interests. [...] When self-interest fails, friendship must also fail' (du Boulay, 1994, p. 85). The apparent conflict between the ideational/normative and the reality of 'cheating' that defined Greek attitudes angered other Europeans, who condemned the Greeks for their ingratitude.

The martyred Greece retained during the nineteenth century the magical ability to 'rise from the grave', like a 'consumed Lazarus of Europe' (Ialemos, 1877). Nineteenth-century narratives of Greek 'Fall' into the Oriental abyss of Ottoman conquest already have a redemptive potential, in that they are followed by the belief that Byzantine subjection allowed the West to flourish intellectually and politically. As happened with other European nations, the modern Greeks expected to be restored by God to their supremacy, to be chosen to fulfill their mission on earth and 'civilize' a 'barbarous humanity' (Pekios, 1880, pp. 18–19). The suggestion was, as Dimitris Ainian (1800–81), ex-secretary of Karaïskakis and self-appointed 'pedagogue of the nation' suggested, that a thoroughly Hellenized Byzantium should 'become the center of all political meetings and … [Constantinople] the holy and inviolable base of Europe' (1876, pp. 19–20). In the same narrative European Westerners bore the stigma of the sinner because their ancestors did not help Constantinople survive the Ottoman siege in 1453 (*Palingenesía*, 9 and 31 March 1878). Thus, the role of Byzantium in the making of European civilization becomes the Greek response to philhellenic accusations of *Neo*hellenic bankruptcy (An Oriental and Former Rayah, 1868, pp. 18–20; Anonymous, 1866, p. 4; *Clio*, 1/13 June, 1868; Ialemos, 1877; *Palingenesía*, 15 July 1867; Pekios, 1880, pp. 16–18).

Such accusations survived the passage of time, and continued to inform twentieth-century Greek self-perceptions (Sutton, 2000, pp. 160–1). They permeated Greek academic discourse, presenting a thoroughly Hellenized Byzantium as the fortress of Europe against the Arab and Ottoman sway (Karayannopoulos, 1993, p. 469). They also impacted on Greek political agendas, encouraging introversion, xenophobia and a reactive nationalist arrogance directed against other European imagined-conversational communities. The 1974 invasion of Turkish Cyprus revived the idea that the 'evil' West plots against Greek sovereign interests. Dismissing the plain fact that the Greek state harbored nationalist sentiments in Cyprus that favored the unification of the island with Greece (especially during the colonel's regime of 1967–74), post-1974 nationalist discourse fostered an argument in which the junta's 'foreign connections' alone precipitated Turkish occupation. Following the invasion of the Yugoslav space by NATO troops in the late 1990s Greece was shaken by anti-war demonstrations. The attack on Serbia by the powerful American allies and the forced commitment of the Greek government to NATO with its military contribution to the 'pacifying cause' angered the Greek public. As the crisis engendered the Greek government's position internally, the state's reaction was to both encourage material aid to the Serbian Orthodox 'brothers' and remind Europe of Greece's 'pacifying and humanitarian role' in the region. It would have been naïve to consider this statement political rhetoric based on contingencies of the moment. The selfsame split attitude manifested itself in the context of the 2004 Olympics, which allegedly marked the return of European heritage to its Greek cradle, Athens. While the Athens Olympic Committee was anxious that Athens would deliver Western standards of security and surveillance during the Games, the demand that Britain returns the Elgian marbles, the usurped Greek heritage, to its true 'home', revived the spirit of nationalist *ressentiment* against the West. This attitude was complemented by the government's discourse on Greece's 'responsibility' to act as a pacifying intermediary in the southeast Mediterranean – a discourse by no means tied to *Athens 2004* exclusively, as it informed both leftist and conservative political agendas throughout the 1990s and beyond (Tzanelli, 2004). To recall Smith, to be elected is to be placed under moral obligations: gradually, pre-Independence narratives of election with a *religious* exterior were integrated into *secular* state discourse.

The 'task' Greece had to accomplish in the nineteenth century was also the nodal point of the Great Idea, the Hellenic civilizing mission in the East. The Greek nation was never truly chosen by God: in the Greek nationalist imagination, the philhellenes *ought* to have chosen the Greek nation to perform this civilizing mission. Ultimately, however, the Greeks had chosen themselves to educate the East *retroactively* (Žižek, 1999, pp. 19, 330–3). The elective affinity of religion with nationalist sentiment takes us back to Weber's (1985) protestant ethic and its ability to shape the social world (Wilkinson, 2004, pp. 61–2). The strong influence of Herder's teaching, according to which every nation had its own, unique *Geist* and its special mission (Bhatt, 2000, p. 30), informed Greek nationalism, so strongly affected by German romanticism (Dimaras, 1983, pp. 419–25; Liakos, 2002, pp. 31–2). The main components of the modern Greek civilizing mission, Christian religion, education and Hellenic civilization appeared entangled in Greek writings on the Great Idea. A retroactive reading of Greek giving in different historical periods enabled a creative 'fusion' of traditions (Alexander, 2006; Brandist, 2002, p. 123), ultimately allowing the nation's symbolic re-admission into the European Eden.

This interpretative fusion bore nevertheless the seeds of a dangerous ecumenical nationalism that stemmed from the very European idea of Edenic happiness (Herzfeld, 1987, pp. 30–1). If Paradise lost is the place of civilized humanity, Paradise reclaimed is the locus of nationalist exclusivity – in other words, the nation provides humanity with a narrative of genesis and flourishing. Consider the idea propagated by Aristarchos Bey, a Constantinopolitan brigadier, who professed that Byzantine universalism was only another version of ancient Greek cosmopolitanism. This cosmopolitanism presented the Greek as the *polítis* of the *kósmos*, the citizen of the world, in the understanding that ancient Athens *was* the civilization of the (known) world. For Bey, to be civilized was to *speak* Greek and *conform* to an Athenian way of living. In the atmosphere of Byzantine humanism of the ninth century, Bey explains, Greek language ceased to be as important as the Greek Christian spirit (Aristarchos Bey, vol. IV, 1876, p. 154). Cyril's admission to the Slavonic tribes by Patriarch Photios in 861 was arranged for their conversion to Christianity – a civilizing mission the nineteenth-century Greeks named the 'dissemination of the good word'. The rhetoric of Christian 'dissemination' was addressed to Balkan peoples the Greeks wanted to incorporate in their new 'empire' (Asklipiadis, 1872, pp. 9, 13). Of course, the emphasis on cultural heritage and ethnic continuity mediated though religion was not a Greek peculiarity: from the eighteenth century onwards, Balkan federalists began to pursue the foundation of supra-national states like that envisaged by the Greeks (Jelavich, 1983; Roudometof, 1999; Stavrianos, 1958).

The idea of the Greek nation's historic mission had already been expressed by C.D. Schinas, the first rector of the University of Athens, during the institution's inaugural ceremony (3 May 1837) (Kitromilidis, 1989, pp. 166–7). The same idea was invoked in Paparhighopoulos' three-stage development of the Greek nation in his *History of the Hellenic Nation* (Carabott, 2005a, p. 23; Clogg, 1992, p. 2; Kitromilidis, 1998, p. 11). According to Paparhighopoulos, the political and intellectual expression of the ancient Hellenes became in the Byzantine era the preservation of the 'Holy Word of God'. Synecdochically, the modern Greek nation, the inheritor of Byzantine culture, 'would be the instigator of ethical and political progress in the East' (Augustinos, 1977, p. 16). This practice was deeply embedded in a reception of classicist education in Greece that fused Christianity with paganism. To invoke the ancient saying of Isocrates Greeks continue to use today (Tzanelli, 2006, pp. 36–8), a Hellene is the one who participates in Greek *paideía* (culture and education). Those who did not were barbarians (Hall, 2002, p. 179). The narrative underscored the inclusion of Macedonia into an imagined 'Hellenic community' from the days of Philip the Macedon and Alexander the Great until 'the "barbaric" invasions of the seventh century' that Fallmerayer 'documented' in his writings (Carabott, 2005a, pp. 23–4). We must not forget how the post-Second World War 'nationalization' of Greek Macedonia echoed such nineteenth-century invocations of a mysteriously Greek 'Holy Gospel' that would exorcise the alleged 'Slavishness' of those populations that inhabited the Greek soil but spoke other languages (Karakasidou, 2002, p. 123).

The 'Holy Word' promoted by Greeks as a vehicle of their civilizing mission was not simply a language. Consider the so-called 'language

controversy' in Greece, which was resolved only after the political restoration of 1974: the co-existence of the *demotic* or folk language with the
katharevousa or artificial, archaic Greek is just another facet of the split
between national self-knowledge and collective self-presentation in the
international political arena (Herzfeld, 1987, p. 114). The manipulation of
language is akin to the institutional production of ideology (Habermas,
1997, p. 360): *demoticism* belonged to the Greek lifeworld before making
its way into literature and school curricula, whereas *katharevousa* was
the hegemonic product of an Europeanized elite that aspired to 'purify'
(*kathaírei*) Greek culture from post-Byzantine cultural corruption. Heteroglot conflicts from below and above (Brandist, 2002, pp. 120–2)
defined modern Greek identity in a profound way. So, when examining
nineteenth-century conceptions of the 'Holy Word' addressed to the 'barbaric tribes' of Europe, we should view language as a combination of
the '*lógos* in the flesh and the *Lógos* of God' (P., 1878, p. 6). At times this
lógos would be identified with the ancient Greek language, which the
'Byzantine Greeks' (a projection of Greekness back to its primordial past)
preserved and disseminated to the Western world – the contribution of
Byzantium to European civilization. For example, it was argued in a
nineteenth-century article on Western Renaissance that 'this is the language of Homer and Hesiod, Herodotus and Thucydides, Plato and Aristotle, Hippocrates and Theophrastus [...] The Logos of the Bible, of Saint
Paul and the Fathers of the Church [...] the language of letters, theology
and legal codes of Byzantine era' (*Clio*, 31/12 August 1864). In this way,
the Aristotelian *lógos*, reason articulated in the act of speaking (Aristotle,
1946, book A, chapter 2), became interchangeable with the Christian
Lógos, the godly *demiurge* (creator) of the world. Modern Greek thought
bore the stamp of Aristotelianism: the idea of a Greek civilizing mission
alluded to a *teleology* that underscored Aristotle's metaphysics. Like all
'things', nations carried within them a *telos*, a purpose and an end. This
was their very essence (*ousía*) that justified their existence (Aristotle, 1924,
vol. I, book B, chapter 8, 198b–199b). It was this unexpected meeting of
Herder's missionary ideas and Aristotle's *teleology* that defined Greek
nationalist thought. For Herder, only community language transformed
humans into social beings – a version of Aristotle's *zóon politikón*. Herder's
argument was that each community had its own language and every
language was the manifestation of unique values and ideas.

Aristotelianism was not alone in influencing modern Greek self-
narration. It would be more precise to follow Dakin's observation that
Aristotelian ideas clashed with the Neoplatonist apparatus of modern
Greek thought (1972, p. 5). Like the rhetorical clash between self-

interested friendship and Christian love, the practicalities of an Aristotelian for the Greek nation were constantly set against a Neoplatonist ideal that questioned the means to this end. The coexistence of these two different levels of being and thinking was inscribed in the humanist anthropocentric vocabulary. The notion of 'human' is encapsulated in two words: *ánthropos* (from *ánō* = up and *thrōskō* = stare at), which denotes a being aspiring to reach the upper level of 'truth', and *vrotós* (*vivrōskomai* = being consumed, perish), which denotes the perishable, malleable side of human nature. Even the post-Byzantine narrative of the Empire's fall was interpreted in Greek nationalist discourse on the basis of the sinful iconoclastic conflict, which began from a heated debate on idols and God's representation (Mango, 1998, pp. 151–5). The consoling legend of 'the chosen' became for the Greek conversational community an imagined transcendence of the Nietzschean 'slave' morality (Nietzsche, 1996, pp. 4–5, 111). To imagine themselves as God's elected was for Greeks the only way to counter the harsh reality of European politics, in which Constantinople was Istanbul and the last Emperor Constantine a distant memory of tragic resistance to the inevitable (Chassiotis, 1981, pp. 63–5; Herzfeld, 1987, pp. 37–9). Nevertheless, to blindly follow Nietzsche would be to miss Durkheim's observation that ceremonies of mourning serve to heal wounds and affirm one's belonging to a human whole (Durkheim in Wilkinson, 2005, pp. 67, 73). Sacrificial giving in nationalist discourses of the weak may still secure a safe place in the European Eden.

Although by untangling the etiological conundrums of redemptive narratives we shed light on their historical development, we also need to stress the significance of their contextual re-emergence (Kearney, 1984, p. 20). My transition here from history to metaphysics and then back may offend historians, but is necessary. To construct a Weberian analytical framework, I argue that all the nations 'Europe' exiles from its political paradise attempt a similar transition by imagining themselves as the 'new chosen people'. This shift from politics to metaphysics must not be dismissed, as it mobilizes the ethical aspects of the idea of the chosen in creative ways. It is not coincidental that in postwar philosophical theory the 'chosen' came to represent a radical form of otherness, what philosophers termed *alterity* (Derrida, 1997, p. 112; Levinas, 1969). Such radical otherness was almost identified with God, whose essence cannot be revealed to the believer, because faith is based on believing without questioning. Yet, to deconstruct this argument, one could claim that the historical background of this philosophy of ethics voiced the trauma of a devastating World War and a genocide that still haunts European memory. Suffering was viewed in terms of a 'terminal aporia', something that defies articulation (Ricoeur, 1995, 2004, p. 89; Wilkinson, 2005, p. 43). The 'banalization' of human suffering (Wilkinson, 2005, p. 87; Yar, 2000, p. 15) often led theorists to see in Judeo-Christian morality an immediately available way to restore our ability to humanize pain. The metaphysics of religion were translated into the politics of suffering.

Likewise, nationalist discourse belongs to geopolitics, and the idea of a national *alterity* that must be respected in its mysticism without question (prior to knowledge) does a great disservice to intercultural communication. Presenting oneself as 'other' can become a clever strategy to avoid questioning and critique that may emerge in dialogic encounters with others. To reach the core of nationalist logic one has to see the idea of the chosen as a symbolic, if not strategic action. In the case of Greek nationalist discourse, the conception of the chosen became the narrative of philhellenism on ancient Greece's cultural uniqueness transformed into modern Greece's radical difference. Such Greek *alterity* could present those who opposed Greek irredentism as sinners against humanity – for, if the Greeks were God's chosen, their choices were part of the ineffable and should remain unchallenged. This counter-conspiracy with heaven allowed Greeks to restructure themselves as a form of 'othering' in their relationship with a judgmental Europe, a performative action with a strong pedagogical element in it: a civilizing mission (Bhabha, 1994).

Undoubtedly, the performative dimension of nationalist othering ceases to look decorative if put in historical and political perspective. The condemnation of Navarino by Greeks and British alike unveils the most unpleasant aspects of political-as-moral accountability. Internalized blaming is always externally projected and internally mobilized, producing a hostile environment in which harmonious coexistence of nations, and multiple ethnic identities *within* nations, becomes impossible. To freely adapt Hutchinson's metaphor (2005), it transforms nations into bloody zones of conflict with numerous victims. The productive nature of moral accountability affected European cultural reciprocities in profoundly damaging ways: not only did it naturalize inequalities in Europe, but performed the same function within the nation-state, transforming systemic discourse into conservative nationalist monologues of unprecedented power. This is the theme of the following chapter.

7
British Patrons and Puerile Greeks: The Dialogics of Self-Presentation

Of families and children: the European politics of interdependency

Why does political patronage masquerade in a gendered language of family unity? Feminist theorists who have worked towards a normative theory of care and of non-contractual values such as trust and responsibility (Deacon, 2007; Kittay, 2001; White, 2003; Williams, 2004) may not be surprised to find that, historically, the language of care was employed to describe unequal political relations on many occasions. The paradox this hides is so striking, that it is easily missed: in replacing the discourse of political control with that of care and unmitigated parental duties, an ethical universalism only Kantians would support becomes auxiliary to a realist 'Weberian power politics', reproducing thus a conflict that stands at the core of *Western* European modernity (Guzzini, 1998, p. 228; Robinson, 1999, pp. 4–6). The chasm between lofty aspirations of 'justice' and the 'good' on the one hand, and the more immanent aspiration of international relations to the maintenance of 'stability' or 'order' (Haslam, 2002; Morgenthau and Thompson, 1984), turn out to be, on closer inspection, two sides of the same coin rather than an intractable opposition. This reminds us in the context of international relations that 'the structures, norms, and practices which govern the global system served to exclude, and to marginalize, certain groups' (Robinson, 1999, pp. 109–10). Like the European system, which excluded certain nation-states from its modernity, nation-states themselves erased boundaries to exclude certain identities from their own modernity. By 'certain identities' in this chapter, I mean *both* women and non-native cultural groups.

As already explained, the political revival of ancient Greece was one of many imperial projects that added to the Victorians' prestige as agents of civilization (Dakin, 1955, pp. 5–6). This tiny Mediterranean state presented a challenge, because it entertained ideas symmetrical to British imperial ambitions. Greek irredentism directed against the Ottoman Empire was a nuisance for Britain: not only did it pose a threat to the fragile political stabilities on the Eastern European border, it also humiliated the magnanimous European protectors of Greece. The British response and the Greek reaction were articulated in a fashion that deserves analysis: in the course of the 1860s and 1870s, one of the rhetorical means Britain employed to chastise the Greek state was to maintain that the country was simply too 'young' and 'feminine' to follow serious ventures like the Great Idea. Conversely, in Greek discourse the nation-state assumed the role of a powerful peda-gogue, destined to 'mother' and 'nourish' the Greeks of the East and the rest of the world. Both sides displayed a tendency to push collec-tive self-presentations further every time they would be antagonized politically. The transposition of social knowledge (of gender and famil-ial relations) into the public political domain aided construction of a formalized 'self' from the messy materials of social intimacy.

The importance of this rhetoric is obscured when we consider it as mere linguistic game. Postcolonial theorists have been accused of unnecessary semiotic obsession time and again, yet their persistence in highlighting the political effectiveness of discursive tropes has broad-ened the horizons of interdisciplinary cultural analysis. Tropes, endur-ing and repetitive formulas of speech that communicate irony, invite substitution and revel in truisms are more than innocent figurative speech when they become implicated in geopolitics – a point already made through Robinson's discourse on the politics and ethics of care. We discover this also from anthropological studies of family and kinship as rhetoric and a social relation. As Herzfeld insists, 'the absence of kinship seems to be one of the defining characteristics of the West's view of itself' (1992, p. 68). Political units' claims to operate on strictly rational, bureaucratic principles sidesteps the dependency of the 'ratio-nal upon the symbolic' (*ibid.*, p. 148; see also Sutton, 2000, p. 175; Schneider, 1977). The symbolic domain of interstate relations can be viewed as a theatrical stage upon which such relations are actualized and constantly reproduced (Schieffelin, 1976) through patterns of reci-procity codified in the language of (not) belonging. In a Maussian twist, social relationships, human beings, values and ideas that change hands in a give-and-take fashion, form an interlocking whole, ulti-mately creating and re-creating each other (Strathern, 1988). The act of reciprocation becomes implicated in the management of meaning as 'a vehicle of social obligation and political manoeuvre' (Schieffelin, 1980, pp. 503, 505; Kapferer, 1976).

When examined cross-culturally, kinship and family relations become potent metaphors of responsibility or indebtedness – metaphors applicable to either party in a relationship (Herzfeld, 2001, p. 231), creating a moral grammar for international relations. To be 'too young' or 'feminine' – two states of being commonly associated in conservative discourse with irrationality – implies a moral inadequacy that limits one's rights to autonomy. If indeed moral responsibility is 'the respectworthy core of the person' (Honneth, 1992, p. 119, 2007, p. 76), its absence stands as a denial of collective recognition. My shift from the individual to the collective extends Honneth's focus on individual rights: strictly speaking, the interchangeability of selfhood and collectivity (as nationhood or Europeanhood) is not mine. It is already omnipresent in the discourses of my social actors. As my nineteenth-century example shows, the selfsame metaphors of familial responsibility and parental mastery of puerile/feminine natures can turn into a centripetal political force when used by the state as part of nation-formation. Hence, although the vocabulary of intimacy is mobilized primarily to consolidate political control, it camouflages an inescapable moral interdependence (Benhabib, 1995): there is no doubt that the ritual application of family, kinship and mothering tropes in national politics corresponds to the exclusiveness of all social connections fostered on the idea of 'blood'. Nevertheless, such tropes are another way to express the need to care and be cared for (Borneman, 1996), and work as an affirmative expression of our humanity. Family evokes 'a relationship that entails affection and love, that is based on cooperation as opposed to competition, that is enduring rather than temporary [...] and that is governed by feeling and morality instead of law and contract' (Collier, Rosaldo and Yanagisako, 1982, p. 34). Family members are expected to offer willingly to each other; when they are denied the opportunity to offer or receive, they feel rejected and excluded (Komarovsky, 1987; Young and Willmott, 1986). Kin relations are defined by a constant communication between substance and code, nature and culture (Schneider, 1979, p. 159). In *Ersatz* families of neighborly environments even the fulfillment of duties *per se* does not bring things to a closure – for, as Bulmer (1986) points out, it leads to the reproduction of the relationship and of giving itself (see also Collier, 1997, p. 216; Schneider, 1979, 1980). Likewise, although gendering political units *prima facie* reflects enduring patterns of social inequality, the practice itself also confirms the intersubjective 'accomplishment' (Connell, 1987, 1995) of hegemonic

identities (Delaney, 1995). Marriage is consolidated in household trans-
actions that secure the structure of communal belonging and moral
co-existence (Mansfield and Collard, 1988). The mutual attribution of
socio-cultural characteristics individuals display from state to state is
never value-free: such political exchanges are carried by political-
as-moral units that remain bound in webs of obligations (Parry, 1986).
Nineteenth-century Greek and British practices of emasculation, val-
orization and infantilization, became symptomatic of European attempts
to repress straightforward reference to 'racial belonging', and both
uncover the dialogical struggles of national identity and present the
origins of the European project as a site of reciprocal political definitions.

On immaturity and patronage

Relationships of patronage are rife with allusions to discipline-as-
pedagogy. Their invariable use by the powerful party in the relationship
also asserts a number of 'manly' attributes that belong to the discourse of
'normative masculinity' (Mosse, 1996): willpower, (self)control, compet-
itiveness, competence and reliability. All these attributes converge behind
a masculinized ideal of liberty, political autonomy and independence
(Bederman, 1995), commonly considered as the outcome of collective
civilizing processes. During the Cretan Insurrection, British allegations
that Greece was unable and unsuitable to partake in the Western European civilizing mission were frequent. Crete, under Ottoman rule, had
repeatedly rebelled against its 'oppressors' and demanded unification
with Greece. Although the Greek metropolis had to declare loyalty to its
European protectors who favored neutrality, it secretly aided the rebels on
many occasions. Even the late British philhellenes retained ambivalent
feelings toward this attitude. In 1867, with the insurrection at a turning
point, a letter signed by a 'Philhellene' in *The Times* analyzed the situation in European Turkey. The 'Philhellene' began his analysis by drawing
attention to the superficial gloss of 'Mohammedan civilization', under
which one still found all the ancient 'vices' of the 'Turkish race': religious
persecution, polygamy, domestic slavery, unequal and oppressive treatment of conquered nations. These references were coupled with comments on the ability of 'Greek Christianity' to make the future of 'the
East' happier. In a radical vein, the 'Philhellene' carried on to say that
the new Kingdom of Greece needed the Greek provinces of Thessaly and
Epirus, then under Ottoman rule, as much as Crete, to regain self-respect.
For 'independence and self-respect are necessary conditions of national
existence. A plaything kingdom, without resources either for internal

improvement or external defense, without any feeling of responsibility, a mere spoilt child of the protecting Powers, Greece has never seriously applied herself to the work of her own regeneration' (*The Times*, 1 January 1867).

Putting aside the conflation of ethnicity with religion that lays the foundations of the 'clash of civilizations' thesis (Huntington, 1993), for the 'Philhellene' Greece appeared to be too 'young' and weak to help itself. The discourse of responsibility is coupled with that of honor and shaming that frequently frames the rhetoric of nationalist movements (McClintock, 1995, pp. 356–7). Nationalism 'has typically sprung from masculinized memory, masculinized humiliation and masculinized hope' (Enloe, 1990, p. 45; Walby, 2006, pp. 124–5). Greece assumes the feminine but childish form in the passage, and remains in need of moral discipline (Nagel, 1998) because it constantly shames its European Protectors. Similar normative takes on masculinity (Connell, 1995, p. 70) continued to circulate in the British press in the 1860s and returned to Greece's suitability for expansion, noting that only Britain had the right to supervise, advise and 'preach Greece' (*The Times*, 8 April 1867), since only Britain helped the country's expansion by granting her the Ionian Islands in 1864. Such gendered reflections highlighted the missing political consistency of Greek nationalist agendas, even though the conditions of national self-realization differed so much for Greece and Britain. British expectations of consistency coded demands for Greek commitment in Anglo-Greek relations, a commitment that would allegedly be based on mutual self-interest (Becker, 1960, p. 34). Despite the call for self-respect and reciprocation, what the British patrons demanded was forced (instilled by preaching), rather than the value commitment (Stebbins, 1970) that normally flourishes in relationships of mutual respect.

Thus the dialogics of Greek 'self-presentation' would emerge whenever British discourse shifted from an analysis of Greek nationalism to speculations on the nature of British control in Greece. After the Dilessi kidnapping, the small Kingdom was likened to 'an offspring of the sympathy of Christian powers', which now 'disgraces her creators' (*The Morning Post*, 28 April 1870) and has a 'perverse and forward childhood' (*The Times*, 26 April 1870). The verdict unveiled a twofold fear: it echoed Victorian psychopathologies concerning the untimely death of nations that are morally degraded – that is, *downgraded* on the ladder of civilization (Bowler, 1989, pp. 9, 193–4; Chamberlin and Gilman, 1985, pp. 290–1). However, such verdicts also mirrored changing Victorian perceptions of childhood: the way Victorian middle-class society viewed children was significantly different from earlier puritan conceptions based upon the firm belief that children were small adults fallen from God's grace (Norton, 1995, pp. 63–4; Aries, 1962). Rousseau's pedagogical ideas, which had a profound impact on the Victorian mind, presented children as innocent creatures who need the chance to understand the natural and social world in their own way. Due to the persistence of puritan ethics, Victorian perceptions of childhood did not evolve evenly: positive images of childhood receded in the early nineteenth century only to return in the mid-Victorian period. Discontinuities in such perceptions were nicely manifested in the discourse on Greece's 'anomaly': its 'development' was described as 'forward and perverse' against the Romantic Victorian image.

Yet, the language of kinship constantly invoked in these texts suggests that the British envisaged the Anglo-Greek relationship in terms of consanguinity: both countries were European and shared a bond of 'blood'. Carrier (1991, p. 127) explains how reciprocal relations are defined in terms of the parties' inalienable attributes: siblings and parents cannot be replaced because of the culturally constructed uniqueness of their 'blood bonding'. Therefore, the rhetoric of failed patronage also articulated the fear that modern Greece 'does not belong' racially – yet another repressed reference to exclusive European practices. For example, speculating on the chasm between Greece's actual condition and the nation's 'sweet belief' in its uniqueness, both Tuckerman and Finlay viewed the Greek state as 'the Oliver Twist of nations [who] had the unblushing temerity "to ask for more"' gifts from Europe (Tuckerman, 1872, p. 125; *The Times*, 31 March 1873). Conceptualizations of the Anglo-Greek 'bond' on the basis of racial affiliation circulated within Greece also. We can read them in an anonymous cartoon published in the 1870s, depicting a boy engaged in a graffiti enterprise: the 'design' of a 'Great Idea' of Turkish–Greek battles on the wall of a house (Figure 7.1). In semiotic terms, this indicates 'untimely' Greek aspirations; perhaps pushed a little further, the way Greece presented political problems for her neighbors (symbolized by the wall, the foreign Ottoman property the cartoon boy damages). The wall however also signified the racial boundaries that 'puerile' Greece disturbed without second thought. The fear of European miscegenation was widespread in the country due to unreasonable European expectations of Greek 'civilized' performance in politics – hence, the cartoon is critical of Greek expansionism.

This critical attitude can be found in other sources of the period: for example, the author of a play published in Kefalonia after the Dilessi Murders presents the unfortunate British captives discussing European progress and Greek irredentist politics. In a scene Greek culture is

Figure 7.1 The Great Idea
T.A. (1974) *Cartoon Album*. Athens.

called 'an infant' that has to 'be taken care of' by the Great Powers. Nevertheless, the author was convinced that the poor Greek nation that 'only yesterday was liberated from the barbarous four-century [Ottoman] bonds...will eventually present signs of progress analogous to those of ancient European nations' (Iatridis, 1870, p. 19). Here the infantilized image of Greece has a double meaning: firstly, it functions as an allegory of historical discontinuity introduced into Greek history after the Ottoman conquest of Byzantium. In this respect, modern Greece will have to become more like its ancient counterpart to fulfill its *telos*. Secondly, the author implied that Greeks accepted the country's collaborative European control, which would ensure the country's safe 'rite of passage' to the European family of nations. Counter-hegemonic games were also present in Greek political commentary: so, for some, Britain might act as patron of a puerile female state, but it seemed to forget 'the womb' it had come from, the womb of the dishonored mother of Europe (Psychas, 1870, p. 7). The need for Britons to see modern Greece 'evolving' into a country 'after their likeness' translated their yearning to see their intellectual/political philehellenic project 'in the flesh'.

The fear of racial contamination would often be codified in a scientific vocabulary that alluded to British 'experimentation' with 'infantile' Greece. But this vocabulary was quite common in British dealings with the Turks also. British involvement in the Eastern Question became very intense due to European expectations about the imminent collapse of the Ottoman Empire. During the Balkan revolutions of the 1870s the Ottoman Empire would figure in British political discourse as a 'Sick Man' in need of the 'family physician' and 'solicitor', an honorary family member in other words who expected the death of the old to secure his 'inheritance [i.e. lands] to his natural heirs, the Christian populations subject to his rule' (Grant Duff, 1876, p. 8; Mill, 1876, p. 6; Farley, 1876, p. 29). Consider also Tuckerman's vitriolic comments on Greece, whom he presents 'as the lame mendicant ... told by Britain that since she has only one leg [the Greek Kingdom], which she cannot use, she should not regret the loss of the other [Greek-speaking parts of the Ottoman Empire]', because she 'would not know how to use it' (Tuckerman, 1872, p. 126).

The languages of experimentation, decline and patronage run parallel lives and were utilized extensively by Greeks on the outbreak of Bulgarian nationalism in the 1870s and the subsequent European support for Bulgarian claims in the Balkans. After accusing some of the 'Constantinopolitan' Greeks of high treason for not opposing the foundation of the Bulgarian Exarchate in 1870, the author of a political monograph proceeded to explore why the Greek nation was so weak at this crucial moment. He explained that nations are like children needing guidance by a good pedagogue. However, the pedagogues of the Greek nation, the Great European Powers, 'against the laws of nature, gave to the child poisoned food'.

That is why, while there is still time, let us try to fight the causes of weakness and degeneration in our society. And those are – with the exception of any inclinations we may have developed – the lack of scientific light and warmth, spiritual progress and the molding of a strong soul. Finally, let us adopt a healthier diet, so that we will not relapse into the same illness (Asklipiadis, 1872, p. 79).

Clinical language could be seen as an insidious sign of subjection to a harsh Western omniscient that nevertheless cares for the patient, like a good parent. The author wonders about the causes of Greece's misery, assuming that the remedy is a Western secret. His speculations correspond to the Greek folk story of the 'ignorant' peasants who thought that their new 'Frankish' dentist's collection of dentures consisted of teeth extracted from the dead to be magically fitted into the mouths of the living (Poole, 1878). Clinical language is based on the logic that the evil West holds a secret Greeks must uncover. Nevertheless, setting the scientific gaze of the Westerner before the desire for it, leads to a deadlock; it is also the Greeks' forgetfulness that excludes their own desire to be treated as patients that produces the impression of subjection. To invoke Žižek, 'the mystery...is to be sought not *beyond* its appearance but in the very *appearance of mystery*' (1991, p. 107). Following Hobbes, one may argue that relationships of political patronage are often based on contractual oblivion. Self-interest informs reciprocal arrangements of political control and subjection, simply because even the weak party can benefit from them without challenging political order.

Simultaneously, the Greek text mirrors an unmistakably Victorian logic concerning ideas of moral physiology (Haley, 1978). The false causal link between morality and bodily disease, not uncommon in the nineteenth century, manifested itself in the context of other, more recent cases, of nationalism. Commenting on the case of Israeli nationbuilding, Roginsky (2006) highlighted the link between bodily politics and the politics of identity. Although the body is a suitable site for the expression of cultural sentiments (Foucault, 1979, vol. I), *like* the ethnic 'essence' of a nation, it remains an indisputable natural property. The body is also traditionally related to irrationality, femininity, sensuality and primitivism – as opposed to the rationality and knowledge of the male Western 'doctor' of the passage. The metaphorical employment of physical properties in relationships of patronage precludes the 'national body' from the sphere of modernity (Handler, 1988; Cowan, 1990; Herzfeld, 2004). Here gender postulates a normative masculinity set against a femininity that is construed as 'lack' or 'aberration' (Butler, 1990). The binary opposites that are produced cast European Britain as a masculine presence, ready to dominate a feminized, 'oriental' Greece.

The interchangeability of gender and racial positions complements crypto-colonial discourse.

Contrast this to the author's use of the 'soul' or the 'spirit' as future visions of salvation for the Greek nation. Soul (*psychí*) and spirit (*pneúma*) are concepts widely used in Greek nationalist discourse even in the present. Bryant (2002) identified the same tropes of spiritual growth in Greek Cypriot nationalist discourse, which uses the word *psychí* to represent the community's kinship with the (home) land in religious terms. The union of 'the people' with the land is depicted thus in spiritual terms and strongly 'resembles the Christian idea of the Immaculate Conception' (*ibid.*, p. 511). *Pneúma* also has religious connotations because it simultaneously describes the breath of life, intelligence *and* the Holy Spirit. This resembles Herder's take on the perennially existing *Volksgeist* (Smith, 2000) and its correspondence to, if not replacement of the ultimate metaphysical authority, God. What acts as a catalyst for the creation of national solidarity is the belief that this solidarity exists magically. When Anderson (1991, p. 11) argued that national sovereignty was achieved with the decline in religious belief he was simply reproducing the old Durkheimian argument (1997 [1893]) on organic solidarity as an autopoetic mechanism. The purity of the 'national soul' presents communal bonding as an esoteric experience of unrefined feminine nature, chaste and needing manly protection from any usurpers. The conclusive conflation of nature with culture (corresponding in Smith's terms [1984, p. 95] to genealogical and conservative national myths respectively) betrays the survival of religious principles in nationalist discourse, notably 'the assumption that the social is founded in a non-social principle, such as an original act of creation or the sanctity of death or loyalty to an absolute principle' (Delanty and O'Mahony 2002, p. 24).

Religious metaphors were present in British understandings of Greek patronage too, but with an emphasis on the creation of Greece by masculine forces. Britain often assumed the role of the benevolent godly 'Father' who gives the much-sought 'breath of life' to the Greek nation, but fails to protect it from tasting the forbidden fruits of freedom. The metaphor was always linked to the Greek state's unwillingness to meet the constitutional requirements for entry into Europe, an obdurate demand on the part of its British patrons. Commenting on the abuse of constitutional principles in Greece, a British journalist said in 1870:

> Perhaps the fault of the failure has lain all along with the Protectors themselves, who said 'Let Greece arise; let us create a kingdom "after

our likeness"' in a land which, however patriotic in guerrilla warfare against the Turks, did not possess even the first elements of a municipality. It was very much as though three rich uncles were to say 'Here is our nephew, a child only five years old, it is true, but for all that, we will make him a man, and he shall be a man at once.'...It was worth trying the experiment, perhaps, just to prove that a Constitution cannot be fitted to a country like a coat to a man's back! (*The Times*, 16 May 1870).

The language is both religious and gendered, linking national and imperial 'honor' to moral consistency and manliness. Yet the religious experiment that Britain has undertaken returns to notions of ethnic innocence and purity. Ethnic Greekness is examined through the orientalist Romantic eyes of the patron as a peripheral entity (Fanon, 1970 [1958]) devoid of spirituality and caged in the physical body. Like women, sexualized creatures lacking rationality and virility, children are uncivilized entities on the evolutionary scale (Yuval-Davis, 1997, p. 8; Sluga, 1998). The tale of the godly uncle and his emasculated nephew – the boy who fails to become 'a man' due to his erratic conduct – was narrated throughout the 1860s and 1870s in many different versions (Benjamin, 1867, p. 232; *The Daily News*, 18 May 1870) and is the secularized counterpart of the language of patronage. This 'forced passage' from innocence to adulthood is haunted by earlier puritan attitudes. Britain is not a benevolent Father here, but a severe pedagogue. Again this implicit reference to pedagogy needs contextualizing, as compulsory schooling was introduced in the 1870s within the framework of the sacralization of childhood in Victorian England (Zelizer, 1994).

Even the Greek side sanctioned British masculine self-presentations. Aristarchos Bey, a Greek appointed by the Ottoman government as a brigadier and an ardent supporter of the Great Idea, produced a massive collection of speeches, articles, Church edicts and parliamentary debates concerning the Bulgarian Question, published in the 1870s. In 1876, when he finished the fourth volume of his work, the revolution in Bosnia and Herzegovina raged, the Serbians had declared war against the Ottoman Empire and the Bulgarians were organizing an anti-Greek campaign in the Balkans. In this climate of general instability, Britain still tried to secure her passage to India via Suez. Among the numerous speeches in Aristarchos Bey's collection there were two by Lord Salisbury and Lord Derby on British policy on Suez. Aristarchos adopted an enthusiastic attitude towards this 'anti-Turkish' British policy, 'for the masculine roads it opened' in international politics (Aristarchos Bey,

1876, p. 121n.). The enduring tradition of depicting the British Empire as male (Mackenzie, 1987) played a significant role in the building of such imageries, in which the 'colonized' is seen as effeminate, degenerate or childish. As Spurr notes, the victory of the colonizer would often be hedged with the rhetoric of protection, in which the threat of distrust or violence remained inherent, but was covered up 'by the mellow language of the restoration of a harmonious order; not that of aboriginal conservatism, but of a more benign one, at once natural and civilized' (Spurr, 1993, p. 34), like the love between father and child.

Even the image of a generous British mother ('Britannia'), which was popular in the metropolis at this time (Bohata, 2004a, 2004b), granted Britain with properties traditionally linked to the imperial image: wisdom (Britannia as the ancient Greek goddess Athena), prestige and virility. In fact, the use of family tropes was not unique to Anglo-Greek reflections. British administrators and colonizers used it to describe their relationship with India; anglicized Indian subjects also mobilized the family vocabulary to describe their country's relationship with a 'benevolent' Britain (*The Empire Review*, May 1924, pp. 488–96). In a series of articles published in the *Revue des Deux Mondes* between 1846 and 1852, French Orientalists used similar patriarchal imageries to describe their relationship with the Oriental Algeria (Gemie, 1998, pp. 58–62). Although Greece was not a British colony, the language employed by both sides unveils a British fantasy in which the Greek Kingdom is already colonized.

The recognition that ethnic-as-racial affiliations have an ambivalent status in European politics, especially when connected to the production of colonial otherness, has been the subject of on-going debate in postcolonial studies (Fanon, 1970 [1958]; Said, 1978; Bhabha, 1990a, 1990c, 1994; Chatterjee, 1993). The constant conflation of gender and racial identities in the Anglo-Greek dialogue facilitated the codification of political dilemmas. As Bhabha (1990a, p. 7) explains, when it comes to the living experience of ambivalence on the part of the subaltern, the tensions between the formalization of identity and its everyday practice can only be resolved by recourse to (self) stereotyping (Bhabha, 1990c). While the masculinization of Britain in Anglo-Greek discourses of patronage remained indisputable, Greece appeared to acquire a split identity enabling the nation and the state to move between two gendered poles, depending on the requirements of the moment and always reflecting back the patron's desire (Butler, 1990, p. 45). It may be incorrect to view this 'masquerade' (Hassan, 2003, p. 310) as a mindless subject interpellation for, as I will explain, its internal resonance was to assert the nation-state's will to autonomy though an *active* control of political self-presentation.

Mothering hegemonic projects

A national community is actualized not solely through a symbolic reproduction of the value systems by which it interprets the world, but also through its ability to simultaneously reflect and act on challenges introduced from outside (Benhabib, 1995, pp. 238–9; Weiner, 1980, p. 71). Since the historical emergence of 'imagined communities', the survival of weak nations has depended on their ability to adapt to external pressures while safeguarding the normative orders they choose to uphold. In other words, the capacity for adaptability would remain dependent on a hermeneutic assessment of the socio-political environment these nations aspire to inhabit: in Greece's case, the 'European ethnic family'. Often the continuation of the struggle for self-preservation would threaten to destroy the space of communication with their significant (political) others. Although 'Europe' has always retained its abstract properties as a collective (moral) designation, it was the imminent relations of weak nations with concrete political powers that defined such international communications (Benhabib, 1987; Honneth, 1992, p. 108). The master-slave nature of such communications blocked the potential for egalitarian reciprocity – and how was Greece to act in the face of such a challenge? Again, gender and kinship relations provided the Greeks with familiar means for political self-presentation.

Following Fanon, Bhabha (1994) claimed that the language of the colonizer re-merges both as mimicry and mockery once it is adopted by the colonized. Bhabha identifies in mimicry the double effect of imitation/parody and subordination/resistance. This ever-present possibility of slippage discredits the colonizer's version of colonized otherness. The two notions of mimesis 'interact and cross continually', producing confusion and subverting roles in colonial discourse (Fuss, 1994, p. 24). I will argue however that mimicry is not the result of colonial oppression exclusively but of any kind of unequal relationship. Feminist studies of work and organization have revealed the omnipresence of bifurcated self-presentations. Ferguson's (1984) comparisons of work and personal life patterns uncover how deep gender stereotypes run in the language of both bureaucratic organization and everyday life. Clients and low-ranking bureaucrats, often effeminized in public discourse, must acquire the necessary skills to cope with work, just like women, who learn the skills of femininity to cope with social challenges.

The 'art' of femininity retains an exquisite ambiguity precisely because of its tendency to both subvert authority and disempower the performer (Ferguson, 1993). Similar insights are offered by Herzfeld's (2004, pp. 152–3) analysis of apprenticeship not just as a 'social skill', but also as a form of social action. The poetics of authority in master-apprentice relations, he argues, harbor subversive attitudes, such as mocking and stealing the secrets of craftsmanship from a jealous master in order to gain respect in his eyes. Although stealing assists apprentices in overcoming their symbolic feminization by a ruthless master, their eventual 'becoming' masters in their turn transforms them into an embodiment of their former tyrant (*ibid.*, p. 92). In Bakhtinian terms (1968), the *carnivalesque* of apprenticeship both broadens the horizons of the human spirit and lays the reproductive foundations of the moribund rituals of power (Clark and Holquist, 1984, p. 302).

At stake for the nineteenth-century Greeks was their solidification as a national unit, but it had proven difficult to circumnavigate the tight control of European political forces since Independence. The response was to both accept and contest their subordinate position, seeking to autonomize the nation's symbolic domain. As we shall see, the Greek rhetoric of patronage gestured towards an inversion of what Herzfeld has termed practical orientalism, 'the translation of hegemonic ideology into everyday practice so that it infiltrates the habitual spaces of ordinary experience' (1997, p. 96). Revising Gellner's modernism (1998, pp. 25–30; Smith, 1971; Hutchinson, 2005, p. 60), it is more pertinent to observe how hegemonic ideologies of nationhood inhabit the spaces of an everyday sociality that defines meaningful human togetherness throughout mankind's history. Modern hegemonies draw upon the same universally recognizable patterns of sociality to organize and legitimize themselves in the eyes of the 'People'. The gendered and kinship images of the nation employed in Anglo-Greek relations would find a new resonance in Greek domestic affairs, as they would now be addressed to a different audience: the Greek state's subjects and the 'unredeemed' Greeks of the Ottoman Empire.

Gendered tropes would assume more currency in nation-defining moments. In 1865, a year after the cession of the Ionian Islands to Greece, the Greek entrepreneur Stefanos Xenos published in London his historical study *East and West*, in which he examined the trajectory of Anglo-Greek relations. The addition of seven islands to the Greek state marked a turning point in Greek self-definitions, as the Ionian State had spent a long time under a series of 'civilized' but hated foreign rulers, including the British. Xenos was opposed to the demolition of fortresses in the Ionian Islands when Britain ceded them to the Greece. Criticizing the British 'despotic attitude' towards the Ionian Greeks, he stated:

> The conduct and dispositions of the Ionians are perfectly intelligible. Let us suppose the case of a respectable mother with her children falling into slavery, and reduced by averse circumstances to extreme want; but one child escapes, and has the good fortune to meet a wealthy patron, who adopts him, for whom he provides every comfort, and who gives him every advantage becoming his new position. But, at length, the mother, with one or two of her other children, after a hard struggle, succeeds in raising her head again in the world and becoming free. She has not been able to recover from her early position – far from it; but she enjoys an independent, though humble, existence. Now, what may we suppose would, under such circumstances, be the natural feelings of the son whom a powerful patron has placed in a position so much superior to that of the rest of his family? Would not his first impulse be a desire to return to his mother, and afford her that aid which the education he had received, and the wealth he had acquired, rendered him so competent to afford her to free his own brothers still in slavery? But should the patron refuse his consent, existence becomes a torture to the protégé, who can think of nothing but his mother's position, and can listen only to the voice of nature (Xenos, 1865, p. 28).

Xenos' readership was both British and Greek and therefore his reflections deserve attention. The passage is replete with ideas from Christian cosmology, ranging from the idea of a secular Edenic Fall to Christ's Resurrection: Greece, the mother of European civilization, becomes a 'poor mother' who has lost her freedom but is somehow awakened and breaks away from centuries-long oriental bondage. The comment on slavery is nicely inserted: having lost her freedom, Greece becomes a woman who is not respected anymore, like the slaves of oriental harems whose status was reduced to that of a concubine. The son-version of Greece of Anglo-Greek relations is transferred to the Ionian Islands, who may be subordinate but more 'civilized' than Greece. Britain is the only persona in the story whose status as the symbolic 'Father' remains unchanged.

The metaphor also draws upon the domestic function of female imagery and the criss-crossing of nationalist and gender discourse. Political theory has recognized the gendered implications carried in the separation of society into two domains: a 'public' domain, the domain of political authority and contestation, and a 'private' realm, associated with family and home (Nussbaum, 2003, p. 5). As Handler explains, nationalist discourse 'naturalizes and objectifies presuppositions that sustain the undeniable existence of a [...] nation' (1988, p. 18). Québecois self-narration is replete with metaphors of the nation as living being, presenting the British conquest as rape (*ibid.*, p. 14). In Greek culture to copulate with the kinswomen of one's enemies equates sexual rivalry with social difference, as the 'rape' of a woman is symbolically a violation of 'the domestic hearth' (Herzfeld, 1987, p. 173; Just, 2000). If the homey façade is the site of manly self-display, the hearth is the familial world of feminine (national) introspection. Since for Xenos the symbolic 'rape' of Greece is conducted not by Britain but Turkey, his metaphor is simultaneously one of British patronage and the narrative of Greek culture's adulteration by the Turkish uncivilized character. The story likens masculine honor, a common theme in Mediterranean societies (Schneider, 1971; Herzfeld, 1985, pp. 232–3; Gallant, 2002, p. 119), to national integrity and autonomy.

There was more, nevertheless, to the Greek rhetoric, since the audience for the Greek metropolis was split into Britons and subjected Greeks. To British readers, such comments might have signified Greek boundedness by moral obligations – a sort of self-reproach akin to those explored in the previous chapter. With the non-native Greeks of the Ottoman Empire in mind, the maternal image of Greece would become that of a skilled matron whom all the 'unredeemed' Greeks ought to love and respect. Let us examine a letter sent to the Greek nationalist newspaper *Palingenesía* by a 'Constantinopolitan' Greek in 1868. The letter was concerned with European, especially British, persistence in keeping Turkey 'alive' by sabotaging the Cretan struggle. For the anonymous Greek, the imminent threat for Turkey was the Great Idea, which contributes to the 'conception and birth of the East'. Greece is suited to play a leading role in the East; its noble aspiration in the Eastern Mediterranean region was to acquire those Ottoman provinces that the Greek center claimed as part of the nation's dominions. 'Europe' is challenged in the letter 'to dare, if she can, abstract forcibly the East from her mother'. Moreover, Greece is asked to use 'her intellectual skills...to succeed Turkey who is still alive only because – to cite European commentary – "there are no able successors". Finally she should prove that Greece is independent and not a European feud' (*Palingenesía*, 4 July 1868). Though in theory the article was addressed to 'Europeans', the actual addressees were British and Greek reader-ships. The image of the 'loving mother', central to this passage, retains its ambiguity: on the one hand, this mother is a dynamic matron. On the other, the reference to feudalism presents the Greek Kingdom's gendered identity as an unexpressed fear of subordination that has already taken place. The letter presents an excellent example of how social intimacy, codified in the language of honor, is mobilized in international political discourse. As Tuckerman noted, an insult on the family's reputation, 'a wound of honor...burns till soothed by the blood of the insulter' (Tuckerman, 1972, p. 240) – Turkey in our case. Despite the informal 'motherly' resonance of the letter, the threat of formalized violence lurks in the background – an inversion of the Eliasian 'civilizing process' that in the British Ionian Islands dictated the separation of everyday masculine violence from the safeguarding of honor (Gallant, 2002, pp. 143–7).

Images of motherhood also appeared in an article on the dinner organized in Manchester for the Cretan struggle, only this time addressed solely to a Greek audience. Markos Renieris, representative of the Cretan Assembly and the Central Committee for the Cretan Insurrection in Athens, claimed in his speech that God himself asked for the union of Crete with Greece, because 'families cannot be separated' (*Clió*, 24, 5 April 1867). Later that year *Clió* revisited the issue of what will happen in Greece if Crete capitulates.

> Internally, Greece will go through a period of insurmountable anomaly, which the wounded honor will magnify [...] In external affairs, Greece's position will be insufferable: the enslaved Greeks will never dare to raise their head again, since they will be taught that Greece might perform the loving mother for a while [...] but would never be disposed to run high risks in crucial moments. Let us not delude ourselves. Greece should not only support the strug-gles of the subordinate children, but also sympathize and suffer with them. Otherwise, what kind of loving mother would she be for the revolting brothers, if, when she senses danger, she transforms herself into an inconsiderate stepmother? (*Clió*, 15/27 September 1867).

The same language was used by the Central Committee for the Cretan refugees at Athens, an organization working as a mediator between the rebels and the Greek government (*Aión*, 28 March 1868). Obviously, the trope had a certain function to fulfill in Greek state discourse. For nineteenth-century Greeks women were destined to participate in the Greek hegemonic project in a guarded way that simply affirmed their status as social subordinates. Women might have been presented as the first pedagogues of young Greeks, but their contribution to the Greek nationalist project had to be performed within the domestic confines (Ainian, 1876, p. 88). Dominant understandings of femininity led to an interpellation, with many middle-class women reproducing these narratives in times of national crisis (Avdela and Psarra, 2005, p. 73). Like women in colonial environments, their role would often be uncertain, as they appeared both as 'subordinates and masters, privileged and restricted, acted upon and acting' (McClintock, 1995, pp. 6, 355; Afshar, 1989; Gittings, 1996, pp. 1–8; Kandiyoti, 1989; Walby, 2006, pp. 120–1). Similar patterns of ambivalent gender positioning can be detected both in Indian and Afrikaner cultures. The 'cult' of 'white motherhood' as a racially/ethnic ideal for example, would often be situated in the 'iconography of domestic service' (McClintock, 1991, pp. 7, 18). Chatterjee (1989, p. 629) identified the same discourses of femininity in nineteenth-century Bengali literature, with women assuming the task of maintaining the cohesiveness of family life and the kin, and by extension of the national kin. Education was supposed to improve women's identity in the private sphere and help them preserve their chastity, cleanliness and sense of personal responsibility. This served to emphasize 'what had in any case become a dominant characteristic of femininity in the new construct of a "woman" standing as a sign for "nation", namely, the spiritual qualities of self-sacrifice, benevolence, devotion, religiosity, and so on' (*ibid.*, p. 630). We note that in Greek tropes of feminized nationhood the ideal of 'woman' is used *in abstracto* and often in relation to religious iconographies; women in the flesh, the site of sexual pollution', are always patronized. As Avdela and Psarra (2005, p. 72) explain, during nineteenth-century political crises, the feminization of nationhood would not dispel social prejudice concerning the dangerousness of collective female action.

The transposition of the language of kinship onto the plain of politics requires further analysis. It would be incorrect to view the inheritance of biological attributes as explanations of ethnic solidarity (van den Berghe, 1978). The conflation bears testimony to the symbolic dimension of kinship as a marker of ethnic belonging (Horowitz, 1985). This language was complicit to Greek nation-building, because it coincided with the debate on Greek citizenship. Following the institutional recognition of Greece, the *autochthone* Greeks (or Greek natives of the Kingdom) had been privileged over the *heterochthones* (or alien, non-indigenous Greeks). The circulation of the infamous erroneous reference to the origins of the Greek debate upon naturalization is telling: as the story goes, the naturalization of *heterochthone* Greeks had coincided with the first use of the term 'Great Idea' in the Greek Parliament by the Greek politicians Kolettis in 1844 (Augustinos, 1976, p. 13; Zakythinos, 1976, p. 193). In reality, the first definition of Greekness on the basis of civic duties comes from the late nineteenth-century historian Epameinondas Kyriakidis (see Carabott, 2005b, p. 139). However, the persistence of this misquote in modern Greek historiography is, in effect, a reliable record of Greek political priorities: in the second half of the nineteenth century, *naturalization* of the non-indigenous Greeks came to be viewed as a prerequisite for the 'nation's' self-fulfillment. However, the privileged position of the metropolitan Greeks as 'natural' architects of the process of nation-building was continually asserted.

One must remember what the process of naturalization comprises to understand the significance of this debate. The state makes non-indigenous peoples *naturalized* citizens – that is, it makes them 'people whose subjectivity conforms to the *nature* of the society that grants them citizenship, *a nature that allows for their subjectivity to be national-ized'* (Gourgouris, 1996, p. 33, emphasis in the text). *Naturalization* (the German *Naturalisierung*) finds its Greek equivalent in *politográfisis*, the inscription upon one of the mark of the citizen (from *polis* and *grafô*, engrave). This process naturalizes the notion of national subjectivity because it makes the subject's nationality appear inherent – yet another contractual form of forgetting that nations do not posses a natural ethic base (Balibar, 1990, p. 349; Hutchinson, 2005, p. 32; Roudometof, 1999; Sassen, 2002a, p. 7, 2002b; Smith, 1981, p. 66, 1995, p. 98; Soysal, 1997).

To this day Greece remains a country that bases conceptions of nationhood on the metaphor of blood lineage, thus linking folk formulas of 'brotherhood' to Eurocentric understandings of racial belonging (Just, 1989). Discursive presentations of 'the Greek nation' as an agnatic group can be found in the centuries old, and still used, term *yénos* or 'race', commonly associated with the period of Ottoman rule (Herzfeld, 2005, p. 77). Perhaps we need recall the more recent dispute over the name of the Republic of Macedonia to recognize the impact symbolic language has in the making of Greek nationhood (Agnew, 2007). As Sutton (2000, pp. 186–7) observes, in questions of heritage/ inheritance names are understood in terms of a tangible connection to ancestors. Put simply, names create a sense of continuity with the past, while adumbrating concerns about the future. Skopje's borrowing of the name 'Macedonia' was equated by the Greek state with 'usurping' part of the national property: Macedonia is, after all, a territory that was nationalized in the twentieth century during the last phase of Greek national integration (1912–13). The dispute resembles the custom of baptism and godfathering, which is sanctioned by the Orthodox Church – another institutionalized marker of Greek nationality. Baptism entails the generation of obligations on the part of the family, the child and the godparents, simultaneously creating a symbolic bond of protection and respect. Likewise, the 'naturalization' of human beings into the Greek nation defines its future development as a moral community, specifying the rights and duties of the state and its newly acquired subjects.

Current concerns about the legal status of migrants in Greece and other parts of Europe echo the prioritization of blood delineation over the civic model of belonging (Herzfeld, 2005, pp. 124, 215), although radical re-conceptualizations of citizenship have begun to emerge (Habermas, 1998; Delanty and Rumford, 2005, pp. 89–91). Nationality and citizenship might represent two different types of membership, but they remain closely connected (Habermas, 1992). The exclusivity of the Greek national community in particular became apparent after the acceptance of over 1,000,000 refugees from Asia after the last Greek-Turkish War (1919–22): despite the fact that unofficially the Greek natives regarded Anatolian refugees with hostility and suspicion as 'aliens', the Greek state granted citizenship rights to all those of Greek descent. The Greek Anatolian expedition was, after all, based on the propaganda of liberating their 'unredeemed brethren' on the other side of the Aegean (Voutira, 2003, p. 148; Hirschon, 1998, p. 10). There is nothing intrinsically European or Greek about this conflation of nature with culture: Cooper and Stoler (1997; Stoler, 1989a) outline the exclusionary mechanisms Western Europeans introduced in the colonies by importing ideas of national citizenship based on a blunt equation of metropolitan elite cultures with human nature. This phenomenon is only a variation of the tendency colonial administrators displayed to export *civilité* codes that allegedly belonged to a distinctively European cultural heritage (Mbembe, 2001, pp. 37–9). Such post-Enlightenment processes created incredible tensions in the colonies because the association of culture with 'race' was used in the consolidation of a brutal colonial rule (Cohn, 1987; Kaplan, 1995; Stoler, 1989a, 1995). European national sovereignties that are legitimated by such conflations are not a far cry from the pitfalls of colonial policies.

The insistence of the nineteenth-century native Greeks upon being regarded as first-class citizens *vis-à-vis* their '*heterochthone* brothers', found its analogue in the language of family bonds: the very language the Greeks of the Kingdom employed in the Anglo-Greek dialogue. Thus the family vocabulary naturalized questions of citizenship and participation of the non-*autochthone* Greeks in Greek politics, while simultaneously asserting the hegemony of the political center, Athens. Its function was to 'cover up' Greek cultural, social and political fragmentation, and to make the 'Greek nation' (a fictional entity comprised by the Greeks of Greece, the 'unredeemed' ones of the Ottoman Empire and those of the Diaspora, whose civil rights in the Greek Kingdom were questioned) appear naturally uniform: like a loving family (Anderson, 1991, pp. 144–5; Gilroy, 1993; Barthes, 1993; Levi-Strauss, 1964, pp. 26–7). The symbolic wailing for the 'subordinate Greek children' is the mark of moral interdependencies between the center and its peripheries, but the language is now applied internally: the political center calls upon a natural bond that defines a system of rights and duties that grants citizens their social status (Balibar, 2006, pp. 13–14). The allusion to the Greek state's mothering also celebrates the fusion of blood and spiritual bonds, especially since the political center's duty is presented in terms of suffering. Having recourse to Christian cosmology, the *Clió* journalist uses the iconography of the Virgin Mary, whose severed bond with her child leaves her devastated. Thus, the miracle of national birth is depicted in terms of an Immaculate Conception and the nation's political losses re-enact the Holy Drama.

Similar discourses of citizenry have emerged in different nation-states in contemporary Europe. The project of European integration, enabling the free movement of populations across member countries, has produced a progressive destabilization of traditional understandings of identity. The reaction is addressed both to European policies and to the specific political others of the national community's past. When in 2006 an Albanian student was denied the 'privilege' of holding the Greek flag during a parade with which Greeks celebrate their Second World War resistance, the Greek press noted the tension between the student's nationality and his desire to be a 'naturalized' Greek (Tzanelli, 2006). A need to link citizenship rights to ethnic belonging was also manifested in the locality in which the episodes took place, betraying how even state-controlled notions of Greek identity are over-determined by informal understandings of Greekness as culturally, historically *and*, by extension, biologically uniform (Tzanelli, 2007c). The Irish seem to follow the same *motif* in so far as they adhere to a new 'cultural nationalism' that bridges the differences of the Irish Republicans and Northern Catholics, but still holds fast to an individualized 'pride' in things 'Irish' (O'Mahony and Delanty, 2001, p. 8). Although the metaphor of kinship is better concealed, it is still present in the language of 'honoring' national bonds. The *jus sanguinis* principle allows preferential treatment to those who desire citizenship in countries such as Greece, Italy, France, Germany and various Eastern European countries – especially following the collapse of the USSR and the Federal Yugoslav Republic that precipitated the emergence of titular national identities (Smith, 1999, p. 260; Brubaker, 1992; Verdery, 1998, p. 301).

Similar practices appear outside Europe. As Schneider explains, the coexistence of the code of 'national' conduct (attained through naturalization) and substance (being born in the 'nation') (Schneider, 2004, p. 264) characterizes American definitions of national belonging. In Japan, the separation of a 'political' conception of the nation (based on institutionalized belonging) from an ethnic (based on a conflation of blood with culture) still has a strong hold on narratives of Japanese identity (Doak, 1997, p. 298). Although brave steps have been made to combat ethnic discrimination against Chinese migrants in Thailand, the history of Thai national integration still dictates preferential treatment of Northern nomadic peoples, traditionally linked to ideas of the Thai *Volksgeist*, over Southern migrant groups, traditionally linked to communist separatism (Callahan, 2003; Herzfeld, 2002b). Thus, citizenship has become the site of a universal struggle for the definition of rights and duties in any polity.

The tropes of family and kinship performed multiple functions in Greek and British politics. British discourse valorized the imperial self-image by representing Greece as a weak British protégé, a crypto-colony. In Greek discourse, it undermined British colonial self-perceptions, but also presented the Greek Kingdom as the center of a Greater Hellenism, which was seeking its self-accomplishment by territorial expansion and amelioration of internal ethnic differences. Allocation of roles on a symbolic level was reciprocal, although the Greeks utilized gender imageries to construct their own language of resistance. Significantly, when we examine the rhetoric of protection from either side individually, we discover that one parent/partner is constantly missing from the implied 'family structure'. The logic of incomplete parenthood could be read as a subtle sign of self-contentment for both sides, and becomes equivalent to Nairn's (1977) recognition of the nation-state's twin, almost gendered, nature both as regressive, war-like, and a cohesive communal force. Putting aside the fact that even Nairn's argument adopts the gendered vocabulary I try to deconstruct, in reality Anglo-Greek theatrical representations concealed the interdependency of roles that make the nuclear family functional. Both Greeks and Britons based their discursive patterns on social experience that governs European social intimacies.

However, despite their evolutionist conception, both Greek and British imageries operated on purely structural principles, because they were static. In the 1860s, thirty years had passed since the birth of the Greek Kingdom, but Greece was still a child. More than thirty years had passed since Britain had assumed the parental role for Greece, but it still remained a vigorous parent. But modern Greek political regeneration, which was always projected into the future, had its negative equivalent, degeneration – an undesirable state of things for the British. The clinical language used in the Anglo Greek dialogue was, therefore, the 'symptom' of this British fear. The idea of birth and re-birth, which asserts the primacy of the natural over the social, has been a major motif of modernity, after all. It is useful therefore to examine the discourse of degeneration and regeneration together in order to understand what was foreclosed from the Anglo-Greek symbolic structure. This was nothing other than British decline, a nightmare that visited Victorians in their sleep ever since Darwin and Gibbon's theories of cyclical historic evolution (Bowler, 1989, pp. 193–5). Not only did the British rhetoric of protection serve to emphasize the order of Anglo-Greek relations, but it also helped to repress reflections on a hideous British future. A static conceptualization of the Anglo-Greek relationship would secure a frozen British imperial self-image and conceal such British anxieties. The British were trapped into an eternal present – a kind of 'Nemesis' for their imperialist desire.

Conclusion

8

Re-Visioning Identity in Europe

I feel like an interloper every time I return to the place that was once home. Former neighbors observe with suspicion the *Evropaía* who visits the village that only administratively became a town in the last decade. *Esý eíse politisméni kséni tóra, den kséreis ti symvaínei sto chorió* (you are a civilized foreigner now, you do not know what happens in the village), explains an aging woman at the local market whenever I offer an opinion exceeding practical questions about the price of vegetables. It took a while to comprehend how the friendly smile that accompanies her words is only a smirk at my willingness to have any opinion on local doings and machinations. If taken seriously (as they should be), her words deliver a verdict of incredible moral weight, displaying all the performative contradictions of Greek political marginality: how dare I, the 'literate' Europeanized apostate, claim understanding of *her* community's dynamics. *She* has to spend their life in a place populated by immigrants who raise their children alongside 'ours'; a place that *Europhile* politicians visit only when they want to improve their popular profile; a place I left behind years ago to embrace bizarre ideas of cultural tolerance and openness.

Being called a *politisméni* rings as an insult of the first degree: *politismós* has the Eliasian resonance of a politicized *civilité* Greeks habitually attribute to highbrow culture. It incorporates the awe of pedagogical exoticism only elites possess and the envy of those who are denied its imagined privileges (i.e. acquisition of social prestige). Many Greek politicians are described as *politisménoi* and *gramatizoúmenoi* (educated, literate); they are, of course, as strange to such Greek localities as any immigrants or European tourists who happen to pass by. Granted, I speak to immigrants who made my village 'home' and, when asked, I frequently speak positively of the fusion of ideas that follow bilateral human mobilities. But new experience has not divested me of all understanding of this locality's social rituals and intimate vocabulary. At other times, my kinship ties re-admit me into this world – as long as I remain silent about politics. I want to believe that I have accepted my fate with some grace: in the old lady's verdict my magically acquired knowledge abroad is automatically coupled with a laughable social ignorance. I cannot help but think that her attitude, which serves to temporarily secure my social outsideness, unwittingly confirms the locality's political and cultural exclusion from 'Europe'.

This is a story about formalized knowledge and intimate understanding, the two sides of a coin that should have more currency in the Europe of today. I am aware that this final essay transports us from the history-land of nineteenth-century nationalism and colonialism to that of contemporary Europe without unanimously recognized academic passports. However, I never claimed to be writing a watertight history; on the contrary, I used events frequently as both structurally and diachronically relevant phenomena. European futures, the exploratory subject matter of this chapter, are overdetermined by European pasts activated in local contexts: thus, my old lady becomes a narrator of historically conditioned cultural insecurities. Our encounter is a tale that outlines the complexities of actually existing cosmopolitanisms, because it hints at the political roots of resentful resistances displayed against any language that advocates the forging of global solidarities. I have met these complexities elsewhere in my shielded 'literate' world: they remind me of Borges' imaginary ethnographic investigator, Fred Murdock, who toils to discover the ritual secrets of Amerindian tribes and finish his doctoral thesis only to discover that he cannot communicate his knowledge to a scientific readership. 'The secret', confesses Murdock to his annoyed university mentor, 'is not as important as the paths that led me to it. Each person has to walk these paths himself [*sic.*]' (Borges, 1998, p. 335).

Borges' allegorical reference to twentieth-century anthropology's turn toward urban areas and elite institutions in modernized societies serves to question the power relation between observer and observed – and by extension, the boundaries between outsiders and natives. More importantly, however, it proffers useful insight into the ontogenetic potential of cultural encounters. These encounters open up ample possibilities to all of us wishing to be reborn as social beings of a global polity – for, as Herzfeld (2005, p. 215) thoughtfully reminds us, 'there no longer are any purely internal affairs' to safeguard, if indeed there ever were. It becomes poignant to see my compatriot struggling to save an imagined local secrecy from someone who knows very well there is no such thing as a local 'secret'. But I have had my share in critiques of local political practices, and feelings may be running a bit high. At least since Geertz's critical interventions in the discipline, ethnography has begun to see the concept of the local as relative, acknowledging that 'there is no innocent political methodology for intercultural interpretation' (Geertz, 1997, p. 19). All we have to do is reverse my positional role and that of Borges' hero: not only was my co-villager communicating the difficulties of disclosing community secrets and problems to someone who ceased to be 'one of their own', she also raised moral barriers to such action. My cultural and geographical extrapolation might have allowed space for the transformation of my intimate social understanding into political knowledge, but it also ensured that the gates of the locality would shut in my face. As far as this Greek lady is concerned, I might as well take my cosmopolitan finesse and go to hell.

Academic talk about the future of an enlarged Europe has never been so animated. University libraries pile up new publications on the post-national future of European politics and scholars are busy envisaging possibilities for the articulation of cosmopolitan futures. Some skeptics unwittingly give credence to my compatriot's suspicion when they distance themselves from such talk – even when they acknowledge the versatility that national commitments and sentiments assume in a new world order that encourages the erosion of fixed political boundaries. There is a very valid argument to be made here, which recuperates the untold fear that the very idea of 'Europe' has submitted to national interests – or, as Hutchinson puts it, 'a European ideal built on collective trauma[s] does not have the "sacred" authority' (2005, p. 189) required for the production of transnational solidarities. Social change itself places the future of democratic principles at stake, because Europe is still controlled by 'moral innovators' who produce the traditions that kept nations as isolated units alive.

How can one resist such a revelation? It matches so well the plain facts of contemporary Europe: the collapse of the Soviet regime and the unleashing of new ethnic differences in Eastern and Central Europe; the break up of Yugoslavia and the emergence of titular nations in its place; the wake of 'Islamophobic' panics in the post 9/11 era; the subsequent enforcement of segregations within multicultural states; and the ideological backlash that immigrations from newly accepted member states and North Africa generate in the receiving countries of the continent. These realities dominate local and national political discourse demoting any talk about cosmopolitan ideals to wishful thinking with which only some dreamy pen pushers would engage (Horowitz, 1985; Hoffmann, 2000). Likewise, my co-villager's criticism of cultural openness communicates an attitude that finds nation-wide appeal in Greece. As luck would have it, the centripetal forces that propel 'recalcitrant nationalisms' of marginalized nations such as the Greek mirror the legend that shrouds Kant's obsession with a round-the-clock precision: since their emergence, these nationalisms had been sustaining the systemic function of European ideology with immaculate but ruthless precision.

It is rumored that even Kant's compulsive punctuality was voluntarily disrupted by the arrival of Rousseau's *Emile* in his house – a novelistic exploration of the human capacity for goodness that supported the development of natural inclinations through interaction with the environment. 'We are born capable of sensation and from birth are affected in diverse ways by the objects around us' (Rousseau in Boyd, 1956, p. 13), explained an imaginary Rousseau to Kant. Humans make rational selections from these interactions, bestowing them with formative, pedagogical value. Though the tension between individual will and the collective good permeated Rousseau's work, his belief in the (positive and negative) powers of interaction to shape our social world was also communicated in his major political work, *The Social Contract*. Kant's 'cosmopolitanism' addressed the same tension, but did so by juxtaposing the state of Hobbesian warfare to the production of inter-state legal order, the pillar of a universal 'civil society'. This imaginary dialogue between the two *philosophes* would become the first draft of a lasting tradition in cosmopolitan writings.

There are good reasons to begin my exploration of better European futures with historical trivia. This sort of gossip often functions as a durable palimpsest upon which we imprint political 'truths', write and re-write our social visions. The same tension between individual and collective will was filtered through the writings of the sociological proponent of solidarity, Durkheim, who, influenced by both Kant and Rousseau, hailed 'universal moral individualism' as the articulation of our humanity 'in the abstract' (Durkheim, 1969 [1898]). It is significant that Durkheim's ethical bipolarity (his distinction between 'patriotism' and 'world patriotism') articulated the trauma of the First World War, which would transform nationalist ideology into the monocultural intellectual tradition of Europe (Durkheim, 1992; Turner, 2006, p. 141; Wolff, 1958, pp. 191–2). Even on the eve of this global devastation, Meinecke (1970) was announcing the decline of cosmopolitanism with the rise of the nation-state.

Durkheim's Kantian renunciation of 'patriotic duty' would replay the Hellenistic farewell to the world of the *polis* and its replacement with the Alexandrian ideal of global imperialism (Inglis and Robertson, 2004, pp. 166–7; Conversi, 2001; Inglis and Robertson, 2005). As argued in Chapter 6, this 'ideal' entered nineteenth-century national cultures and transmogrified European nationalisms into a pseudo-universal political program often rehearsed in contemporary European politics (Roudometof, 1999; Tzanelli, 2006). Even the Habermasian alternative of 'constitutional patriotism' would accommodate Durkheim's traumatic discourse, recasting it into the context of institutionalized memories of the Holocaust. From his grave, Kant would continue to dictate the intellectual agenda of cosmopolitanism with a political philosophy that remained related to the nation-state. There is a woeful comment to make on Enlightenment philosophy: the formalization of any global social contract (Kant's implicit suggestion) both 'legalizes' an inherently socio-political condition and submerges the *kosmopolítis* as such into universalist abstraction.

Should we talk about cosmopolitanism *in abstracto*? The history of European systemic violence teaches us that any 'cosmopolitan' respect for human diversity that promotes solidarity on a global scale cannot be achieved solely through formalized agreement; it also demands the development of moral sensitivity for specific *cultural* contexts. The moral make-up of European cosmologies, the center of this book's substantive historical analysis, should be taken seriously if we are to solve the ideational and pragmatic riddles of cosmopolitanism. I therefore set out to analyze a phenomenon with strong cultural dimensions (Hannerz, 1990; McGrew, 1992; Smith, 1990, 1995) that transcends, but does not dismiss the tradition of nationalism. Mann (1997) has gone to great lengths to show how cosmopolitan currents were present in the intellectual and political realms of European societies even as nationalism was beginning to gain popular support – although the Western Eurocentric take of his examples should not be overlooked. Similar points were made by various theorists who today relate cosmopolitanism to globalization (Archibugi *et al.*, 1998; Cheah and Robbins, 1998; Vertovec and Cohen, 2002). As Herder's vision of an individualized humanity was becoming real, Enlightenment universalism was still working its way underground. But Mann's discourse remains indifferent to the ways in which cosmopolitan currents may emerge today in villages at the margins of Europe. Being infiltrated by global telecommunications and bilateral global migrations, even such places reluctantly began to operate as sites of cross-cultural *rendezvous* (Herzfeld, 2005, p. 217).

By this comment I wish to move away from republican discourses of civic belonging, which remain related to the national ideal (Nielsen, 2002, pp. 158–9). Also, I do not endorse a 'statocentric' model of cosmopolitanism that relates nation-state and EU political structures to conceptualize a new cultural *Weltanschauung* (Delanty and Rumford, 2005, p. 188). At the same time, however, an attachment to a 'universal whole' (Nussbaum, 1996, pp. 11–12) or a rigidly moralized discourse of 'civic patriotism' (Habermas, 1996, p. 495) dismisses our need to retain emotional and social anchorage and remain connected to our significant others in culturally specific ways. The 'either-or' of this debate reactivates the opposition between Gadamer's 'hermeneutics of recovery' and Derrida's 'hermeneutics of suspicion' (Dallmayr, 1996, chapter 2), splitting a Heideggerian urgency to escape European 'logocentrism' into two opposing halves. The cosmologies of nationalist exclusivity and the discourse of universal solidarity are equally valuable sides of human communication and they exist – and *must* coexist – as *inter*dependent responses to particular needs and social challenges. The right question to ask is how we can establish stable patterns of interaction with other actors in the social field 'who do not share (overtly at least) our values and norms [… This is] the cosmopolitan dilemma of the structure of social action' (Turner, 2006, p. 138).

Perhaps social theory should depart on a new search for the ideational base of cosmopolitanism. A search for ideational grounding takes into account intersubjective principles that are irreducible to individuals but serve to construct the identities of social actors. Although the argument has gained credibility in the field of International Relations (Adler, 1997; Ruggie, 1998; Price and Reus-Smit, 1998), I am more interested in its mobilization outside state norms for the construction of cosmopolitan action. Cosmopolitanism cannot be simply seen as a condition of diversity but 'a conceptualisation of the social world as an open horizon in which new cultural models take place' (Delanty, 2006, p. 27). This 'critical' version of cosmopolitanism is actualized in moments of open interaction between self, other and world. A Kantian universalism must be replaced by conceptions of openness; subsequently, the social theorist's task becomes the analysis of the cultural modes of communication that shape the social locally and globally at any given time (Beck, 2002). But *how* is this supposed to happen? Should we follow Benhabib's lead and see this mediation in the 'law of hospitality' that secures good relations between state and strangers? The 'project of mediations' (Benhabib, 2006, p. 20) through which cosmopolitan norms eventually acquire a positive legal status certainly acknowledges the active (moral) role of citizens in the preservation of global democracy.

Benhabib does not dismiss Habermas out of hand, but argues for a context-specific understanding of transcultural ethics that does not equate general with universal interests (Benhabib, 1990, pp. 345–6). But the much-needed cultural specificity for the realization of cosmopolitics is still not defined outside legal norms, despite Benhabib's overall commitment to multicultural ethics and the promotion of inter-communal solidarity (Benhabib, 2004). Benhabib advocates the establishment of communicative solidarity across and within communities, but she does not explain why citizens should be expected to internalize cosmopolitan 'laws'. She tries to move away from the discourse of the nation-state to defend open forms of post-national belonging that vie for recognition of minority rights without neglecting however the role of active civic participation in post-national environments. As is the case with defenders of human rights in global contexts (Soysal, 1994; Balibar, 2004), her thesis becomes an attempt to re-vision a European society free of prejudice, war and hatred.

The cultural mechanics of such transformation – the contexts and histories of social change – do matter a lot, however. They provide the contours of a 'diatopical hermeneutics' of difference based on processes of reciprocal learning in cross-cultural encounters (Dallmayr, 1996, p. 61). The move to a prejudice-free European world can only be achieved through open dialogue and bias-free interaction between cultures that developed in different spaces (or *topoi*) independent modes of philosophizing and reaching intelligibility. This rudimentary observation, which I qualify below, has both theoretical and practical implications. Theoretically, to define the interaction of the universal order of the cosmos and the human order of the polis as cosmopolitanism presupposes an understanding of the interdependencies that bind the global and the local (Appadurai, 1996; Tzanelli, 2007b). I consider the analytical difference between Europeanization and globalization in terms of scale rather than substance: just like the move from a social to a cultural idiom, which has been largely the consequence of the emergence of European nationalisms (Herzfeld, 1992, p. 68), Europeanization is just another variant of socio-cultural dialogues and changes that take place at local, national and transnational levels. Even the Greek local's grudging attitude towards my ideas acknowledges – indeed, sanctions – the transformative potential of an exchange that happened despite her resentful reactions.

We should also consider the possibility that such dialogues have been taking place for centuries *because of such resentful reactions*. I am suggesting this because the practical consequences of this type of social change take us back to the history of nation-building. There is no doubt that my use of Herzfeld's term 'cultural intimacy' in the analysis of different modalities of national self-presentation within Europe revealed a picture of cross-cultural encounters governed by prejudice and inequality. In any case, 'cultural intimacy' involves a common form of protected self-presentation mobilized by both disenfranchised communities and state power to counter externally sanctioned forms of morality – including European discourses that denigrate peripheral identities (Herzfeld, 1997b, 2005). In Part I, I explained how imperial discourses constructed weak nations as another version of inferior and disorderly colonial difference, only to produce a backlash of negative imperial images within the national domain. Imperial hegemonies led to the emergence of national hegemonies: the nation communicated a coherent self-image to its European significant others at the expense of internal cultural difference. Part II revealed how the battle for cultural self-recognition in everyday encounters with European others paralleled the 'exegetic stance' promoted in formalized academic discourse in the nation-state. This 'exegetic stance' mobilized the inconsistencies of the nation's lifeworld, but turned them into an essential aspect of self-narration to 'Europe' *and* the members of the national community alike. Part III examined the ways in which European discourses of political dependency were clothed in the language of unilateral debt and indebtedness only to be challenged by nationalist discourses of interdependency that employed the vocabulary of care, reciprocity and sacrificial giving to Europe. If European history is governed by such reciprocal backlashes, what kind of cosmopolitan program can we outline?

An answer lies within the ambivalent role of 'cultural intimacy' in cross-cultural (rather than cross-state) encounters. I do not want to suggest that intimacies of this type are freely available to significant others – such a claim would counter Herzfeld's definition. Perhaps my theoretical model draws more on the sister notion of 'social poetics' that 'allows us to analyze strategic or tactical deployment of ideal types – stereotypes, laws and regulations, representations of culture, nostalgic folklore' (2005, p. 47) to understand the complexities of cultural intimacy. What I mean by this is that challenging intimate selves often produced dialogical communication. In the course of European history, such *intimations* might have contributed to the implosion of cultural embarrassment, allowing European critics of other 'nations' to express dissatisfaction about their political 'performance', but they also contributed to an interactive articulation of cultural identities. This articulation remained topographically and temporally specific and had more than one internal and external addressee. It is significant that fully articulated resentful intimations would be appropriated by centralized power. To draw parallels between Herzfeld's social poetics in the nation-state and Habermasian communicative theory (Habermas, 1989b), the shift from national lifeworld to systemic state self-narration is equivalent to a shift from the backstage chaos of nation-building (the birthplace of cultural intimacies) to the frontstage of national self-presentation in international politics (formalized 'social poetics'). As Herzfeld explains, if we examine the phenomenon within the 'nation', such political shifts are constitutive of interactions that take place at the local level (Herzfeld, 1997b, p. 91). National and global politics reiterate local patterns of multiple interactions with significant others, revealing how even systemic power has to rely on 'peasant' vocabularies to achieve social mobilization. Just cosmopolitan action must be located in our attempts to secure a sound, but *critical*, environment for this *poetic* shift from backstage to frontstage cultural intimations that are clearly not exclusively tied to the nation-state but are the creative material of inter-communal conversations.

So, I will not argue that systems ('Europe') and subsystems (nation-states) are inherently 'evil': the problem is not in the shift itself, but the conditions under which it takes place. There is no doubt that redistributive inequalities, the everyday reality of contemporary continental (and global) politics, are the legacy of damaged European reciprocities that promoted cultural closure alongside openness. This is understandable: to move Honneth's theory of recognition from the individual to a collective level, when cultural vulnerabilities are turned into material for denigration, criticism and derision, collective self-relations are damaged (Fraser and Honneth, 2003, p. 175; Thompson, 2006, pp. 108–10; Benhabib, 1992, p. 5). On an ideal level, we must therefore situate positive self-relations in the generation of a global horizon of value, which will allow the recognition of all cultural backstages in their own right. Despite the ubiquitous lack of cross-cultural trust in Europe, 'the medium of reciprocity in the social field' (Turner, 2006, p. 135), cultural *intimations* (rather than intimacies) continue to exist, constantly trying to open up local and national cosmologies to significant others. Although such communications must be properly acknowledged, they must also be followed by constructive criticism (Turner, 2001): an uncritical acceptance of radical difference will only repeat the errors of Levinassian metaphysics-as-politics. *Kosmotheoría*, an impassionate viewing of other worlds that allows space for engagement with them in their specificity, becomes the prerequisite of cosmopolitics, infusing spectatorship-as-action with moral meaning (Bakhtin, 1990, p. 26; Villa, 1996, p. 103; Yar, 2000). An impassionate viewing of the world integrates ontological questions (who I am, who others are for me and what I am for) into a quest for ethical action towards others (how should I act) (Bakhtin, 1990, p. 88; see also Nielsen, 1995, p. 806; Nielsen, 2002, p. 47). Perhaps this is what Herzfeld means in the context of professional ethics when he refers to the 'charge' of anthropologists to make pragmatic judgments that they can follow through 'when they have unintended consequences' (Herzfeld, 2005, p. 214).

It is therefore naïve to claim that this type of ethical commitment to difference will eliminate dialogical conflict. It will, however, allow space for cross-cultural fertilizations: in moments of world openness cultural interlocutors become answerable to each other, while retaining their uniqueness as social actors. As Bakhtin would have it, regardless of whether two or more discourses contradict each other, they must come into 'inner contact' (1984, p. 188). This contact zone, creates a third space for the *just* articulation of cultural intimacies, and presents identities as an on-going answerable event that exceeds rational planning. An investment of different cultural interlocutors in discourse ensures the preservation of the dialogic fabric of human life, 'the world symposium' (*ibid.*, p. 293) of cosmopolitics. When cultural interlocutors begin to acknowledge the creative unpredictability of their encounter (the 'residue' of their dialogues), they are more likely to develop dialogical respect for each other.

Obviously, the creativity of cross-cultural encounters presents the expression of difference as something more than rationally oriented 'communicative action'. To the satisfaction of die-hard Habermasian theorists, I argue that such creative expressions of cosmopolitanism can only be located in reciprocities involved in face-to-face interactions; to their disappointment, I do not separate the local embodiment of solidary subjectivities from universal articulations of justice (Benhabib, 1992, p. 186). My equation of lifeworld communications with the space of cultural intimacy aims to overcome the problems of Kantian abstraction. This thesis does not sidestep the fact that public dialogues are 'not external, but constitutive of power relations' (Benhabib, 1990, p. 353) – put bluntly, my old lady's resentments are not irrational peasant moaning but an acknowledgement of Greece's global political impotence, and an honest acknowledgment of her fear that I, as an once upon a time insider, possess the power to disclose what would rather be kept private. But to assume that speech acts are fully understood by interlocutors even when unforced agreements are achieved would be to ignore how communication is based on imagined responses that might misrecognize the intentions of our interlocutor (Bernard-Donals, 1994, p. 57). Because each of us, and each cultural world we inhabit, is unique, all encounters have to be understood and respected as unrepeatable (Bakhtin, 1993, p. 40). We all look to an understanding listener, awaiting interpretation of our worldview into an alien conceptual system (Bakhtin, 1981, p. 82) – a point that reminds us that what *we think* of ourselves to be and what *we aspire* to become for ourselves and our significant others, the grand question of *anthropopoiésis* (Smith, 2007, pp. 252–5), is an intersubjective venture. To move the discussion to the collective level: the irreplaceable, rather than relative, value of each lifeworld presents our support of any monologic view of the world as the ultimate unethical act. No European world-system has place in this cosmopolitan future.

Such observations put the initial suggestion that we re-vision identity in Europe under critical scrutiny for a number of reasons: first of all, it makes no sense to talk about unitary 'identity' within any imagined-conversational community, because national cultures are inherently polyvocal. As Brubaker has persuasively explained, because nationhood is 'a contingent event or happening', we 'should refrain from using the analytically dubious notion of "nations" as substantial enduring events' (1998, p. 21). By this reference I do not want to have recourse to an extreme constructivism that denies the ontogenetic, emotive and cohesive importance of nation-building. I am just arguing that the polyvocality of imagined-conversational communities (see also Benhabib, 2002, p. 25) may also relocate processes of answerability *within* them: different ethnic pasts and identities constantly face each other in national politics. This already suggests that nation-building is an open event that *ought* to be governed by internal reciprocities. Even the defenders of liberal nationalism have argued that the universal can be seen in certain particulars 'so a cosmopolitan may be intensely partial to a particular nation or group while at the same time having committed to the whole of humanity' (Nielsen, 1999, p. 120; Kymlica, 2001; Nielsen, 2003; Tan, 2004, p. 99; Taylor, 1994). To reiterate my previous comments on systemic violence, no nationalism is inherently evil, though it may contingently become so.

Nor can we talk about a single 'identity' in relation to a single notion of 'Europe': European history, culture and politics are characterized by a plethora of different, and often conflicting, modernities (Faubion, 1993; Roudometof, 1999). This book's example is telling in this respect, as the idea of 'Greece' produced different understandings of modernity in different regions of the continent (not to mention the rest of the world). The political reality of coexisting modernities was nicely encapsulated by my historical actors, who tried to relate different modernities in multiple discursive frameworks: Greece became Ireland, India, Abyssinia, Mexico, 'Christianity', 'civilization' and Europe by turns. Europe, has always been an incredibly malleable concept because of its geopolitical expansion eastwards. And yet, the 'Euro-Mediterranean border' seems to act as a deterrent when it comes to migrations from the African continent. Dallmayr's call to 'exit Orientalism' by transcending established categories 'in favor of a freer recognition of alien life forms' (1996, p. 130) finds some rhetorical use in current political talk to admit new states and cultural forms in Europe including one embodiment of the Oriental other, Turkey. And yet, the relationship between core and periphery still follows the rationale of a Wallersteinian world-system, even though new peripheries emerge. Immigrations into developed member states may be relocating peripheral identities into the 'core', but such identities become marginalized and demonized in nationalist discourse.

My attempt to narrate the history of European nation-building from the nineteenth-century margins of Europe has a critical solidary rationale. The nineteenth-century peasants were as modern as the foreign observers who studied them and the elite Greek writers, pedagogues and statesmen of the same bygone era who were busy enacting visions of *modern* Greece. The dialogics of failed European reciprocities were *still* dialogics with unpredictable poetic consequences. Likewise, we, the intellectual elite of contemporary Europe, are not the only ones who qualify to re-vision European *identities*: this is happening every day by the anonymous actors of the European space in different conversational contexts. Thus, although the old lady of my story and myself are unique as interlocutors, we are functionally replaceable. What cannot be replaced is the experiential dimension of modernity that we communicate from our unique perspectives. Why can we both not do this in a safe shared space? It is the living experience of dialogue – a dialogue that should be infused with respect for our significant others – that transforms us into viewers of, and actors in, the world. This is the future of actually existing cosmopolitanisms.

Bibliography

Books, pamphlets and travel books

About E. (1990) *The King of the Mountains* (in Greek). Athens: Tolidi Bros.

Abu-Lughod L. (1993) *Writing Women's Worlds*. Berkeley and Los Angeles: University of California Press.

Adler E. (1997) 'Seizing the Middle Ground: Constructivism in World Politics', *European Journal of International Relations*, 3, 3, 319–63.

Adorno T.W. (1986) 'What Does Coming to Terms with the Past Mean?', translated by T. Bahti and G. Hartman, in *Bitburg in Moral and Political Perspective*. Bloomington, IN: Hartman.

Afshar H. (1989) 'Women and Reproduction in Iran', in N. Yuval-Davis and F. Anthias (eds) *Woman/Nation/State*. Basingstoke: Macmillan, 110–25.

Agnew J. (2007) 'No Borders, No Nations: Making Greece in Macedonia', *Annals of the Association of American Geographers*, 97, 2, 398–422.

Ainian D. (1876) *On the Eastern Question* (in Greek). Athens: private.

Alexander J. (1982) 'Differentiation Theory: Problems and Prospects', in J. Alexander and P. Colomy (eds) *Differentiation Theory and Social Change*. New York: Columbia University Press, 1–15.

Alexander J.C. (2006) 'Cultural Pragmatics: Social Performance Between Ritual and Strategy', in J.C. Alexander, B. Giesen and J.L. Mast (eds) *Social Performance, Symbolic Action, Cultural Pragmatics and Ritual*. Cambridge: Cambridge University Press, 29–89.

Allen T. (1994) *The Invention of the White Race*, I. London and New York: Verso.

Althusser L. (1994) 'Ideology and Ideological State Apparatuses', in S. Žižek (ed.) *Mapping Ideology*. London and New York: Verso, 100–40.

An Oriental and Former Rayah (1868) *The East and the West*. Athens: Ethnikon Typografeion.

Anderson B. (1991) *Imagined Communities*, rev. edn. London and New York: Verso.

Angelomatis-Tsougarakis H. (1990) *The Eve of the Greek Revival*. London and New York: Routledge.

Anon. (1867) *Some Notes on Turkey*. London: William Ridgway.

Anonymous (1866) *East and West* (in Greek). Ermoupolis Syra: Melistagis Makedonas.

Anonymous (1867) *Turkey and the Christians under her Rule* (in Greek). Athens: Mavromatis.

Anonymous (1878) *Collection of Cretan Correspondence in the Local Dialect* (in Greek). Athens: Efimimeris ton Syzitiseon.

Ansted D.T. (1863) *The Ionian Islands in the Year 1863*. London: H. Allen.

Antonopoulos D. (1870) *Reflections on a Successful Persecution and Elimination of our Country's Demise, Brigandage* (in Greek). Athens: private.

Appadurai A. (1981) 'The Past as a Scarce Resource', *Man* N.S., 16, 2, 201–19.

Appadurai A. (1986) 'Towards an Anthropology of Things', in A. Appadurai (ed.) *The Social Life of Things*. Cambridge: Cambridge University Press, 3–63.

Appadurai A. (1996) *Modernity at Large*. Minneapolis, MN: University of Minnesota Press.

Archibugi D., D. Held and M. Köhler (eds) (1998) *Re-Imagining Political Community: Studies in Cosmopolitan Democracy*. Cambridge: Polity.

Ardener E. (1989) *The Voice of Prophecy and Other Essays*. Oxford: Basil Blackwell.

Arendt H. (1973) *The Origins of Totalitarianism*. New York: Harcourt.

Aries P. (1962) *Centuries of Childhood*, translated by R. Baldick. New York: Alfred A. Knopf.

Aristarchos D. Bey (1875–6) *The Bulgarian Question and the New Schemes of Panslavism in the East* (in Greek), III–IV. Athens: unknown.

Aristotle (1924) *Metaphysics*, translated by W.D. Ross. Oxford: Clarendon.

Aristotle (1946) *Politics*, translated by E. Barker. Oxford: Clarendon.

Asad T. (1973) 'Introduction', in T. Asad (ed.) *Anthropology and the Colonial Encounter*. Atlantic Highlands, NJ: Humanities, 9–20.

Asklipiadis Th. (1872) *Changes in the East owing to Bulgarian conduct* (in Greek). Athens: Peris Bros.

Augustinos G. (1977) *Consciousness and History: Nationalist Critics of Greek Society, 1897–1914*. New York: Columbia University Press.

Avdela E. (2000) 'The Teaching of History in Greece', *Journal of Modern Greek Studies*, 18, 2, 239–53.

Avdela E. and A. Psarra (2005) 'Engendering "Greekness": Women's Emancipation and Irredentist Politics in Nineteenth-Century Greece', *Mediterranean Historical Review*, 20, 1, 67–79.

Bagdon Reverend J.O. (1868) *The Brigands of Morea: A Narrative of the Captivity of Mr. Soteropoulos*, I–II. London: Saunders, Otley.

Bagdon Reverend J.O. (1869) *A Brief Comparison of the Fundamental Doctrines of the Anglican and Greek Churches*. London: J.T. Hayes.

Bakalaki A. (1997) 'Students, Natives, Colleagues: Encounters in Academia and in the Field', *Cultural Anthropology*, 12, 4, 502–26.

Bakhtin M.M. (1968). *Rabelais and His World,* translated by H. Isowolsky. Cambridge, MA: MIT Press.

Bakhtin M.M. (1981) *The Dialogic Imagination*, edited by M. Holquist. Austin, TX: Texas University Press.

Bakhtin M.M. (1984) *Problems of Dostoevski's Poetics*, edited and translated by C. Emmerson. Manchester: Manchester University Press.

Bakhtin M.M. (1986) *Speech Genres and Other Essays*, edited by C. Emmerson and M. Holquist, translated by V.W. MaGee. Austin, TX: University of Texas Press.

Bakhtin M.M. (1990) *Art and Answerability*, edited by M. Holquist, translated by V. Liapunov. Austin, TX: University of Texas Press.

Bakhtin M.M. (1993) *Toward a Philosophy of the Act*, edited by V. Liapunov and M. Holquist, translated by V. Liapunov. Austin: University of Texas Press.

Balibar É. (1990) 'The Nation Form: History and Ideology', *Review*: Fernard Braudel Center, 13, 329–61.

Balibar É. (1991) 'Racism and Nationalism', in É Balibar and I. Wallerstein, *Race, Nation, Class*. London: Verso, 37–67.

Balibar É. (1994) *Masses, Classes, Ideas*, translated by J. Swenson. London and New York: Routledge.

Balibar É. (2004) *We, the People of Europe*. Princeton, MA: Princeton University Press.

Balibar É. (2006) 'Strangers as Enemies: Further Reflections on the Aporias of Transnational Citizenship', *Globalization and Autonomy Online Compedium*. Online. http://www.globalautonomy.co/global1/article.jsp?index=RA_Balibar_ Strangers.xml (consulted: 14 March 2007).

Balibar É. and I. Wallerstein (1991) *Race, Nation, Class*. London: Verso.

Ball C. (1981) *The History of Indian Mutiny*. New Delhi: Master Publishers.

Barth F. (1969) 'Introduction', in F. Barth (ed.) *Ethnic Groups and Boundaries*. Boston: Little, Brown & Co., 7–38.

Barth F. (1981) *Process and Form in Social Life*, I. London: Routledge and Kegan Paul.

Barth F. (1994) 'Enduring and Emerging Issues in the Analysis of Ethnicity', in H. Vemeulen and C. Govers (eds) *Anthropology of Ethnicity: Beyond 'Ethnic Groups and Boundaries'*. Amsterdam: Het Spinhuis, 11–32.

Barthes R. (1993) *Mythologies*. London: Vintage.

Bataille G. (1988) *The Accursed Share*, I. London: Urzone.

Baudrillard J. (1988) *Selected Writings*, edited by M. Poster. Stanford, CA: Stanford University Press.

Bauman Z. (1995) *Life in Fragments*. Oxford: Blackwell.

Baumann C.E. (1973) *Diplomatic Kidnappings: A Revolutionary Tactic of Urban Terrorism*. The Hague, Netherlands: Martinus Nijhoff.

Beames M. (1983) *Peasants and Power: The Whiteboy Movements and the Control in Pre-Famine Ireland*. New York: St. Martins Press.

Beck U. (2002) 'The Cosmopolitan Society and its Enemies', *Theory, Culture and Society*, 19, 1, 17–44.

Becker H. (1960) 'Notes on the Concept of Commitment', *The American Journal of Sociology*, 66, 1, 32–40.

Bederman G. (1995) *Manliness and Civilization: A Cultural History of Gender and Race in the United States 1880–1917*. Chicago, IL: University of Chicago Press.

Belich J. (1986) *The New Zealand Wars and the Victorian Interpretation of Racial Conflict*. Auckland: Auckland University Press.

Bell D. (1991) 'Reciprocity as a Generating Process in Social Relations', *Journal of Quantitative Anthropology*, 3, 251–60.

Bell M.M. and M. Gardiner (1998) 'Bakhtin and the Human Sciences: A Brief Introduction', in M.M. Bell and M. Gardiner (eds) *Bakhtin and the Human Sciences*. London: Sage, 1–12.

Ben-Amos D. (1998) 'The Name is the Thing', *Journal of American Folklore*, 111, 441, 257–80.

Benhabib S. (1987) 'The Generalized and Concrete Other', in S. Benhabib and D. Cornwell (eds) *Feminism as Critique: Essays on the Politics of Gender in Later Capitalist Societies*. Minneapolis, MN: University of Minnesota Press, 77–95.

Benhabib S. (1990) 'Afterward: Communicative Ethics and the Current Controversies in Practical Philosophy', in S. Benhabib and F. Dallmayr (eds) *The Communicative Ethics*. Cambridge, MA: MIT Press, 330–69.

Benhabib S. (1992) *Situating the Self: Gender, Community and Postmodernity*. New York: Routledge.

Benhabib S. (1995) 'Cultural Complexity, Moral Interdependence and the Global Dialogical Community', in M.C. Nussbaum and J. Glover (eds) *Women, Culture and Development*. Oxford: Clarendon Press, 235–55.

Benhabib S. (2002) *The Claims of Culture*. Princeton: Princeton University Press.

Benhabib S. (2004) *The Rights of Cultures*. Cambridge: Cambridge University Press.

Benhabib S. (2006) 'The Philosophical Foundations of Cosmopolitan Norms', in R. Post (ed.) *Another Cosmopolitanism*. New York: Oxford University Press, 13–44.

Benjamin S.G.W. (1867) *The Turk and the Greek: or Creeds, Races, Societies and Scenery in Turkey, Greece, and the Isles of Greece*. New York and London: Hurd & Houghton.

Benjamin W. (1989) 'The Work of Art in the Age of Mechanical Reproduction', in D. Richter (ed.) *The Critical Tradition*. New York: St. Martin's Press.

Benjamin W. (1992) *Illuminations*. London: Fontana Press.

Bennett R. (2000) 'National Allegory or Carnivalesque Heteroglossia?', in San Diego Bakhtin Circle, *Bakhtin and the Nation*. London and Toronto: Associated University Press, 177–94.

Bennett T. (1995) *The Birth of the Museum: History, Theory, Politics*. London and New York: Routledge.

Berking H. (1999) *Sociology of Giving*, translated by P. Gamiller. London, Thousand Oaks and New Delhi: Sage.

Bernal M. (1991) *Black Athena: The Afroasiatic Roots of Classical Civilisation*, I. London: Vintage.

Bernal M. (1995) 'Greece: Aryan or Mediterranean? Two Contending Historiographical Models', in S. Federici (ed.) *Enduring Western Civilization*. London and Westport, CT: Praeger, 3–12.

Bernard-Donals M.F. (1994) *Mikhail Bakhtin: Between Phenomenology and Marxism*. Cambridge: Cambridge University Press.

Bhabha H.K. (1990a) 'DissemiNation', in H.K. Bhabha (ed.) *Nation and Narration*. Westport CT, London and New York: Routledge, 291–322.

Bhabha H.K. (1990b) 'Narrating the Nation', in H.K. Bhabha (ed.) *Nation and Narration*. Westport CT, London and New York: Routledge, 1–7.

Bhabha H.K. (1990c) 'The Other Question: Difference, Discrimination and the Discourse of Colonialism', in R. Ferguson, M. Gevr, T.T. Min-Ha and C. West (eds) *Out There: Marginalization and Contemporary Cultures*. Cambridge, MA: MIT Press, 71–87.

Bhabha H.K. (1994) *The Location of Culture*. London and New York: Routledge, 1994.

Bhatt C. (2000) 'Primordial Being: Enlightenment, Schopenhauer and the Indian Subject of Postcolonial Theory', *Radical Philosophy*, 100, 28–41.

Billig M. (1995) *Banal Nationalism*. London: Sage.

Bleicher J. (1980) *Contemporary Hermeneutics: Hermeneutics as Method, Philosophy and Critique*. London and New York: Routledge.

Blinkhorn M. (2000) 'Liability, Responsibility and Blame: British Ransom Victims in the Mediterranean Periphery, 1860–1881', *Australian Journal of Politics and History*, 1, 3, 336–56.

Bohata K. (2004a) 'En-gendering a New Wales: Female Allegories, Home Role and Imperialism 1890–1910', in A. von Rothkirch and D. Williams (eds) *Beyond the Difference: Welsh Literature in Comparative Contexts*. Cardiff: University of Wales Press.

Bohata K. (2004b) *Postcolonialism Revisited*. Cardiff: University of Wales Press.

Bok S. (1978) *Lying: Moral Choice in Public and Private Life*. Brighton: Harvester Press.

Borges J.L. (1998) *Collected Fictions*, translated by A. Huxley. New York: Viking.

Borneman J. (1996) 'Until Death do us Part: Marriage/Death in Anthropological Discourse', *American Ethnologist*, 23, 2, 215–35.

Bourdieu P. (1977) *Outline of a Theory of Practice*, translated by R. Nice. Cambridge: Polity Press.

Bourdieu P. (1984). *Distinction: A Social Critique of the Judgement of Taste*, translated by R. Nice. Cambridge: Harvard University Press.

Bourdieu P. (1994) 'Rethinking the State: On the Genesis and Structure of the Bureaucratic Field', *Sociological Theory*, 12, 1, 1–19.

Bourdieu P. (1998) *Practical Reason*, translated by R. Johnson. Cambridge: Polity.

Bourdieu P. (1999) *Language and Symbolic Power*, trans. G. Raymond and M. Adamson. Cambridge: Polity Press.

Bowler P.J. (1989) *The Invention of Progress: The Victorians and the Past*. Oxford: Blackwell.

Boyce D.G. (1988) *The Irish Question and British Politics 1868–1986*. London: Macmillan.

Boyd W. (1956) *Émile for Today*. London: Heinemann.

Brandist C. (2002) *The Bakhtin Circle: Philosophy, Culture and Politics*. London and Sterling, Virginia: Pluto.

Brown K. and Theodossopoulos D. (2004) 'Other's Others: Talking About Stereotypes and Constructions of Otherness in Southeast Europe', *History and Anthropology* 15, 1, 3–14.

Brubaker R. (1992) *Citizenship and Nationhood in France and Germany*. Cambridge, MA: Harvard University Press.

Bruner M.L. (2005) ' Rhetorical Theory and the Critique of National Identity Construction', *National Identities*, 7, 3, 309–27.

Bryant R. (2002) 'The Purity of Spirit and the Power of Blood: A Comparative Perspective on Nation, Gender and Kinship in Cyprus', *Journal of the Royal Anthropological Institute*, 8, 3, 509–30.

Bugge P. (2003) 'A European Cultural Heritage? Reflections on a Concept and a Programme', in R. Shannan-Peckham (ed.) *Rethinking Heritage*. London: I.B. Tauris, 61–73.

Bull M. (1997) 'Overlapping and Competing Identities in the Frankish First Crusade,' *La Concile de Clermont de 1095 et l' Appel a la Croisade. Actes du Colloque Universitaire International de Clermont*. École Franc[,]aise de Rome Palais Farnèse, 195–211.

Bulmer M. (1986) *Neighbours*. Cambridge: Cambridge University Press.

Burrow J.W. (1966) *Evolution and Society: A Study of Victorian Social Theory*. Cambridge: Cambridge University Press.

Butler J. (1990) *Gender Trouble*. New York: Routledge.

Callahan W. (2003) 'Beyond Cosmopolitanism and Nationalism: Diasporic Chinese and Neo-Nationalism in China and Thailand', *international Organization*, 57, 3, 481–517.

Campbell D. (1877) *Turks and Greeks: Notes on a Recent Excursion*. London: Macmillan.

Campbell J.K. (1964) *Honour, Family and Patronage: A Study of Institutional and Moral Values in a Greek Mountain Community*. Oxford: Oxford University Press.

Campbell Sir G.D. (1876) *A Handy Book on the Eastern Question*. London.

Cannadine D. (2002) *Ornamentalism*. Oxford: Oxford University Press.

Carabott P. (2005a) 'Aspects of Hellenization of Greek Macedonia ca. 1912–ca. 1959', *Κάμπος: Cambridge Papers in Modern Greek*, 13, 21–61.

Carabott P. (2005b) '"In Keeping with Modernity": Historical Writing on Greece in the Modern Era', *Southeast European and Black Sea Studies*, 5, 1, 135–44.

Carabott P. (2006) 'A Country in a "State of Destitution" Labouring under "An Unfortunate Regime": Crete at the Turn of the 20th Century', *Creta Antica*, 7, 39–53.

Carrier J. (1991) Gifts, Commodities and Social Relations: A Maussian View of Exchange', *Sociological Forum*, 6, 1, 119–36.

Casson S. (1943) *Greece and Britain*. London: Collins.

Castoriadis C. (1987) *The Imaginary Institution of Society*, translated by K. Blamey. Cambridge, MA: Cambridge University Press.

Chadjiskos D. (1871) *Speech Delivered by D. Chadjiskos, MP for Phthiotis* (in Greek). Athens: Koinovoulio.

Chamberlin E. and S.L. Gilman (eds) (1985) *Degeneration: The Dark Side of Progress*. New York: Columbia University Press.

Chassiotis I. (1981) 'The European Powers and the Question of Greek Independence from the Fifteenth to the Beginning of the Nineteenth Century' (in Greek), in *Greece: History and Civilization*, V. Thessaloniki: Estia.

Chatterjee P. (1986) *Nationalist Thought and the Colonial World*. Minneapolis, MN: University of Minnesota Press.

Chatterjee P. (1993) *The Nation and its Fragments*. Princeton, NJ: Princeton University Press.

Cheah P. and B. Robbins (eds) (1998) *Cosmopolitics*. Minneapolis, MN: University of Minnesota Press.

Clark K. and M. Holquist (1984) *Mikhail Bakhtin*. Cambridge: Harvard University Press.

Claudio P. (2002) 'The Two Levels of Public Use of the Past', in J. Revel and G. Levi (eds) *Political Uses of the Past*. London: Frank Cass, 74–86.

Clifford J. (1986) 'On Ethnographic Analogy', in J. Clifford and G. Marcus (eds) *Writing Culture: The Poetics and Politics of Ethnography*. Berkeley: University of California Press, 98–121.

Clifford J. (1988) *The Predicament of Culture*. Cambridge, MA: Harvard University Press, 215–51.

Clogg R. (1992) *A Concise History of Modern Greece*. Cambridge: Cambridge University Press.

Clogg R. (2002) *A Concise History of Modern Greece*, 2nd edn. Cambridge: Cambridge University Press.

CNN (28 September 1997) 'EU Ban on Animal Parts Upsetting Greek Appetites'. Online. http://www.cnn.com/WORLD/9709/28/greece.edible.eyes/ (consulted: 25 February 2008).

Cochran C.E. (2002) 'Joseph and the Politics of Memory', *The Review of Politics*, 64, 3, 421–44.

Cochran W. (1887) *Pen and Pencil in Asia Minor*. London: Sampson Law.

Cohen E. (1996) 'A Phenomenology of Tourist Experiences', in Y. Apostolopoulos, S. Leivadi and A. Yannakis (eds) *The Sociology of Tourism*. London: Routledge, 90–114.

Cohen G.A. (1972) 'Karl Marx and the Withering Away of Social Science' *Philosophy and Public Affairs*, 1, 2, 182–203.

Cohn B. (1987) 'Social Structure and Objectification in South East Asia', in B. Cohn, *An Anthropologist Among the Historians and Other Essays*. Delhi: Oxford University Press, 224–54.

Colbeck A. (1887) *A Summer's Cruise in the Waters of Greece, Turkey, and Russia*. London: unknown.

Collier J.F. (1997) *From Duty to Desire: Remaking Families in a Spanish Village*. Princeton, NJ: Princeton University Press.

Collier J.F., M.Z. Rosaldo and S. Yanagisako (1982) '"Is There a Family?" New Anthropological Views', in B. Thorne and M. Yalom (eds) *Rethinking the Family*. New York: Longman, 25–39.

Comaroff J. (1985) *Body of Power, Spirit of Resistance*. Chicago: University of Chicago Press.

Comerford R.V. (1998) *The Fenians in Context*. Dublin: Wolfhound Press.

Connell R.W. (1987) *Gender and Power*. Stanford, CA: Stanford University Press.

Connell R.W. (1995) *Masculinities*. Berkeley, CA: University of California Press.

Connerton P. (1989) *How Societies Remember*. Cambridge: Cambridge University Press.

Conversi D. (2001) 'Cosmopolitanism and Nationalism', in A. Leoussi, (ed.) *The Companion Guide to Nationalism*. New Brunswick, NJ: Transaction Publishers.

Cooper F. and Stoler A. (1997) *Tensions of Empire: Colonial Cultures in a Bourgeois World*. Berkeley, CA: University of California Press.

Cowan J. (1990) *Dance and the Body Politic in Northern Greece*. Princeton, NJ: Princeton University Press.

Cowan J.K. (1988) 'Folk Truth: When the Scholar Comes to Carnival in "Traditional" Community', *Journal of Modern Greek Studies*, 6, 2, 245–60.

Crawshaw C. and J. Urry (1997) 'Tourism and the Photographic Gaze', in J. Urry and C. Rojek (eds) *Touring Cultures*. London and New York: Routledge, 176–95.

Curtis L.P. (1971) *Apes and Angels: The Irishman in Victorian Caricature*. New York: Smithsonian Institution Press.

Dakin D. (1955) *British and American Philhellenes During the War of Independence, 1821–1833*. Thessaloniki: Institute for Balkan Studies.

Dallmayr F. (2001) *Beyond Orientalism*. New Delhi, Rawat.

Damianakos S. (1987) *Tradition of Revolt and Folk Culture* (in Greek). Athens: Plíthron.

Daphnis G. (1980) 'The Attitude of the Greek State toward the Cretan Insurrection' (in Greek), in *History of the Greek Nation*, XIII. Athens: Ekdotiki Athinon, 277–89.

Dastur K.J. (May 1924) 'Is India Fit for Home Rule?', *The Empire Review*, 39, 280, 488–96.

David S. (2003) *The India Mutiny: 1857*. London: Penguin.

Davies N. (1997) 'Polish National Mythologies', in G. Hosking and G. Scöpflin (eds) *Myths and Nationhood*. New York: Routledge, 141–57.

Davis J. (1987) 'Family and State in the Mediterranean', in D. Gilmore (ed.) *Honor and Shame and the Unity of the Mediterranean*. Washington: American Anthropological Association, 22–34.

de Certeau M. (1985) 'What We Do when We Believe', in M. Blonsky (ed.) *On Signs: A Semiotic Reader*. Baltimore, MD: Johns Hopkins University Press, 192–202.

de Certeau M. (1986) *Heterologies: Discourse on the Other*, translated by B. Massumi. Manchester: Manchester University Press.

de Certeau M. (1988) *The Writing of History*, translated by T. Conley. New York: Columbia University Press.

de Peuter J. (1998) 'The Dialogics of Narrative Identity', in M.M. Bell and M. Gardiner (eds) *Bakhtin and the Human Sciences*. London: Sage, 30–48.

Deacon A. (2007) 'Civic Labour or Doulia? Care, Reciprocity and Welfare', *Social Policy and Society*, 6, 4, 481–90.

Delaney C. (1995) 'Father State, Motherland and the Birth of Modern Turkey', in S. Yanagisako and C. Delaney (eds) *Naturalizing Power: Essays in Feminist Cultural Analysis*. New York: Routledge, 177–99.

Delanty G. (1995a) *Inventing Europe*. Basingstoke: Macmillan.

Delanty G. (2002) 'Models of European Identity: Reconciling Universalism and Particularism', *Perspectives on European Politics and Society*, 3, 3, 345–59.

Delanty G. and P. O'Mahony (2002) *Nationalism and Social Theory*. London: Sage.

Delanty G. and C. Rumford (2005) *Rethinking Europe*. London and New York: Routledge.

Derrida J. (1976) *Of Grammatology*. Baltimore: Johns Hopkins University Press.

Derrida J. (1997) *Writing and Difference*, translated by A. Bass. London: Routledge.

Dhima A. (1994) 'Ethnical Anthropology of Albania', *Homo*, 45, 2, 127–58.

Diamantouros N. (1983) 'Greek Political Culture in Transition', in R. Clogg (ed.) *Greece in the 1980s*. London: Macmillan, 43–69.

Dickie J. (1993) 'A Word at War: The Italian Army and Brigandage 1860–1870', *History Workshop Journal*, 33, 1, 1–24.

Dickie J. (1999) *Darkest Italy*. New York: St. Martin's Press.

Dimakos I. and K. Tasiopoulou (2003) 'Attitudes towards Immigrants: What do Greek Students Think about their Immigrant Classmates?', *Intercultural Education*, 14, 3, 307–16.

Dimaras A. (1972) 'The Other British Philhellenes', in R. Clogg (ed.) *The Struggle for Greek Independence*. London: Macmillan, 200–23.

Dimaras K. (1983) *Greek Romanticism* (in Greek). Athens: Ermis.

Dimitrijević N. (1999) 'Words and Death: Serbian Nationalist Intellectuals', A. Bozóki (ed.) *Intellectuals and Politics in Central Europe*. Budapest and New York: Central European University Press, 119–50.

Doak K.M. (1997) 'What Is a Nation and Who Belongs? National Narratives and Ethnic Imagination in Twentieth-Century Japan', *The American Historical Review*, 102, 2, 283–309.

Douglas M. (1993) *Purity and Danger: An Analysis of the Concepts of Pollution and Taboo*. London: Routledge.

Douglas M. and A. Wildavsky (1982) *Risk and Culture*. Berkeley, CA: University of California Press.

du Boulay J. (1994) *Portrait of a Greek Mountain Village*. Evia: Harvey.

Dubisch J. (1995) *In a Different Place: Pilgrimage, Gender, and Politics at a Greek Island Shrine*. Princeton: Princeton University Press.

Duijzins G. (2000) *Religion and the Politics of Identity in Kosovo*. New York: Columbia University Press.
Durkheim E. (1969 [1898]) 'Individualism and the Intellectuals', translated by J. Lukes, *Political Studies* 17, 1, 19–30.
Durkheim E. (1992) *Professional Ethics and Civic Morals*. London: Routledge.
Durkheim E. (1997 [1893]) *The Division of Labour in Society*. New York: Free Press.
Eleftheriadis P. (1999) 'Political Romanticism in Modern Greece', *Journal of Modern Greek Studies*, 17, 1, 41–61.
Eley G. (2000) 'Culture, Nation and Gender', in I. Blom, K. Hageman and C. Hal (eds) *Gendered Nations*. New York: Berg, 27–40.
Elias N. (1982) *The Civilising Process: State Formation and Civilisation*, II. Oxford: Blackwell.
Elias N. (1996) *The Germans: Power Struggles and the Development of Habitus in the Nineteenth and Twentieth Centuries*, translated by E. Dunning and S. Mennell. New York: Columbia University Press.
Elias N. (2006) *The Court Society*, translated by E. Jephcott. Dublin: University College Dublin Press.
Enloe C. (1990) *Bananas, Beaches and Bases: Making Feminist Sense of International Politics*. Berkeley, CA: University of California Press.
Fabian J. (1983) *Time and the Other: How Anthropology Makes its Object*. New York: Columbia University Press.
Fabian J. (1990) *Power and Performance*. Madison: University of Wisconsin Press.
Fabian J. (1991) *Time and the Work of Anthropology*. Reading, Berks: Harwood Academic Publishers.
Fabian J. (2007) *Memory Against Culture*. Durham and London: Duke University Press.
Fanon F. (1965) *A Dying Colonialism*, translated by H. Chevalier. New York: Grove Weidenfeld.
Fanon F. (1967) *The Wretched of the Earth*. Harmondsworth: Penguin.
Fanon F. (1970 [1958]) *Black Skin, White Masks*. London: Paladin.
Farley L.J. (1876) *Turks and Christians*. London: Simpkin, Marshall & Co.
Farrer R.R. (1882) *A Tour in Greece, 1880*. Edinburgh and London: Blackwood and Sons.
Faubion J. (1993) *Modern Greek Lessons*. Princeton, NJ: Princeton University Press.
Federici S. (1995) 'The God that Never Failed: The Origins and Crises of Western Civilisation', in S. Federici (ed.) *Enduring Western Civilisation*. London and Westport, CT: Praeger, 63–90.
Felton C.C. (1867) *Greece, Ancient and Modern, Lectures Delivered before the Lowell Institute*, I–II. Boston: Ticknor and Fields.
Ferguson K. (1984) *The Feminist Case Against Bureaucracy*. Philadelphia: Temple Press.
Ferguson K. (1993) *The Man Question*. California: University of California Press.
Finlay G. (1973) *History of the Greek Revolution* (in Greek), I–II, translated by A. Georgouli. Athens: Toldi Bros.
Finlay G., Manuscript Drafts of Articles to *The Times*.
Forrest G.W. (2006) *A History of the Indian Mutiny 1857–58*, I–III. New Delhi: Asian Educational Services.

Foster R.F. (1988) *Modern Ireland, 1600–1972*. London: Allen Lane.

Foucault M. (1979) *The History of Sexuality*, I, trans by Robert Hurley. London: Allen Lane.

Foucault M. (1980) *Power/Knowledge*. New York: Pantheon.

Foucault M. (1986) 'Of Other Spaces', *Diacritics*, 16, 1, 22–7.

Foucault M. (1991) *Discipline and Punish: the Birth of the Prison*. Harmondsworth, MX: Penguin Books.

Foucault M. (1997) *The Archaeology of Knowledge*, translated by A.M. Sheridan Smith. London: Routledge.

Frangoudaki A. and T. Dragonas (1997) '"What Could be Our Country?" Ethnocentrism in Education' (in Greek). Athens: Alexandria.

Fraser N. and A. Honneth (2003) *Redistribution or Recognition?* London: Verso.

Fuss D. (1994) 'Interior Colonies: Frantz Fanon and the Politics of Identification', *Diacritics*, 24, 2–3, 19–42.

Gallant T.W. (1997) 'Greek Exceptionalism and Contemporary Historiography: New Pitfalls and Old Debates', *Journal of Modern Greek Studies* 15, 2, 209–16.

Gallant T.W. (1999) 'Brigandage, Piracy, Capitalism, and State-Formation: Transnational Crime from a Historical World-Systems Perspective', in J. McC. Heyman (ed.) *States and Illegal Practices*. Oxford and New York: Oxford Berg 1999, 25–61.

Gallant T.W. (2000) 'Honor, Masculinity, and Ritual Knife Fighting in Nineteenth-Century Greece', *The American Historical Review*, 105, 2, 359–82.

Gallant T.W. (2001) *Modern Greece*. London: Arnold.

Gallant T.W. (2002) *Experiencing Dominion*. Notre Dame, IN: University of Notre Dame Press.

Gardiner M. (1992) *The Dialogics of Critique: M.M. Bakhtin and the Theory of Ideology*. London: Routledge.

Gardiner M. (1997) 'A Postmodern Utopia? Heller and Fehér's Critique of Messianic Marxism', *Utopian Studies*, 8, 1, 89–122.

Garelick R.K. (1999) *Rising Star: Dandyism, Gender and Performance in the Fin-de-Siècle*. Princeton, NJ: Princeton University Press.

Geertz C. (1963) 'The Integrative Revolution: Primordial Sentiments and Civil Policies in the New States', in C. Geertz (ed.) *Old Societies and New States*. Glencoe, IL: Free Press, 105–57.

Geertz C. (1980) *Negara*. Princeton, NJ: Princeton University Press.

Geertz C. (1997) *Routes: Travel and Translation the Late Twentieth Century*. Cambridge, MA: Harvard University Press.

Gefou-Mandianou D. (1993) 'Mirroring Ourselves through Western Texts: The Limits of an Indigenous Anthropology', in H. Driessen (ed.) *The Politics of Ethnographic Reading and Writing*. Saarbrucken, Belgium: Verlag Breitenbach, 160–77.

Gefou-Mandianou D. (1999) 'Cultural Polyphony and Identity Formation: Negotiating Tradition in Attica', *American Ethnologist*, 26, 2, 412–39.

Gellner E. (1983) *Nations and Nationalism*. Oxford: Blackwell.

Gellner E. (1998) *Nationalism*. London: Phoenix.

Gemie S. (1998) 'France, Orientalism and Algeria: 54 Articles from the *Revue des Deux Mondes*, 1846–1852', *The Journal of Algerian Studies*, 3, 58–62.

Gennadios J. (1870) *Notes on the Recent Murders by Brigands in Greece*. London: private.

Gennadios, J. (1871) *Notes on the Recent Murders by Brigands in Greece...* (in Greek). Athens: Ethnikon Typografeion (unfinished translation).

Gerth H.H. and W. Mills (1948) *From Max Weber: Essays in Sociology*. London: Routledge and Kegan Paul.

Gheorghe N. (1997) 'The Social Construction of Romani Identity', in T. Acton (ed.) *Gypsy Politics and Traveller Identity*. Hatfield: University of Hertfordshire Press, 153–63.

Giddens A. (1985) *A Contemporary Critique of Historical Materialism*, II. Cambridge: Polity.

Gilmore D. (1987) *Aggression and Community: The Paradoxes of Andalusian Culture*. New Haven: Yale University Press.

Gilmore D. (ed.) (1987) *Honor and Shame and the Unity of the Mediterranean*. Washington: American Anthropological Association.

Gilroy P. (1987) *There Ain't No Black in the Union Jack*. London: Routledge.

Gilroy P. (1993) 'It's a Family Affair: Black Culture and the Trope of Kinship', in P. Gilroy (ed.) *Small Acts: Thoughts on the Politics of Black Cultures*. London: Serpent's Tail, 192–207.

Gittings C. (ed.) (1996) *Imperialism and Gender*. New Lambton: Dangaroo Press.

Goffman E. (1987) *The Presentation of Self in Everyday Life*. Middlesex: Penguin Books.

Gouldner A.W. (1960) 'The Norm of Reciprocity: A Preliminary Statement', *American Sociological Review*, 25, 161–78.

Gouldner A.W. (1973) 'The Importance of Something for Nothing', in R.C. Jr Hinkle and G.J. Hinkle (eds) *For Sociology*. New York: Basic Books, 260–99.

Gourgouris S. (1992a) 'Modern Greece in the "Third World"', *Journal of the Hellenic Diaspora*, 18, 99–112.

Gourgouris S. (1992b) 'Nationalism and Oneirocentrism: Of Modern Hellenes in Europe', *Diaspora*, 2, 43–71.

Gourgouris S. (1996) *Dream Nation: Enlightenment, Colonization and the Institution of Modern Greece*. Stanford, CA: Stanford University Press.

Graham C. (2000) 'Epic, Nation and Empire', in San Diego Bakhtin Circle, *Bakhtin and the Nation*. London and Toronto: Associated University Press, 84–100.

Grant Duff Mountstuart (Mountstewart) (1876) *The Eastern Question*. Edinburgh: unknown.

Greenberg O. (1993) 'When They Read what the Papers Say We Wrote', in C. Brettell (ed.) *When They Read What We Write*. Westport, CT: Bergin & Garvey, 107–18.

Greenfeld L. (1990) 'The Formation of the Russian National Identity: The Role of Status Insecurity and Ressentiment', *Comparative Studies in Society and History*, 32, 549–91.

Greisman H. (1977) 'Social Meanings of Terrorism', *Contemporary Crises*, 1, 303–18.

Grey W. (1870) *Journal of a Visit to Egypt, Constantinople, the Crimea, Greece &c.* London: private.

Gudeman S. (1986) *Economics as Culture*. London: Routledge Kegan Paul.

Guzzini S. (1998) *Realism in International Relations and International Political Economy*. London: Routledge.

200   *Bibliography*

Habermas J. (1972) *Knowledge and Human Interests*, translated by J. Shapiro. Boston: Beacon Press.

Habermas J. (1977) ' A Review of Gadamer's *Truth and Method*', in F. Dallmayr and T. McCarthy (eds) *Understanding and Social Enquiry*. Notre Dame, IN: University of Notre Dame Press.

Habermas J. (1983) 'Hannah Arendt: On the Concept of Power', *Philosophical/ Political Profiles*, London: Heinemann.

Habermas J. (1984) *The Theory of Communicative Action*, I: *Reason and the Rationalisation of Society*. London: Heinemann.

Habermas J. (1987) *The Philosophical Discourse of Modernity*. Cambridge, MA: MIT Press.

Habermas J. (1989a) *The New Conservatism*, edited and translated by S.E. Nicholsen. Cambridge, MA: MIT Press.

Habermas J. (1989b) *The Theory of Communicative Action*, II: *Lifeworld and System*. Boston, MA: Beacon Press.

Habermas J. (1991) *The Structural Transformation of the Public Sphere*, translated by T. Burger. Cambridge, MA: MIT Press.

Habermas J. (1992) 'Citizenship and National Identity', *Praxis International*, 12, 1, 1–19.

Habermas J. (1996) *Between Facts and Norms*, translated by W. Rehg. Cambridge, MA: MIT Press.

Haley B. (1978) *The Health Body and Victorian Culture*. Cambridge, MA: Cambridge University Press.

Hall S. (1992) 'The West and the Rest: Discourse and Power', in S. Hall and B. Gieben (eds) *The Formation of Modernity*. Cambridge: Polity, 275–332.

Handler R. (1988) *Nationalism and the Politics of Culture in Quebec*. Madison: University of Wisconsin Press.

Hannerz U. (1990) 'Cosmopolitans and Locals in World Culture', *Theory, Culture and Society*, 7, 2, 237–51.

Hansen T.B. and F. Stepputat (2006) 'Sovereignty Revisited', *Annual Review of Anthropology*, 35, 295–315.

Harris M. (1969) *The Rise of Anthropological Theory*. London: Routledge and Kegan Paul.

Haslam J. (2002) *No Virtue like Necessity: Realist Thought in International Relations since Machiavelli*. New Haven, CT: Yale University Press.

Hassan W.S. (2003) 'Gender (and) Imperialism: Structures of Masculinity in Tayeh Sahib's Season of Migration to the North', *Men and Masculinities*, 5, 3, 309–24.

Hay D. (1968) *Europe: the Emergence of an Idea*, rev. edn. Edinburgh: Edinburgh University Press.

Hedetoft U. (1993) 'National Identity and the Mentalities of War in Three EC Countries', *Journal of Peace Research*, 30, 281–300.

Herzfeld M. (1982) *Ours Once More*. Austin, TX: University of Texas Press.

Herzfeld M. (1985) *The Poetics of Manhood*. Princeton, NJ: Princeton University Press.

Herzfeld M. (1987) *Anthropology through the Looking-Glass*. Cambridge: Cambridge University Press.

Herzfeld M. (1991a) 'Silence, Submission and Subversion: Towards a Poetics of Womanhood', in P. Loizos and E. Papataxiarchis (eds) *Contested Identities:*

Gender and Kinship in Modern Greece. Princeton: Princeton University Press, 79–97.

Herzfeld M. (1991b) *A Place in History*. Princeton, NJ: Princeton University Press.

Herzfeld M. (1992) *The Social Production of Indifference*. Oxford: Berg.

Herzfeld M. (1995) 'Hellenism and Occidentalism: Permutations of Performance in Greek Bourgeois Identity', in J. Carrier (ed.) *Occidentalism*. Oxford: Clarendon, 218–33.

Herzfeld M. (1997a) 'Anthropology and the Politics of Significance', *Social Analysis*, 4, 3, 107–38.

Herzfeld M. (1997b) *Cultural Intimacy*. New York: Routledge.

Herzfeld M. (2001) *Anthropology*. Oxford: Blackwell.

Herzfeld M. (2002a) 'Ethnographic Phenomenology of the Greek Spirit', in J. Revel and G. Levi (eds) *Political Uses of the Past*. London, Portland Or: Frank Cass, 13–26.

Herzfeld M. (2002b) 'The Absent Presence: Discourses of Crypto-Colonialism', *South Atlantic Quarterly*, 101, 4, 899–926.

Herzfeld M. (2004) *The Body Impolitic*. Chicago, IL: University of Chicago Press.

Herzfeld, M. (2005) *Cultural Intimacy*, 2nd edn. New York and London: Routledge.

Hess H. (2003) 'Like Zealots and Romans: Terrorism and the Empire in the 21st Century', *Crime, Law and Social Change*, 39, 4, 339–57.

Hirschkop K. (1990) 'Heteroglossia and the Civil Society: Bakhtin's Public Square and the Politics of Modernity', *Studies in the Literary Imagination*, 23, 1, 65–75.

Hirschon R. (1998) *Heirs of the Catastrophe*. Oxford: Berghahn.

Hitchcock P. (1993) *Dialogics of the Oppressed*. Minneapolis, MN: University of Minnesota Press.

Hobsbawm E. (1959) *Primitive Rebels*. Manchester: Manchester University Press.

Hobsbawm E. (1972) *Bandits*. London: Weidenfeld and Nicolson.

Hobsbawm E. (2000) *Bandits*, new edn. London: Weidenfeld and Nicolson.

Hoffmann S. (2000) 'Nationalism and World Order', in K. Goldmann, U. Hannerz and C. Westin (eds) *Nationalism and Internationalism in the Post-Cold War Era*. London: Routledge, 197–215.

Holt J.C. (1989) *Robin Hood*. London: Thames and Hudson.

Honneth A. (1992) *The Struggle for Recognition*. Cambridge: Polity.

Honneth A. (2001) 'Recognition or Redistribution? Changing Perspectives on the Moral Order of Society', *Theory, Culture and Society*, 18, 2/3, 43–55.

Honneth A. (2007) *Disrespect*. Cambridge: Polity.

Honneth A. and H. Joas (1988) *Social Action and Human Nature*, translated by R. Meyer. Cambridge: Cambridge University Press.

Hoppen T.K. (1998) *Mid-Victorian Generation, 1846–1881*. Oxford: Clarendon Press.

Horowitz D. (1985) *Ethnic Groups in Conflict*. California, LA: University of California Press.

Huntington S. (1993) 'The Clash of Civilizations', *Foreign Affairs*, 72, 3, 22–49.

Hutchinson J. (2004) 'Myth against Myth: The Nation as Ethnic Overlay', in M. Guibernaeu and J. Hutchinson (eds) *History and National Destiny*. Oxford: Blackwell, 109–24.

Hutchinson J. (2005) *Nations as Zones of Conflict*. London: Sage.

Ialemos O. (1877) *Rights and Duties of the Greeks* (in Greek). Athens: Efimeris ton Syzitiseon.

Iatridis P.E. (1870) *The Oropos Captivity and the Dilessi Massacre* (in Greek). Kefallonia: Kephallonia Printing Office.

Ignatiev N. (1995) *How the Irish became White*. London and New York: Routledge.

Independence Greque (23 May 1870).

Inglis D. and R. Robertson (2004) 'Behind the Gates of the *Polis*: Reconfiguring Sociology's Ancient Inheritance', *Journal of Classical Sociology*, 4, 2, 165–89.

Inglis D. and R. Robertson (2005) 'The Ecumenical Analytic: "Globalization", Reflexivity and the Revolution in Greek Historiography', *European Journal of Social Theory*, 8, 2, 99–122.

Ivy M. (1995) *Discourses of the Vanishing: Modernity, Phantasm, Japan*. Chicago: University of Chicago Press.

James P. (2006) 'Theorizing Nation Formation in the Context of Imperialism and Globalism', in G. Delanty and K. Kumar (ed.) *The Sage Handbook of Nations and Nationalism*. London: Sage, 369–81.

Jay M. (1984) *Adorno*. Cambridge, MA: Harvard University Press.

Jay M. (1993) *Downcast Eyes: The Denigration of Vision in Twentieth-Century French Thought*. Berkeley: University of California Press.

Jebb Sir R.C. (1880) *Modern Greece, Two Lectures Delivered before the Philosophical Institution of Edinburgh*. London, Glasgow: Macmillan and Co.

Jelavich B. (1983) *History of the Balkans*, I–II. Cambridge: Cambridge University Press.

Jenkins B.M. (1974) *Terrorism and Kidnapping*. Santa Monica: R.AN.D. Corporation.

Jenkins R. (1998) *The Dilessi Murders*. London: Prion.

Jenkyns R. (1980) *The Victorians and Ancient Greece*. Oxford: Blackwell.

Just R. (1989) 'The Triumph of the Ethnos', in E. Tonkin, M. McDonald and M. Chapman (eds) *History and Ethnicity*. London: Routledge and Kegan Paul, 71–88.

Just R. (1995) 'Cultural Certainties and Private Doubts', in W. James (ed.) *The Pursuit of Certainty*. London: Routledge, 285–308.

Just R. (2000) *A Greek Island Cosmos: Kinship and Community on Meganisi*. Oxford: James Currey.

Kallighas P. (1987) *Thanos Vlekas* (in Greek). Athens: Nefeli.

Kandiyoti D. (1989) 'Women and the Nation-State: Political Actors or Symbolic Pawns?', in N. Yuval-Davis and F. Anthias (eds) *Woman/Nation/State*. Basingstoke: Macmillan, 126–49.

Kapferer B. (ed.) (1976) *Transaction and Meaning*. Philadelphia: Institute for the Study of Human Issues.

Kaplan M. (1995) 'Panopticon in Poona: An Essay on Foucault and Colonialism', *Cultural Anthropology*, 10, 1, 85–98.

Kapllani G. and N. Mai (2005) '"Greece Belongs to the Greeks!" The Case of the Greek Flag in the Hands of an Albanian Student', in R. King, N. Mai and S. Schwandner Sievers (eds) *The New Albanian Migration*. Brighton: Sussex Academic Press, 153–72.

Karakasidou A. (1994) 'Sacred Scholars, Profane Advocates: Intellectuals Shaping National Consciousness in Greece', *Identities: Global Studies in Culture and Power*, 1, 1, 35–62.

Karakasidou A. (1997) *Fields of Wheat, Hills of Blood: Passages to Nationhood in Greek Macedonia 1870–1990*. Chicago: University of Chicago Press.

Karakasidou A. (2000) 'Transforming Identity, Constructing Consciousness: Coercion and Hegemony in Northwestern Greece', in V. Roudometof (ed.) *The Macedonia Question*. Boulder, CO: Columbia University Press, 55–97.

Karakasidou A. (2002) 'Cultural Illegitimacy in Greece: The Slavo-Macedonia "Non-Minority"', in R. Clogg (ed.) *Minorities in Greece*. London: Hurst & Co., 122–64.

Karayannopoulos J. (1993) *The Byzantine State* (in Greek). Thessaloniki: Vanias.

Karydis V. (1996) *Immigrants' Criminality in Greece* (in Greek). Athens: Papazisis.

Kearney M. (1995) 'The Local and the Global: The Anthropology of Globalisation and Transnationalism', *Annual Review of Anthropology*, 24, 547–65.

Kearney R. (1984) *Dialogues with Contemporary Thinkers: The Phenomenological Heritage*. Manchester: Manchester University Press.

Kelly J.D. and M. Kaplan (1990) 'History, Structure and Ritual', *Annual Review of Anthropology*, 19, 119–50.

King R. and N. Mai (2002) 'Of Myths and Mirrors: Interpretations of the Albanian Migration to Italy', *Studi Emigrazione*, 39, 145, 161–200.

King R. and N. Mai (2004) 'Albanian Immigrant in Lecce and Modena: Narratives of Rejection, Survival and Integration', *Population, Space and Place*, 10, 455–77.

Kirkwall Viscount (1864) *Four Years in the Ionian Islands*. London: Chapman and Hall.

Kitromilidis P. (1989) '"Imagined Communities" and the Origins of the National Question in the Balkans', *European History Quarterly*, 19, 2, 166–7.

Kitromilidis P. (1996) *Neohellenic Enlightenment* (in Greek). Athens: Morfotiko Idrima Ethnikis Trapezis.

Kitromilidis P. (1998) 'Europe and the Dilemmas of Greek Conscience', in P. Carabott (ed.) *Greece and Europe in the Modern Period: Aspects of a Troubled Relationship*. Centre for Hellenic Studies: King's College London, 1–15.

Kittay E.F. (2001) 'A Feminist Public Ethic of Care Meets the New Communitarian Family Policy', *Ethics*, 111, 523–47.

Kofos E. (1980) 'The Period of Withdrawal (1869–1870)' (in Greek), in *History of the Greek Nation*, XIII. Athens: Ekdotiki Athinon, 305–43.

Kojève A. (1969) *Introduction to the Reading of Hegel*. New York: Basic Books.

Kokoretsi.org (2007) 'Welcome to Kokoretsi.org' Online: http://kokoretsi.org/jpage/ index.php?option=com_content&task=view&id=1&Itemid=1 (consulted: 25 February 2008).

Koliopoulos J.S. (1987) *Brigands with a Cause: Brigandage and Irredentism in Modern Greece 1821–1912*. Oxford: Clarendon.

Koliopoulos J.S. (1988) *Brigands* (in Greek). Athens: Ermis.

Koliopoulos J.S. and T.M. Veremis (2002) *Greece: The Modern Sequel, from 1831 to the Present*. London, Hurst & Co.

Komarovsky M. (1987) *Blue-Collar Marriage*, 2nd edn. New Haven, CT: Yale University Press.

Koronaios P. (1870) *Addressed to the English State* (in Greek). Athens: Psylliakos & Co.

Kössler R. (2003) 'The Modern Nation State and Regimes of Violence: Reflections on the Current Situation', *Ritsumeikan Annual Review of International Studies*, 2, 15–36.

Koukoudis A.I. (2003) *The Vlachs: Metropolis and Diaspora*. Thessaloniki: Zitros.

Kuklick H. (1991) *The Savage Within: The Social History of British Anthropology*. Cambridge: Cambridge University Press.

Kumar K. (2000a) 'Englishness and English National Identity', in D. Morley and K. Robins (eds) *British Cultural Studies*. Oxford: Oxford University Press, 41–55.

Kumar K. (2000b) 'Nation and Empire: English and British National Identity in Comparative Perspective', *Theory and Society*, 29, 5, 575–608.

Kumar K. (2003) *The Making of English National Identity*. Cambridge: Cambridge University Press.

Kurti L. (1996) 'Homecoming: Affairs of Anthropologists in and of Eastern Europe', *Anthropology Today*, 12, 3, 11–15.

Kuzmics H. (1997) 'State Formation, Economic Development and Civilization in North-Western and Central Europe. A Comparison of Long-Term Civilizing Processes in Austria and England', *Geschichte und Gegenwart*, 16, 2, 80–91.

Kymlicka W. (2001) *Politics in the Vernacular*. Oxford: Oxford University Press.

Kyriakidís S. (1948[1938]) 'What is Folklore?' (in Greek), *Laografía*, 12, 15–19.

Kyriakidou-Nestoros A. (1975) 'Modern Greek Folklore in Modern Dimension' (in Greek), *Folklore Studies*. Athens: Olkos.

Kyriakidou-Nestoros A. (1976) *Modern Greek Studies* (in Greek). Athens: Nea Synora.

Kyriakidou-Nestoros A. (1981) 'Folk Culture' (in Greek), in *Greece: History and Civilization*. Thessaloniki: Estia, 264–78.

Laclau E. and C. Mouffe (1985) *Hegemony and Socialist Strategy: Towards a Radical Democratic Politics*. New York and London: Verso.

Lazaridis G. and E. Wickens (1999) '"Us" and the "Others." Ethnic Minorities in Greece', *Annals of Tourism Research*, 26, 3, 632–55.

Lazaridis G. and M. Koumandraki (2001) 'Deconstructing Naturalism: The Racialisation of Ethnic Minorities in Greece', in R. King (ed.) *The Mediterranean Passage*. Liverpool: Liverpool University Press, 279–301.

Le Goff J. (1993) *The Civilization of Medieval West* (in Greek), translated by Benveniste Rika. Thessaloniki: Vanias.

Leech H.H. (1869) *Letters of a Sentimental Idler from Crete, Turkey, Egypt, Nubia and the Holy Land*. New York: D. Appleton.

Leontis A. (1995) *Topographies of Hellenism*. Ithaca, NY and London: Cornell University Press.

Leoussi A. (2004) 'The Ethno-Cultural Roots of National Art', in M. Guibernaeu and J. Hutchinson (eds) *History and National Destiny*. Oxford: Blackwell, 143–59.

Letters of Mr. Frank Noël Respecting the Murder by Brigands of the Captives of Marathon and the Prosecution by the Greek Government (1871). Edinburgh: private.

Levinas E. (1969) *Totality and Infinity*. Pittsburgh: Duquesne University Press.

Lévi-Strauss C. (1953) 'Social Structure', in A. Kroeber (ed.) *Anthropology Today*. Chicago: Chicago University Press, 524–33.

Lévi-Strauss C. (1964) *Totemism*, translated by N. Rodney. London: Merlin Press.

Lévi-Strauss C. (1967) *Structural Anthropology*. New York: Doubleday.

Lévi-Strauss C. (1971) 'Race and History' (in Greek), translated by M. Voutiras, in D. Maronitis (ed.) *The Fear of Freedom*. Athens: Papazisis, 171–213.

Lévi-Strauss C. (1972[1962]) *The Savage Mind*. London: Weidenfeld and Nicolson.
Lewis B. (1993) *The Arabs in History*, new edn. Oxford: Oxford University Press.
Liakos A. (2002) 'The Construction of National Time', in J. Revel and G. Levi (eds) *Political Uses of the Past*. London, Portland Or: Frank Cass, 27–42.
Löfgren O. (1989) 'The Nationalisation of Culture', *Ethnologica Europaea*, 19, 1, 5–24.
Luhmann N. (1982) *The Differentiation of Society*. New York: Columbia University Press.
Luhmann N. (1990) 'The Paradox of System Differentiation and the Evolution of Society', in J. Alexander and P. Colomy (eds) *Differentiation Theory and Social Change*. New York: Columbia University Press, 409–40.
Luhmann N. (1995) *Social Systems*. Stanford, CA: Stanford University Press.
Lyons F.S.L. (1971) *Ireland since the Famine*. London: Weidenfeld and Nicolson.
MacKenzie G.M.M. and A.P. Irby (1877) *Travels in the Slavonic Provinces of Turkey in-Europe*, II. London: Daldy, Ibister.
Mackenzie J. (1987) 'The Imperial Pioneer and Hunter and the British Masculine Stereotype in Late Victorian and Edwardian Times', in J.A. Mangan and J. Walvin (eds) *Manliness and Amorality: Middle-Class Masculinity in Britain and America, 1800–1940*. Manchester: Manchester University Press, 176–98.
Mackenzie J. (1993) 'Occidentalism: Counterpoint and Counter-Polemic', *Journal of Historical Geography*, 19, 3, 339–44.
Mackenzie J. (1995) *Orientalism*. Manchester: Manchester University Press.
Mackenzie J. (1997) *Empires of Nature and the Nature of Empires*. East Linton: Tuckwell Press.
Mahaffy J.P. (1876) *Rambles and Studies in Greece*, 3rd edn. London: Macmillan.
Malinowksi B.C. (1916) 'Baloma: Spirits of the Dead in the Trobriand Islands', *Journal of the Research of the Anthropological Institute*, 46, 353–430.
Malinowski B. (1948) *Magic, Science and Religion, and Other Essays*. Boston: Beacon.
Malinowski B. (1967) *A Diary in the Strict Sense of the Term*. New York: Harcourt.
Mango C. (1998) *Byzantium*. London: Phoenix Giant.
Mani L. and R. Frankenberg (1985) 'The Challenge of Orientalism', *Economy and Society* 14, 2, 174–92.
Mann M. (1997) 'Has Globalization Ended the Rise and Rise of the Nation-State?', *Review of International Political Economy* 4, 3, 472–96.
Mannheim K. (1968 [1936]) *Ideology and Utopia: An Introduction to the Sociology of Knowledge*, translated by L. Wirth and E. Shils. New York: Harcourt, Brace & World.
Mansfield P. and J. Collard (1988) *The Beginning of the Rest of Your Life: A Portrait of Newly-Wed Marriage*. London: Macmillan.
Mansfield P. and C. Jean (1988) *The Beginning of the Rest of your Life?* Basingstoke: Macmillan.
Marcus M.A. (1987) '"Horsemen are the Fence of the Land": Honor and History Among the Ghiyata of Eastern Morocco', in D. Gilmore (ed.) *Honor and Shame and the Unity of the Mediterranean*. Washington: American Anthropological Association, 49–59.
Mauss M. (1954) *The Gift*, translated by I. Cunnison. London: Cohen & West.
Mazower M. (2000) 'Three Forms of Political Justice: Greece, 1944–1945', in M. Mazower (ed.) *After the War was Over: Reconstructing the Family, the Nation and the State, 1943–1960*. Princeton, NJ: Princeton University Press, 24–41.

Mbembe A. (2001) *On the Postcolony*. Berkeley, CA: University of California Press.

McCall D.F. (1980) 'Radcliffe-Brown vs. Historical Ethnology: The Consequences of an Anthropological Dispute for the Study of Africa's Past', *The International Journal of African Historical Studies*, 13, 1, 95–102.

McCannell D. (1973) 'Staged Authenticity: Arrangements of Social Space in Tourist Settings', *American Journal of Sociology* 79, 3, 589–603.

McClintock A. (1991) 'No Longer in Future Heaven: Women and Nationalism in South Africa', *Transition*, 51, 104–23.

McClintock A. (1995) *Imperial Leather: Race, Gender and Sexuality in the Colonial Context*. New York: Routledge.

McEnroe J.C. (2002) 'Cretan Questions: Politics and Archaeology 1898–1913', in Y. Hamilakis (ed.) *Labyrinth Revisited*. Oxford: Oxbow Books, 61–71.

McGee M. (1975) 'In Search of "the People": A Rhetorical Alternative', *Quarterly Journal of Speech*, 61, 235–49.

McGrew T. (1992) 'A Global Society', in T. McGrew, D. Held and S. Hall (eds) *Modernity and its Futures*. Oxford: Polity Press and Open University, 62–113.

McGrew W. (1985) *Land and Revolution in Modern Greece 1800–1881*. Kent, OH: Kent State Press.

McVeigh R. (1997) 'Theorising Sedentarism', in T. Acton, *Gypsy Politics and Traveller Identity*. Hatfield, University of Hertfordshire, 7–25.

Means J. (1970) 'Political Kidnapping and Terrorism', *North American Review*, 255, 16–19.

Meinecke F. (1970) *Cosmopolitanism and the National State*. Princeton, NJ: Princeton University Press.

Melosi D. (2000) 'Changing Representations of the Criminal', *British Journal of Criminology*, 40, 2, 296–320.

Meltzer B.N. and G.R. Musolf (2002) ' Resentment and *Ressentiment*', *Sociological Inquiry*, 72, 2, 240–55.

Metcalf S. (2002) *They Lie, We Lie*. New York: Routledge.

Milisis G. (1871) *Two Speeches by G. Milisis, MP for Ermionis, Delivered in Parliament* (in Greek). Athens: Koinovoulio.

Mill J. (1876) *The Ottomans in Europe*. London: Weldon & Co.

Miller A.H. (1980) *Terrorism and Hostage Negotiations*. Boulder, CO: Westview Press.

Montenyohl E.L. (1988) 'Andrew Lang's Contributions to English Folklore Narrative Scholarship', *Western Folklore*, 47, 4, 269–84.

Moore B. (1978) *Injustice: The Social Bases of Obedience and Revolt*. New York: Macmillan.

Moorehead A. (1970) *The Blue Nile*. London: Hamilton Press.

Morgenthau H.J. and K.W. Thompson (1984) *Politics Among Nations*. New York: Alfred A. Knopf.

Moskonisios A. (1869) *The Mirror of Brigandage in Greece* (in Greek). Ermoupolis: unknown.

Mosse G.L. (1995) 'Racism and Nationalism', *Nations and Nationalism*, 1, 2, 163–73.

Mosse G.L. (1996) *The Image of Man*. New York: Oxford University Press.

Murray J. (1872) *A Handbook for Travellers in Greece*, 4th edn. London: John Murray.

Nagel J. (1998) 'Masculinity and Nationalism: Gender and Sexuality in the Making of Nations', *Ethnic and Racial Studies*, 21, 2, 242–69.

Nairn T. (1977) *The Break-Up of Britain*. London: New Left Books.

Newton C.T. (1865) *Travels and Discoveries in the Levant*, I–II. London: Day & Son.

Nielsen G. (1995) 'Bakhtin and Habermas: Toward a Transcultural Ethics', *Theory and Society*, 24, 6, 803–35.

Nielsen G. (2002) *The Norms of Answerability*. New York: SUNY.

Nielsen K. (1999) 'Cultural Nationalism: Neither Ethnic nor Civic', in R. Beiner (ed.) *Theorizing Nationalism*. Albany: SUNY, 119–30.

Nielsen K. (2003) 'Toward a Liberal Socialist Cosmopolitan Nationalism', *International Journal of Philosophical Studies*, 11, 4, 437–63.

Nietzsche F.W. (1980) *On the Advantage and Disadvantage of History for Life*. Indianapolis, IN: Hacket.

Nietzsche F.W. (1996) *On the Genealogy of Morals*, translated by S. Douglas. Oxford: Oxford University Press.

Norton D.E. (1995) *Through the Eyes of A Child*. Cleveland, OH: Prentice-Hall.

Nussbaum M. (1996) 'Patriotism and Cosmopolitanism', in J. Cohen (ed.) *For Love of Country*. Boston, MA: Beacon Press, 2–17.

Nussbaum M. *et al.* (2003) *Essays on Gender and Governance*. New Delhi, India: United Nations Development Programme.

O'Mahony P. and G. Delanty (2001) *Rethinking Irish History*. Basingstoke: Palgrave.

O'Neill J. (1999) 'Economy, Equality and Recognition', in L. Ray and A. Sayer (eds) *Culture and Economy after the Cultural Turn*. London: Sage, 76–91.

P. (1878) *Fantasy and Truth or The Great Idea of Hellenism and the Course of Things* (in Greek). Athens: unknown.

Pantazidis I. (1876) *Inaugural Speech* (27 February 1876) (in Greek). Athens: Ermis.

Parry J. (1986) '*The Gift*, the Indian Gift and the "Indian Gift"', *Man* N.S., 21, 3, 453–73.

Parsons T. (1971) *The System of Modern Societies*. Englewood C., NJ: Prentice Hall.

Parsons T. (1977) *Social Systems and the Evolution of Action Theory*. New York: Free Press.

Peckham R.S. (2001) *National Histories, Natural States: Nationalism and the Politics of Place in Greece*. London and New York: I. B. Tauris.

Pedro-Ruiz T. (2002) ' Political Uses of History in Spain', in J. Revel and G. Levi (eds) *Political Uses of the Past*. London: Frank Cass, 95–116.

Pekios A.I. (1880) *A Spiritual View of Greece under the Turkish Rule, or a Sketch of the Intellectual condition of the Greek Race under the Ottoman Yoke* (in Greek). Constantinople: Zellitch.

Pemberton J. (1994) *On the Subject of 'Java'*. Ithaca, NY: Cornell University Press.

Pešić V. (1995) *Serbian Nationalism and the Origins of the Yugoslav Crisis*. Washington: US Institute for Peace.

Pickel A. (2004) 'Homo Nationis: The Psychosocial Infrastructure of the Nation-State Order', *Paper presented at the annual meeting of the American Sociological Association, San Francisco, CA*. Online. http://www.allacademic.com/meta/p109061_index.html (consulted: 21 September 2007).

Polítis N. (1909) 'Folklore' (in Greek), *Laografía*, 1, 10–14.

Poole S.L. (ed.) (1878) *The People of Turkey: Twenty Years Residence among Bulgarians, Greeks, Albanians, Turks and Armenians, by a Consul's Daughter and Wife*, I. London: John Murray.

Poulantzas N. (1978) *State, Power, Socialism*. London: New Left.

Poulantzas N. (1973) *Political Power and Social Classes*. London: New Left.

Price R. and C. Reus-Smit (1998) 'Dangerous Liaisons? Critical International Relations Theory and Constructivism', *European Journal of International Relations*, 4, 3, 259–94.

Psomiades H.J. (1976) 'The Character of the New Greek State', in N.P. Diamandouros (ed.) *Hellenism and First Greek War of Liberation*. Thessaloniki: Institute for Balkan Studies, 147–57.

Psychas N. (1870) *A Revolutionary Portrait of Crete* (in Greek). Athens: unknown.

R(ikakis) A. (1870) *Thoughts on the Suppression of Brigandage* (in Greek) Athens: Ermis.

Rapport N. (2002) 'Best of British! An Introduction to the Anthropology of Britain', in N. Rapport (ed.) *British Subjects: An Anthropology of Britain*. Oxford: Berg, 3–26.

Ray L. (1996) *Social Theory and the Crisis of State Socialism*. Cheltenham: Edward Elgar.

Ray L. (1999) 'Memory, Trauma and Genocidal Nationalism', *Sociological Research Online*, 4, 2. Online. http://www.socresonline.org.uk/socresonline/4/2/ray.html (consulted: 20 January 2007).

Renan E. (1990) 'What is a Nation?' [1882] in H.K. Bhabha (ed.) *Nation and Narration*. Westport CT, London and New York: Routledge, 8–22.

Rhighopoulos T. (1979[1881) *Memoirs from the Beginning of the Revolution until the Year 1881* (in Greek). Athens: unknown.

Richardson M. (1990) 'Enough Said: Reflections on Orientalism', *Anthropology Today*, 6, 4, 16–19.

Ricoeur P. (1995) 'Evil, a Challenge to Philosophy and Theology', in P. Ricoeur (ed.) *Figuring the Sacred*. Indianapolis, IN: Fortress, 249–61.

Ricoeur P. (1999) 'Memory and Forgetting', in R. Kearney and M. Dooley (eds) *Questioning Ethics*. London: Routledge, 5–12.

Ricoeur P. (2004) *Memory, History, Forgetting*. Chicago: University of Chicago Press.

Robinson F. (1999) *Globalizing Care: Ethics, Feminist Theory, and International Relations*. Boulder, CO: Westview Press.

Robinson R. and J. Gallagher (1967) *Africa and the Victorians: The Official Mind of Imperialism*. New York: Macmillan.

Roginsky D. (2006) 'Nationalism and Ambivalence: Ethnicity, Gender and Folklore as Categories of Otherness', *Patterns of Prejudice*, 40, 3, 237–58.

Rosoux V.-B. (2001) 'National Identity in France and Germany: From Mutual Exclusion to Negotiation', *International Negotiation*, 2, 175–98.

Roudometof V. (1999) 'Nationalism, Globalization, Eastern Orthodoxy: "Unthinking" the "Clash of civilizations" in Eastern Europe', *European Journal of Social Theory*, 2, 2, 233–47.

Roving Englishman (1877) *Turkey being Sketches from Life*. London and New York: Routledge & Sons.

Ruggie J.G. (1998) 'What Makes the World Hang Together? Neo-Utilitarianism and the Social Constructivist Challenge', *International Organization*, 52, 855–87.

Sahlins M. (1965) 'On the Sociology of Primitive Exchange', in M. Banton (ed.) *The Relevance of Models for Social Anthropology*. London: Tavistock, 139–236.

Sahlins M. (1972) *Stone Age Economics*. Chicago: Aldine.

Said E. (1978) *Orientalism*. London: Penguin.

Said E. (1994) *Culture and Imperialism*. London: Vintage.

Sampson E. (1993) *Celebrating the Other: A Dialogic Account of Human Nature*. Boulder, CO: Westview Press.

Sangiovanni A. (2007) 'Global Justice, Reciprocity and the State', *Philosophy and Public Affairs*, 35, 1, 3–39.

Sassen S. (2002a) 'The Repositioning of Citizenship: Emergent Subjects and Spaces for Politics', *Berkeley Journal of Sociology*, 46, 4–25.

Sassen S. (2002b) 'Towards a Post-National and Denationalized Citizenship', in E.F. Isin and B.S. Turner (eds) *Handbook of Citizenship Studies*. London: Sage, 277–92.

Sayer A. (1999) 'Valuing Culture and Economy', in L. Ray and A. Sayer (eds) *Culture and Economy after the Cultural Turn*. London: Sage, 53–75.

Scheler M. (1961) *Ressentiment*, translated by W.W. Holdheim. New York: Free Press.

Schieffelin E.L. (1976) *The Sorrow of the Lonely and the Burning of the Dancers*. New York: St. Martin's Press.

Schieffelin E.L. (1980) 'Reciprocity and Construction of Reality', *Man N.S.*, 15, 3, 502–17.

Schneider D.M. (1977) 'Kinship, Nationality and Religion: Toward a Definition of Kinship', in J. Dolgin, D. Kemnitzer and D.M. Schneider (eds) *Symbolic Anthropology*. New York: Columbia University Press, 63–71.

Schneider D.M. (1979) 'Kinship, Community and Locality in American Culture', in A. Lichtman and J. Challinor (eds) *Kin and Communities*. Washington, DC: Smithsonian University Press, 155–74.

Schneider D.M. (1980) *American Kinship: A Cultural Account*, 2nd edn. Chicago: University of Chicago Press.

Schneider D.M. (2004) 'What is Kinship All About?', in R. Parkin and L. Stone (eds) *Kinship and Family*. Oxford, MA: Blackwell, 257–74.

Schneider J. (1971) 'Of Vigilance and Virgins: Honor, Shame and Access to Resources in Mediterranean Societies', *Ethnology*, 1, 1–24.

Scott J. (1986) 'Everyday Forms of Peasant Resistance', in J. Scott and B. Kerkvleit (eds) *Everyday Forms of Peasant Resistance in Southeast Asia*. London: Cass, 5–35.

Seremetakis N. (1996) 'In Search for Barbarians: Borders in Pain,' *American Anthropologist*, 98, 3, 488–91.

Seremetakis N. (ed.) (1994) *The Senses Still: Memory as Material Culture*. Boulder, CO: Westview.

Sheridan G. (1987) 'Pearse's Sacrifice: Christ and Cuchulain Crucified and Risen in Easter Rising 1916', in J. Obelkevich, L. Roper and R. Samuel (eds) *Disciplines of Faith: Studies in Religion, Politics and Patriarchy*. London and New York: Routledge and Kegan Paul, 479–97.

Skinner H.E.I. (1868) *Hardships in Crete during 1867* (in Greek), translated by T.G. Dixon. Athens: Ethnikon Typografeion.

Skopetea E. (1988) *The 'Model Kingdom' and the Great Idea: Aspects of the National Problem in Greece (1830–1880)* (in Greek). Athens: Polytypo.

Skopetea E. (1992) *The East Sets in the West: Images from the End of the Ottoman Empire* (in Greek). Athens: Gnosi.

Skopetea E. (1999) *Fallmerayer: Tricks of the Rival Awe* (in Greek). Athens: Themelio.

Skultans V. (1998) *The Testimony of Lives: Narrative and Memory in Post Soviet Latvia.* London and New York: Routledge.

Sloan R. (2000) *William Smith O'Brien and the Young Ireland Rebellion of 1848.* Portland, OR: Four Courts Press.

Slobodin R. (1978) *W.H.R. Rivers.* New York: Columbia University Press.

Sluga G. (1998) 'Identity, Gender and the History of European Nationalism', *Nations and Nationalism*, 4, 1, 87–111.

Smith A.D. (1971) *Theories of Nationalism.* London: Duckworth.

Smith A.D. (1981) *The Ethnic Revival in the Modern World.* Cambridge: Cambridge University Press.

Smith A.D. (1984) 'National Identity and Myths of Ethnic Descent', *Research in Social Movements, Conflict, Change*, 7, 95–130.

Smith A.D. (1990) 'Towards A Global Culture?', *Theory, Culture & Society*, 7, 2, 171–91.

Smith A.D. (1995) *Nations and Nationalism in a Global Era.* Cambridge: Polity Press.

Smith A.D. (1999) *Myths and Memories of the Nation.* Oxford and New York: Oxford University Press.

Smith A.D. (2000) *The Nation in History.* Hanover, NH: University Press of New England.

Smith A.D. (2004) 'History and National Destiny: Responses and Clarifications', in M. Guibernaeu and J. Hutchinson (eds) *History and National Destiny.* Oxford: Blackwell, 195–209.

Smith D. (1989) 'Sociological Theory: Writing Patriarchy in Feminist Texts', in R. Wallace (ed.) *Feminism and Sociological Theory*, Newbury Park, CA: Sage, 34–64.

Smith D. (1998) 'Bakhtin and the Dialogic of Sociology: An Investigation', in M.M. Bell and M. Gardiner (eds) *Bakhtin and the Human Sciences.* London: Sage, 63–77.

Smith R. (2007) *Being Human.* New York: Columbia University Press.

Sotiropoulos S. (1866) *Thirty-six Days of Captivity and Consort with the Brigands* (in Greek). Athens: private.

Soulier G. (1978) 'European Integration and the Suppression of Terrorism', *Review of Contemporary Law*, 2, 2, 21–45.

Soysal Y.N. (1994) *Limits of Citizenship.* Chicago: University of Chicago Press.

Soysal Y.N. (1997) 'Changing Parameters of Citizenship and Claims-Making: Organized Islam in European Public Spheres', *Theory and Society*, 26, 4, 509–27.

Spohn W. (2005) 'National Identities and Collective Memory in an Enlarged Europe', in K. Eder and W. Spohn (ed.) *Collective Memory and European Identity.* Aldershot: Ashgate, 1–16.

Spratt Captain T.A.B. (1865) *Travels and Researches in Crete*, I. London: John Van Voorst.

Spurr D. (1993) *The Rhetoric of Empire.* Durham and London: Durham University Press.

St Clair W. (1977) 'The Philhellenes and the War of Independence', in J.T.A. Koumoulides (ed.) *Greece in Transition.* London: Zeno, 272–82.

Stavrianos L. (1958) *The Balkans Since the Nineteenth Century*. New York: Harper.

Stearns F.P. (1905) *Cambridge Sketches*. Philadelphia, Pennsylvania: J.B. Lippincott.

Stebbins R.A. (1970) 'On Misunderstandings of the Concept of Commitment: A Theoretical Clarification', *Social Forces*, 48, 4, 526–9.

Stevens C. (1989) *Ransom and Murder in Greece: Lord Muncaster's Journal, 1870*. Cambridge: Lutterworth Press.

Stewart C. (1991) *Demons and the Devil*. Princeton: Princeton University Press.

Stocking G.W. (1987) *Victorian Anthropology*. New York: Free Press.

Stocking G.W. Jr. (1983) 'The Ethnographer's Magic: Fieldwork in British Anthropology from Tylor to Malinowski', in G.W. Stocking (ed.) *Observers Observed: Essays on Ethnographic Fieldwork*. Madison: University of Wisconsin Press, 70–120.

Stocking G.W. Jr. (1996) *After Tylor*. London: Athlone.

Stoler A.L. (1989a) 'Making Empire Respectable: The Politics of Race and Sexual Morality in Twentieth-Century Colonial Cultures', *American Ethnologist*, 16, 4, 634–60.

Stoler A.L. (1989b) 'Rethinking Colonial Categories: European Communities and the Boundaries of Rule', *Comparative Studies in Society and History*, 31, 1, 134–61.

Stoler A.L. (1995) *Race and the Education of Desire*. Durham, NC: Duke University Press.

Strathern M. (1988) *The Gender of the Gift*. California, LA: University of California Press.

Strickland E. (1863) *Greece: Its Conditions, Prospects and Resources*. London: The London Review.

Šuber D. (2006) 'Myth, Collective Trauma and War in Serbia: A Cultural-Hermeneutical Appraisal', *Anthropology Matters*, 8, 1, 1–9. Online. http://www.anthropology matters.com (consulted: 22 April 2007).

Sutton D.E. (2000) *Memories Cast in Stone: The Relevance of the Past in Everyday Life*. Oxford, New York: Berg.

Svoronos N. (1991) *A History of Modern Greece* (in Greek). Athens: Themelio.

Swindal J. (1999) *Reflection Revisited*. New York: Fordham University Press.

Symonds R. (1986) *Oxford and Empire: The Last Lost Cause?* Oxford: Clarendon.

T.A. (1974) *Cartoon Album* (in Greek). Athens: unknown.

Tan K.C. (2004) *Justice Without Borders*. Cambridge: Cambridge University Press.

Tannenbaum F. (1966) *Peace by Revolution: Mexico After 1910*. New York and London: Columbia University Press.

Taylor C. (1989) *Sources of the Self*. Cambridge: Cambridge University Press.

Taylor C. (1994) *Multiculturalism*. Princeton, NJ: Princeton University Press.

Taylor C. (1995) *Philosophical Arguments*. Cambridge, Mass: Harvard University Press.

The Oxford English Dictionary (1933), IV. Oxford: Clarendon.

Theodossopoulos D. (2003) 'Degrading Others and Honouring Ourselves: Ethnic Stereotypes as Categories and as Explanations', *Journal of Mediterranean Studies* 13, 2, 177–88.

Theodossopoulos D. (2004) 'The Turks and their Nation in the Worldview of Greeks in Patras', *History and Anthropology* 15, 1, 29–45.

Thomas N. (1994) *Colonialism's Culture: Anthropology, Travel and Government*. London: Polity Press.

Thomas N. (1996) *Out of Time: History and the Evolution in Anthropological Discourse.* Michigan: Michigan University Press.

Thompson E.P. (1971) 'The Moral Economy of the Crowd in the Eighteenth Century', *Past and Present*, 50, 76–136.

Thompson J. (1994) *Mercenaries, Pirates and Sovereigns: State-Building and Extraterritorial Violence in Early Modern Europe.* Princeton, NJ: Princeton University Press.

Thompson S. (2006) *The Political Theory of Recognition.* Cambridge: Polity.

Thongchai W. (1994) *Siam Mapped: A History of the Geo-Body of the Nation.* Honolulu, HI: Hawaii University Press.

Tilly C. (1975) 'Reflections on the History of European State-Making', in C. Tilly (ed.) *The Formation of National States in Europe.* Princeton NJ: Princeton University Press, 3–83.

Tilly C. (1984) *Big Structure, Large Processes, Huge Comparisons.* New York: Russel Sage Foundation.

Tilly C. (1993) *European Revolutions: 1492–1992.* Oxford: Blackwell.

Tilly C. (2003) *The Politics of Collective Violence.* Cambridge: Cambridge University Press.

Todorova M. (1997) *Imagining the Balkans.* Oxford: Oxford University Press.

Towner J. (1985) 'The Grand Tour: A Key Phase in the History of Tourism', *Annals of Tourism Research*, 12, 3, 293–333.

Townshend C. (1983) *Political Violence in Ireland.* Oxford: Clarendon.

Tozer H.F. (1869) *Researches in the Highlands of Turkey*, I–II. London: John Murray.

Tozer H.F. (1873) *Lectures on the Geography of Greece.* London: John Murray.

Tozer H.F. (1890) *The Islands of the Aegean.* Oxford: Oxford University Press.

Trevor-Roper H. (1986) 'The Invention of Tradition: the Highland Tradition of Scotland', in E. Hobsbawm and T. Ranger (eds) *The Invention of Tradition.* Cambridge: Cambridge University Press, 15–41.

Trey G. (1992) 'Communicative Ethics in the Face of Alterity: Habermas, Levinas and the Problem of Post-Conventional Universalism', *Praxis International*, 11, 4, 412–27.

Triantafyllidou A. (1998) 'National Identity and the "Other"', *Ethnic and Racial Studies*, 21, 4, 593–612.

Tricha L. (1991) *Diplomacy and Politics* (in Greek). Athens: Eteria Ellinikou Loghotekhnikou ke Istorikou Archeiou.

Tsingos A. (1983) 'Language Shift Among the Albanian Speakers of Greece', *Anthropological Linguistics*, 25, 288–308.

Tsoukalas C. (2002) 'The Irony of Symbolic Reciprocities: The Greek Meanings of 'Europe' as a Historical Inversion of the European Meaning of 'Greece', in M. af Malmborg and B. Stra[o]th (eds) *The Meaning of Europe*, Oxford: Berg, 27–50.

Tuckerman C. (1872) *The Greeks of Today.* London: Sampson Low.

Tuckerman C. (1877) *The Greeks of Today* (in Greek), translated by A. Zyghomalas. Athens: Filokalia.

Turner B.S. (2001) 'Cosmopolitan Virtue: On Religion in a Global Age', *European Journal of Social Theory*, 4, 2, 131–42.

Turner B.S. (2006) 'Classical Sociology and Cosmopolitanism: A Critical Defense of the Social', *The British Journal of Sociology*, 57, 1, 133–51.

Turner V. (1967) *The Forest of Symbols*. Ithaca, NY: Cornell University Press.
Turner V. (1969) *The Ritual Process: Structure and Anti-Structure*. New York: Aldine De Gruyter.
Tylor E.B. (1964[1878]) *Researches into the Early History of Mankind and the Development of Civilization*. Chicago: University of Chicago Press.
Tzanelli R. (2004) 'Giving Gifts (and then Taking Them Back): Identity, Reciprocity and Symbolic Power in the Context of *Athens 2004*', *The Journal of Cultural Research*, 8, 4, 425–46.
Tzanelli R. (2006) '"Not MY Flag!" Citizenship and Nationhood in the Margins of Europe (Greece, October 2000/2003)', *Ethnic & Racial Studies*, 29, 1, 27–49.
Tzanelli R. (2007a) 'Solitary Amnesia as National Memory: From Habermas to Luhmann', *International Journal of Humanities*, 5, 4, 253–60.
Tzanelli R. (2007b) *The Cinematic Tourist: Explorations in Globalization, Culture and Resistance*. London: Routledge.
Tzanelli R. (2007c) 'The Politics of "Forgetting" as Poetics of Belonging: Between Self-Narration and Reappraisal (Michaniona, October 2000/2003)', *Nations and Nationalism*, 13, 4, 1–20.
Tziovas D. (1985) 'The Organic Discourse of Nationalistic Demoticism: A Tropological Approach', in M. Alexiou and V. Lambropoulos (eds) *The Text and its Margins*. New York: Pella, 253–77.
Urry J. (1990) *The Tourist Gaze*. London and New Delhi: Sage.
Urry J. (1996) 'Tourism, Culture and Social Inequality', in Y. Apostolopoulos, S. Leivadi and A. Yannakis (eds) *The Sociology of Tourism*. London: Routledge, 114–33.
Van den Berghe P. (1978) 'Race and Ethnicity: A Socio-Biological Perspective', *Ethnic and Racial Studies*, 4, 4, 401–11.
Van Dijk T.A. (1993) 'Analysing Racism Through Discourse Analysis', in J. Stanfield (ed.) *Race and Ethnicity in Research Methods*. Newbury Park, CA: Sage, 92–134.
Van Kreuren D.K. (1989) 'Cabinets and Culture: Victorian Anthropology and the Museum Context', *Journal of the History of Behavioural Sciences*, 25, 26–39.
Van Lennep Reverend H.J. (1862[1962]) *The Oriental Album*. New York: Anson D. Randolph.
Van Lennep Reverend H.J. (1870) *Travels in Little Known Parts of Asia Minor*, I. London: John Murray.
Verdery K. (1998) 'Transnationalism, Nationalism, Citizenship and Property: Eastern Europe since 1989', *American Ethnologist*, 25, 2, 291–306.
Veremis T. (1990) 'From the National State to the Stateless Nation', in M. Blinkhorn and T. Veremis (eds) *Modern Greece*. Athens: Eliamep, 9–22.
Verney S. (2002) 'Challenges to Greek Identity', *European Political Science*, 1, 2, 12–16.
Vertovec S. and R. Cohen (2002) *Conceiving Cosmopolitanism*. Oxford: Oxford University Press.
Villa D.R. (1996) *Arendt and Heidegger: The Fate of the Political*. Princeton, NJ: Princeton University Press.
Vitti M. (1990) *Military Life in Greece* (in Greek). Athens: Ermis.
Vitti M. (1991) *Ideological Function of Greek Ethography* (in Greek). Athens: Odysseas.

Vournas T. (1990) 'The Domination of Brigandage' (in Greek), Preface in E. About, *The King of the Mountains*. Athens: Tolidi Bros.

Voutira E. (2003) 'When Greeks Meet other Greeks: Settlement Policy Issues in the Contemporary Greek Context', in R. Hirschon (ed.) *Crossing the Aegean*. New York and Oxford: Berghahn, 145–59.

Walby S. (2006) 'Gender Approaches to Nations and Nationalism', in G. Delanty and K. Kumar (eds) *The Sage Handbook of Nations and Nationalism*. London: Sage, 118–28.

Walker M. (1864) *Through Macedonia to the Albanian Lakes*. London: Chapman & Hall.

Wallerstein I. (1974) *The Modern World System*, I. New York: Academic Press.

Wallerstein I. (1980) *The Modern World System*, II. New York: Academic Press.

Weber M. (1978a) *Economy and Society*. Berkeley, CA: University of California Press.

Weber M. (1978b) *Selections in Translation*, edited by W.G. Runciman and translated by E. Matthews. Cambridge: Cambridge University Press.

Weber M. (1985) *The Protestant Ethic and the Spirit of Capitalism*, translated by T. Parsons. London: Unwin Hyman.

Weber M. (2002) ' Basic Sociological Terms', in C. Calhoun *et al.* (eds) *Classical Sociological Theory*. Oxford: Blackwell.

Weiner A. (1980) 'Reproduction: A Replacement for Reciprocity', *American Ethnologist*, 7, 1, 71–85.

Weiner A. (1992) *Inalienable Possessions*. Berkeley, CA: University of California Press.

White H. (1973) *Metahistory*. Baltimore: Johns Hopkins University Press.

White H. (1978) *Tropics of Discourse*. Baltimore: Johns Hopkins University Press.

Wilkinson I. (2005) *Suffering*. Cambridge: Polity.

Williams F. (2004) *Rethinking Families*. London: Calouste Gulbenkian Foundation.

Williams K. (1997) 'National Myths in the New Czech Liberalism', in G. Hosking and G. Scöpflin (eds) *Myths and Nationhood*. New York: Routledge, 132–40.

Winnifrith T. (1987) *The Vlachs*. London: Duckworth.

Winnifrith T. (1992) *Perspectives of Albania*. London: Macmillan.

Wintle M. (1998) 'Europe's Image: Visual Representations of Europe from the Earliest Times to the Twentieth Century', in M. Wintle (ed.) *Culture and Identity in Europe*. Aldershot: Ashgate, 52–95.

Wolff K. (1958) 'The Challenge of Durkheim and Simmel', *The American Journal of Sociology*, 63, 590–6.

Wolffe J. (1994) *God and Greater Britain*. London and New York: Routledge.

Wolin S.S. (1989) *The Presence of the Past*. Baltimore, MD: John Hopkins University Press.

Wyse Sir T. (1871) *Impressions of Greece*. London: Hurst & Blackett.

Xenos S. (1865) *East and West: The Annexation of the Ionian Islands to the Kingdom of Greece*. London: Trübner & Co.

Xenos S. (1881) *The Demure Koumoundouros* (in Greek). Athens: private.

Yar M. (2000) 'From Actor to Spectator: Hannah Arendt's "Two Theories" of Political Action', *Philosophy and Social Criticism*, 26, 2, 1–27.

Yar M. (2001) 'Beyond Nancy Fraser's "Perspectival Dualism"', *Economy and Society*, 30, 3, 288–303.

Young J.F. (1876) *Five Weeks in Greece*. London: Sampson Low.
Young M. and P. Willmott (1986) *Family and Kinship in East London*, rev. edn. London: Routledge and Kegan Paul.
Yuval-Davis N. (1997) *Gender and Nation*. London: Sage.
Zakythinos D.A. (1976) *The Making of Modern Greece*. Oxford: Blackwell.
Zelizer V.A. (1994) *Pricing the Priceless Child*. Princeton, NJ: Princeton University Press.
Žižek S. (1988) 'The Object as a limit of Discourse: Approaches to the Lacanian Real', *Prose Studies*, 11, 3, 94–121.
Žižek S. (1991) *For they Know Not What They Do*. New York and London: Verso.
Žižek S. (1999) *The Ticklish Subject*. London and New York: Verso.

Greek and British periodical press (selected articles, 1864–1881)

Aión.
Clió.
Cornhill Magazine, 126, June 1870.
Levant Herald.
Méllon.
Palingenesía.
Pall Mall Gazette.
Rescued Works of the Greek Philological Society in Constantinople (in Greek), (December 1865 to May 1870), IV, Constantinople.
Philological Society 'Parnassos' (in Greek), I, Pamphlet 1, April 1870.
The Daily News.
The Daily Telegraph.
The Morning Post.
The Scotsman.
The Times.

Index

About, E., 112, 113
  The King of the Mountains (1990), 112
abstraction, 24, 72
Abyssinia, 41–2, 44
Abyssinian episode (1860s), 30
academic debates, 5, 79
academic disciplines, 76
Achmetaga, 94
affiliations, 5, 156, 162
affinities, 7, 16, 35, 129, 146
  dialogical interpretations, 129
affirmative action, 41, 138
agency, 10, 13, 36
Ainian, Dimitris (1800–81), 145
Aión, (Greek pro-government
  newspaper), 35, 51, 54, 123
áksestoi Vláchoi, 58
Albanian Epos (1940–1941), 64
Albanian(s), 26, 49, 50, 52, 54, 56, 57,
  58, 59, 60–4, 66, 78
  brigands, 66
  of Greece, 50, 54, 56, 58
  of Illyrian origin, 50
Albanian-Vlach-brigands, 54
Albanian-Vlachs, 52, 53, 56
Alexander the Great, 147
aliens/alien elements, 5, 47, 49, 60,
  64, 66, 82, 91, 169, 170, 187,
  188
alterity, 149–50
Altertumswissenschaft (science of
  'ancient civilizations'), 7
Althusserian resonance, 23
amateur anthropologists, 81, 90–1
ambiguities, 10, 14, 24, 31, 33, 38, 44,
  53, 79, 106, 114, 164, 167
  in Albanian identity and Greekness,
  62
  and brigands, 55
  cultural, 66
  and dandyism, 79
ambivalence, 1, 9, 17, 79, 109, 118,
  162, 168, 184

of British philhellenes, 154
of Greek cosmology, 113
amnesty, 31, 37, 55, 56
Anatolian generations, 59
Anatolian refugees, 170
Anderson, B., 6, 9, 10, 11, 23, 46, 47,
  160
  Imagined Communities (1991[1989]),
  9
Anglo-Greek encounters, 6, 76, 78, 138
'Anglos', 31
anomaly, 2, 156, 167
Anonymous, 40–1
  Some Notes, 40–1
Ansted, D.T., 84, 85, 86
anthropological encounters *see*
  anthropology/anthropological
anthropological epistemology *see*
  anthropology/anthropological
Anthropological Institute, 90
anthropological intimacy *see*
  anthropology/anthropological
anthropology/anthropological, 5, 16,
  18, 71–2, 75–6, 104, 109–10, 178
  and colonizers, 75–6
  discourse, 77, 78, 98, 99, 109–10
    heterotopias, 109
  encounters, 17, 71–6
    cultural intimacy, 94–9
  ethno-history, 78–88
  origins and growth of, 90–3
  epistemology, 84
    practice, 77–89
  travel accounts, 75–6
  folklore, 96–8
  practice, 77–89
  reflexivity, 89
  social relation, 152–4
  'wars', 46–7
  see also proto-anthropology/
    protoanthropological
anthropopoiésis, 187
anti-brigand laws, 58

brigands, 18, 23–45, 49, 50, 51, 52,
53–4, 55, 57, 66, 101, 103, 106,
110, 113, 114, 116, 123, 126, 130
  Albanian, 54, 66
  and ambiguities, 55
  Arvanitakis band, 31
  attire of, 118
  banditry, 101, 105, 118, 123
  bands, 26, 31, 50, 55, 56, 62
  chiefs, 27, 52, 112
  crime, 48–9
  disorder, 57
  excommunication of, 57
  Greek, 18, 42, 43, 54, 57, 110, 111,
116, 118
  hideouts of, 50
  and *klephtic* ballads, 111
  mythistories of, 105–9
  origins of, 56, 61–2
  raids, 27, 42
  see also brigandage; Greek brigand-
    Klephts; *klephtism*; *listeía*
brigands-*listés*, 30, 34
Britain, 3, 5–8, 27–8, 33–5, 37, 42, 52,
57, 66, 81, 90, 111, 125, 134–7,
139, 146, 152, 159–62, 165–6, 173
  Anglo-Greek relations, 155–8
  class consciouness, 82–3
  and Greek irredentism, 152
  relationship with Greece, 130–2
  and Indian 'disorder' of 1857, 43
*British Association for the Advancement
of Science*, (BAAS), 90, 91
British colonial self-perceptions, 172
British Empire, 28, 33–4, 36, 39, 44,
90, 162
British *ethnohistorical* discourses, 102
British honor/British imperial honor,
35, 37, 42, 136, 161
British imperialism, 8, 37, 39, 44, 152,
173
British political discourse, 158
British travel writing, 87, 103, 116–25
British travelers, 76–8, 83, 85, 86, 93,
94–9, 110, 112, 114, 134, 136
Brubaker, R., 187
Bryant, R., 160
Bulgaria/Bulgarian, 50, 60, 62, 63,
133, 158, 161

Bulgarian Exarchate (1870), 74, 158
Bulgarian Question, 161, 190
Bulwer, Sir Henry, 135
bureaucracy/bureaucratic, 3, 31, 32,
75, 92, 100, 152, 163
Burnouf, Émile, 51, 52
Byron, Lord, 116, 139
Byzantium/Byzantian, 4, 7, 50, 59,
60, 65, 113, 142, 144, 145, 146,
147, 148, 149, 158
  heritage, 65

Calvinism, 2
Campbell, Sir George, 42, 43, 53, 81,
110
Canada, 33
capitalism, 2–3, 23, 29, 100
carnivalesque, 18, 79, 96, 164
Castoriadis, C., 132
Celtic Red Branch, 111
Center for Social Research, 64
centripetal political force, 15, 153,
180
Cervantes, Miguel de, 112
  Don Quixote, 112
Chadji-Stavros (Greek brigand chief),
112–13
Chambers of Greece, 53
Chámidhes, 63
change, 6, 32, 136
  historical, 80, 129
  social, 7, 100, 179, 183, 184
Chatterjee, P., 10
children, 64, 116, 151–73, 177
China, 143
'the chosen', 14, 130–2, 141–9
Christian *agápe*, 144
Christianity, 1, 4, 147, 154, 188
chronicle time, 2
chronological time, 2
citizenries, 49, 53, 171
citizenship, 1, 65, 169, 170, 171, 172
civil conflict, 38–9
civilité, 37, 170, 177
civilization/civilizational, 2, 5, 7, 16,
143, 147, 152, 155, 188
'civilizing process', 24, 76, 104, 154,
167
Clifford, J., 89, 124

clinical language, 159, 173
Clió (Cretan newspaper), 42, 167, 171
Clogg, R., 24
Cochran W., 123
  Turkish irregular forces, 123–4
Cochran, C.E., 118
coexistence, 4, 6, 7, 14, 67, 73, 81, 97, 108, 149, 172, 182, 188
  and anthropocentric vocabulary, 149
  Evolutionist and Romantic modes of, 78, 102
  of nations, 150
coexisting modernities, 188
cohesion, 2, 3, 19, 24, 168, 173, 187
Cold War era, 5
collectivity
  imaginations, 125
  interlocutors, 12–13
  self-narration, 9, 11, 14
  self-presentation, 148
  self-recognition, 11
colonialism, 1–2, 4, 10, 17, 25, 39, 49, 67, 72–3, 82, 84, 98, 131, 152, 168, 170–1, 178
  and 'anthropological wars', 46–7, 75–7, 80, 93
  and 'civilizing process', 104–5
  discourse, 5, 17, 23–9, 125, 163; and British self-perceptions, 172; and irredentist violence, 30–40
  and ethnographic survey, 91–3
  and governance, 4, 25 *see also* governance
  and Greek brigandage, 43–4, 105–8, 125
  'occulocentric' technique of 'domination' of, 83
  and otherness, 162–3
  symbolic *habitus* of, 40–5
colonization/colonizers, 3–4, 8, 13, 38, 75, 97, 162–3
  European political discourse and, 24–6
  and European-Hellenic superiority, 131–2
  restoration of order by, 43–4

communication, 9, 13, 94–5, 130, 150, 182, 186, 187
  dialogical, 184–5
  and kin relations, 153
  with significant (political) others, 163–4
communicative action, 12, 13, 138
comparative evolutionism, 81, 91, 114
conflicts, 1, 7, 10, 30, 39, 41, 42, 105, 148, 149, 186
  civil, 38–9
  class, 82
  ethnic, 65, 150
  Greek-Albanian (1940), 63, 64
  zones of conflict, 7, 150
consolidation, 4, 11, 28, 141, 171
Constantine, Emperor, 149
Constantinople, 4, 89, 145, 149
  see also Istanbul
continuities, 46, 60, 61, 63, 64, 66, 89, 170
'conversational communities', 12–13, 16, 66, 100, 187
Cooper, F., 170
corruption, 27, 81, 95, 107, 142, 143, 148
cosmology
  European, 30
  Greek, 16, 86, 113, 132, 142
  orders, 77, 86
cosmopolitanism, 170
cosmopolitics, 183
counter-hegemonies/counter-hegemonic, 2, 14, 76, 158
  agendas, 2
  games, 2, 158
  narratives, 14
  nationalism, 131
  nationhood, 76
creative irreverence, 11
credit, 135
credo, 135
Cretan Insurrection (1866–69), 6, 34, 41, 56, 98, 134, 154, 167
Cretan Question, 34, 42 *see also* 'Eastern Question'
Cretans, 34, 41, 74, 80, 138

denigration, 4, 105, 107, 184–5
Derby, Lord, 161
Derrida, J., 46, 182
destabilization, 28, 30, 75, 171
de-symbolization, 136–7
diachronicity/diachrony/diachronica,
    6, 53, 67, 93, 97, 101, 108, 132,
    172
diachrony *see* diachronicity/diachrony/
    diachronical
dialogues/monologism, 3, 13, 25, 54,
    130, 71, 72–4, 98, 138, 150, 180,
    183, 186, 188
  Anglo-Greek, 40, 162, 171
  cross-cultural, 3, 98
  dialogic relation, 3–4
  dialogical self, 15
  inter-cultural, 18
  intratextual, 71
  on nation-building, 12, 184
  of reciprocity, 9–16, 17, 183, 188
  of self-presentation, 163–72
  socio-cultural, 183–4
Diamantouros, N., 5
  'underdog culture', 5
dictatorship, 5, 63
diffusionism, 91, 93
Dilessi (Marathon) Murders (1870)
    see Dilessi Murders
Dilessi affair, 134 *see also* Dilessi
    Murders
Dilessi band, 52, 55, 118
  pictures of, 119–22
Dilessi Murders, 31–2, 35–6, 43, 45,
    51, 54, 105, 114, 135, 156–7
  damage to tourism in Greece by, 44
  and Greece's national image, 112
  Pantazis' analysis of, 109
Dilessi/Marathon Murders (1870)
    see Dilessi Murders
Dilthey, W., 72
  reflexive humanism, 72
dirt/dirty, 31, 48, 58, 60, 64, 113, 114,
    118
disciplinary archaeologies, 71–7
disciplinary scholarship, 71–7
discontinuities, 6, 46, 76, 89, 92, 106,
    156
  historical, 157

disemia, 142
'dishonoring', 58
disorder, 4, 17, 40–5, 57, 58, 60, 101,
    184
  brigand, 57
  British, 37
  and crime, 23–30
  Greek, 32, 38, 39
  Indian, 43
  internal, 17, 28
  Irish, 37, 40
  Irish-Greek, 107
  irredentist violence and, 30–9
  political, 2, 39, 61
  social, 58
Disraeli, Benjamin, 142
domestic problems, 28, 61
domination, 15, 24, 46, 72, 83, 107
  'occulocentric' technique of, 83
doxa, 87
Dragonas, T., 64
Durkheim, E., 71, 149, 180, 181
  ethical bipolarity, 180
  Kantian renunciation of 'patriotic
    duty', 181
  objectification of social phenomena,
    71
Durkheimian argument, 160
Durkheimian debates, 9
Durkheimian thesis, 93

Easter Rising (1912, Ireland), 143
Eastern Mediterranean region, 166
'Eastern Question', 34, 75, 84, 89, 158
    see also Cretan Question
Eastern Thrace, 50
economic interests, 4, 75, 134
EDES (Greek irredentist resistance
    group), 63
eghoismós (Greek masculinity), 104,
    108
Egypt, 32
Elias, N., 25, 28, 177
elites, 11, 40, 62, 162, 138, 148, 170,
    177, 178, 188
emancipation, 30, 72, 125
  Catholic, 35
emergent nation, 3
emotional blackmail, 134

pre-Hellenic European humanity, 80
pre-Independence bandits-*Klephts*, 30
print-capitalism, 9
problématique, 50, 78
processes, 6, 25, 34, 78, 154, 187
  inclusive, 52
  of modern Greek tradition, 95–6
  nation-building, 6–7
  post-Enlightenment, 170
  reciprocal learning, 183
  ritual, 78
progress/progressive, 2, 38, 55, 59, 82,
    90, 137, 139, 141, 147, 156–7
  socio-political, 2
proksenió, 85
protection, 18, 28, 30, 108, 160, 162,
    170, 172–3
proto-anthropology/proto-
    anthropological, 17, 18, 73, 74, 80,
    90, 93, 96, 98, 100, 101–12 *see also*
    anthropology/anthropological
psychí (soul), 160
public discourse, 47, 163
public insecurity, 2, 58
'public sphere', 13, 47
purification, 47, 67, 85
Puritanism, 79, 155, 156, 161

racism/racist/racial, 9, 47, 60, 61, 142
  language criteria, 63–4
  and purity, 64
Radcliffe-Brown, 83, 91, 92, 93
  The Andaman Islanders (1922), 93
rape, 166
rationalization, 13, 17, 25, 27, 73,
    76–7, 100–1, 107, 108, 130
reciprocity, 3–4, 30, 46–7, 48, 77, 114,
    130, 131, 154, 155, 159, 163,
    172–3, 184, 185, 186, 187
  Anglo-Greek consanguinity, 156–8
  character of European-Greek
      encounters and, 141–4
  concomitants of self-interest in,
      159
  cultural intimacy and, 94–6
  dialogics of, 9–16, 17, 183, 188
  glorification of *klephti*, 107–8
  and moral accountability, 150
  philhellenism and, 135–6, 146

  Maussian dimensions of, 137,
      152–3
  symbolic resources of, 29–30
reciprocity-as-recognition, 17, 29
recognition, 6, 9, 10, 11, 13, 15, 17,
    18, 29, 30, 44, 47, 48, 61, 64, 66,
    101, 110, 173, 185
  of ethnic-as-racial affiliations, 162–3
  from individual to a collective level,
      185
  of Greece by its European protectors,
      61
  of Greece, institutionally, 168–9
  minority rights and , 183
  and obliteration of certain social
      groups, 48
reconstruction, 77
redemption, 6
  and sacrifice, 141–50
  territorial, 6
redemptive narratives, 149–50
redemptive potential, 141, 144
redistribution, 15, 33, 137, 141
reflexivity, 72, 76
Regency (Greece, 1833–35), 7
regeneration, 51, 59, 155, 173
relationships, 3, 9, 11, 29, 35, 42, 56,
    59, 63, 65, 88, 108, 125, 135,
    138–9, 142, 143, 150
  Anglo-Greek, 6, 131, 138, 155–6,
      164, 165, 173
  between Albanians and Greeks, 54,
      62, 79–80
  between Britain's relationship and
      Greece, 130
  brigand crime, 109
  British, with Greece, 130–2
  dialectical, 72, 76
  and Greek relationship with Europe,
      150
  Greek-European, 34, 141
  imbalanced symbolic exchange in,
      15
  inequality/equality in, 109, 131,
      137, 141, 163, 188
  international, 151, 153, 182
  master-slave relationships, 3
  patronage, 154–62
  racial rift, 46

relativity, 59, 102
Renaissance, 143
Renan, E., 16, 47
Renieris, Markos, 167
representativeness, 125
Republic of Macedonia, 169
resistance, 9, 13, 14, 26, 38, 63, 75,
    96, 106, 116, 163, 172
  anticolonial, 72, 104, 107
  ethnic, 67
  foreign elements and, 75, 99, 107
  and hegemonic modes of
      representation, 11
  Indian, 43
  mechanism, 96, 107
  Ottoman 'tyranny' and, 56, 80,
      102, 103, 107, 149
  of peasantry, 17
  in Second World War, 64, 171
ressentiment, 137, 138, 146
restoration of order, 43, 59
revolt, 27, 29, 30, 77, 107, 138, 167
revolution/revolutionary, 35, 52, 72,
    82, 108, 110, 113, 130, 134, 161
  anthropological, 72
  Mexico (1810–21), 42
  revolutionary Irish, 40
Revue des Deux Mondes, 51–2
Rhallis Brothers (London), 36
  Notes, 36
rhetoric/rhetorical, 1, 18, 28–9, 35,
    47, 51, 134, 149, 152–3, 156
  British, 173
  devices, 59
  Greek, 164, 166
  in nationalist movements, 155
  patriotic, 35
  political, 145–6
  protection, 18, 162, 172
rhetorical tropes, 18
Ribbonmen, 33
Ridgeway, William, 91
Rikakis, Antonios, 54
Risorgimento, 143
Rivers, W.H.R.(President of the BAAS),
    91, 92
  'Cambridge Method' of research,
      91
Rob Roy, 106–7

Robin Hood, 102–3 *see also* gentleman-
    cateran
Robinson, F., 152
Rocaguinarda (bandit in *Don Quixote*),
    112
Roginsky, D., 159
role making., 82
Roma, 60
Romania, 32
Romantic conceptions, 18, 79
Romanticism, 1, 8, 15, 18, 34, 78, 79,
    80, 81, 82, 90, 156, 161
romanticization/romantic, 26, 34, 79,
    81, 90, 102, 118
  brigandage, 105–8, 110, 116
  British otherness, 80
  kléphticism, 26, 111–12, 116, 125
Romiossíni, (shameful feminized
    Greece), 58
Rousseau, Jean-Jacques, 156, 180
rural Greeks, 81, 82

sacrifice, cult of, 130, 141–50
Said, E., 4, 14, 44, 131
  Orientalism, 43
Salisbury, Lord, 161
Sarajevo, 65
Sarakatsans, 49–50, 53
savage customs, 90, 92
savagery, 41, 51, 100
savages, 42, 49, 53, 78, 81, 87, 90, 91,
    109
scapegoating, 15, 60
Schinas, C.D., 147
Schneider, J., 172
scientific investigation, 60, 108
scourge , 27, 51, 57, 61, 66
Second World War, 5, 63, 64, 65, 147,
    171
secular theodicy, 3
secularization, 3, 23, 130, 146, 161,
    165
selective amnesia, 47, 65
self-blame, 134–41
  treachery, 134–41
self-civilizing processes, 48
self-consciousness, 72
self-determination, 10
self-election, 132